T0327900

'Brilliant, revelatory and compelling. The legendary Reg Seekings was an iconic figure in SAS operations of WWII. A highly decorated Original, a warrior almost without compare, an elite soldier with a touching humanitarian side, this book does his memory full justice, demonstrating how powerfully the legacy endures.'

DAMIEN LEWIS

'This is a vital addition to the history of the SAS. Reg Seekings was a formative member of L Detachment, David Stirling's SAS, but had joined special forces as a Commando, and continued to serve in both the Special Raiding Squadron, then in A Squadron 1 SAS during operations in France and into Germany. As such he saw more wartime service than most ranks, and his story is not only a personal journey but an account of the wartime SAS from its inception. Rushmer has done a great job of pulling the various strands of both known archives, but many hereto unseen accounts to flesh out this biography of a remarkable man.'

TOM PETCH, former Troop Commander in 22 SAS and author of *Speed. Aggression. Surprise. The Untold Secret Origins of the SAS*

'Reg Seekings is the great unsung hero of the wartime SAS. Countless words have been written about David Stirling and Blair Mayne but, as the power behind their thrones, Seekings' importance can hardly be overstated. Here, at last, is a biography that does him justice. In Tony Rushmer's skilful hands, Seekings' remarkable story leaps from the pages. But this book is more than a biography. It is the story of the Special Air Service from its pre-existence to its post-war termination, told through a little-remembered man who experienced every moment. It is a thrilling - and important - new angle on a frequently told story.'

JOSHUA LEVINE, author of No. 1 bestseller *Dunkirk*

'The book has been a gift we never expected ... a story that is now written down and which will not be lost in the passage of time.'

Maj (Ret'd) KERRY SEEKINGS, MBE, the Parachute Regiment

SAS
DUTY BEFORE GLORY

THE TRUE WWII STORY
OF SAS ORIGINAL
REG SEEKINGS

**TONY
RUSHMER**

Michael O'Mara Books Limited

First published in Great Britain in 2024 by
Michael O'Mara Books Limited
9 Lion Yard
Tremadoc Road
London SW4 7NQ

Copyright © Tony Rushmer 2024

All rights reserved. You may not copy, store, distribute, transmit, reproduce or
otherwise make available this publication (or any part of it) in any form, or by
any means (electronic, digital, optical, mechanical, photocopying, recording
or otherwise), without the prior written permission of the publisher. Any
person who does any unauthorized act in relation to this publication may be
liable to criminal prosecution and civil claims for damages.

A CIP catalogue record for this book is available from the British Library.

This product is made of material from well-managed, FSC®-certified forests
and other controlled sources. The manufacturing processes conform to the
environmental regulations of the country of origin.

ISBN: 978-1-78929-672-3 in hardback print format
ISBN: 978-1-78929-719-5 in trade paperback format
ISBN: 978-1-78929-673-0 in ebook format

1 2 3 4 5 6 7 8 9 10

Cover design by Ana Bjezancevic, using photographs supplied by courtesy of
the SAS Regimental Association and the Cooper family
Designed and typeset by D23
Maps by David Woodroffe
Printed and bound by CPI Group (UK) Ltd, Croydon, CR0 4YY

www.mombooks.com

CONTENTS

AUTHOR'S NOTE

There have been countless times during the research and writing of this book that I wished I could sit down and chat just once with Reg Seekings. I would have loved to pick his brains on the detail of some of the big moments from history in which he was involved.

However, it was my good fortune that Seekings recorded many hours of audio that are held by the Imperial War Museum. In the same vein, he also filled a series of notebooks with reflections on the Special Air Service's operations in North Africa. These handwritten accounts proved to be an absolute treasure trove of information and give valuable new insights into early SAS operations.

The audio reels and private papers have provided the framework for me to write in-depth about Seekings' war years. But to provide the context for his involvement in SAS operations, I have conducted extensive research at a series of archive centres (referenced in 'Acknowledgments') to try and put together the pieces of the jigsaw more than eighty years after events occurred. Also, I've studied many books, not least the original SAS War Diary held by the SAS Regimental Association. This unique volume is a collection of reports, orders, letters and photographs documenting the regiment's war years. I've read autobiographies written by soldiers involved in the events they describe and enjoyed a long list of SAS-related works by other authors. One of the most illuminating sources was

SAS legend Mike Sadler, whom I was privileged enough to visit a number of times.

What became evident to me through the research process is that on occasion it is difficult to be categoric about exactly what happened and when. I realized that accounts can differ in terms of details and timelines. Hence, I have attempted to present events as diligently and faithfully as possible. If I have made any errors in doing so, I am happy to be notified to enable corrections to be applied to future editions of the book.

I am very grateful to all those who have supplied material to assist with my work. I have taken considerable time requesting the appropriate permissions, albeit this has presented the odd challenge. Every attempt has made been made to ensure all sources for written content have been listed in a chapter-by-chapter breakdown at the end of this book. I would be pleased, in future editions, to address any omissions or mistakes.

Seekings' handwritten notes were a great asset when it came to documenting his first days in the SAS through to the point of victory in North Africa. For ease of flow, appropriate grammar has been applied, but his words have been reproduced almost to the letter as he wrote them. In Seekings' extensive audio recordings, he refers to the words of others and on occasion I have reproduced these as attributed quotes. This has been done both for ease of accessibility and to maintain pace.

Lastly, at certain points, information is given within brackets and, in a very few instances, provided as footnotes. These have been used so that the story is interrupted as few times as possible.

PREFACE

I came across Reg Seekings' name for the first time during a spot of television channel-hopping. Landing on an episode of *SAS Rogue Warriors*, tales of Second World War derring-do piqued my interest, but almost more absorbing were the accompanying interviews with some of those involved. The archive footage had been recorded more than forty years after the conflict's end, and the lines on their faces as well as greying hair reinforced how time had caught up with these SAS 'Originals'. However, age had in no way diminished the spirit or characteristics of the men. David Stirling's dark beady eye pierced the camera as he spoke. Johnny Cooper's composure and easy charm were evident, likewise Pat Riley's openness and sense of camaraderie. Jim Almonds impressed with his measured words and thoughtfulness.

And then there was Seekings. Deep into his sixties with clipped moustache and swept-back, slightly untidy hair, he appeared no nonsense, brusque – almost intimidating. But at the same stage, there was something compelling about the man. A quick internet search revealed that he had been born just a couple of miles from where I sat watching the television; maybe it had been the familiar accent that initially prompted me to find out more. 'He gets into you,' Johnny Cooper once said of his fellow Special Air Service Original. Certainly, Seekings had made an impression on me.

Further reading underlined Seekings' courage. He received high-level gallantry honours for his actions in North Africa and Europe. His physical prowess – he was a pre-war amateur boxer – also featured in historical coverage. However, to some, it seemed that Seekings was not much more than a hard-nosed bastard who was handy with his fists or a Tommy gun. But the deeper I researched, the more complex a man I discovered. Wiliness accompanied street-fighter survival instincts; ambition matched bravery. Officers sought his opinion, even relied on him on occasion. Seekings possessed brains as well as brawn. And when it came to actually confronting the enemy, men wanted to fight alongside him. They recognized that it increased their own chances of staying alive.

Never afraid to speak his mind, ever ready to back his own judgement, Seekings may not have always made for the easiest company. But SAS commanders David Stirling and Paddy Mayne saw the rare qualities that he possessed – both men promoted him. Stirling, who personally recruited Seekings as a twenty-one-year-old for his newly minted L Detachment, grew to trust implicitly both him and Johnny Cooper. He referred to them as 'utterly dependable' and able to 'laugh easily regardless of the circumstances'. This was the lesser-known lighter side of Seekings, just another element in the make-up of one of the Special Air Service's most fascinating individuals.

For the last two years or so, I have lived with thoughts of Reg Seekings. It's a place that's kept me on my toes. What started out as a pursuit of a few simple facts turned into a quest to present a rounded depiction of the man.

• ● •

Reg Seekings was forced to take a short count from the referee. He had been rocked by a swift right-hand cut by his older, slightly heavier opponent – but Seekings was not the type of man to take a backward step in the face of adversity. He was compelled to push on. Attack.

It was early 1939, and Seekings had made his way across the flood-ravaged Cambridgeshire Fens to Wisbech to represent Ely Amateur Boxing Club in an eighteen-fight programme at the town's Women's Institute. Boxing was tremendously popular and the hall was rammed with eager fans of the sport.

The eighteen-year-old Reg faced up to a powerfully-framed police constable in a light heavyweight bout. Constable Riley, born in the US state of Wisconsin but now a local beat bobby, was Seekings' senior by five years and enjoyed vociferous home support. Riley had already landed that telling first-round shot, eluding his opponent's defences to send glove thudding into jaw.

With the young visitor down so early, the enthusiastic crowd could have been forgiven for thinking their man was to make short work of Seekings. However, Reg had shown in previous fights that he was no quitter. At close to 6 foot tall and weighing 12 stone 6 pounds, he knew he possessed the ammunition to fight back. In round two he began to do just that. Drawing Riley in, he began to 'mix it', street-brawler fashion, before unleashing a thunderous straight right that dropped his opponent to his knees. The tide had turned – this was now a battle of equals.

In the third and final round, Riley once more found his range and knocked the younger man's head back with a left lead. Seekings refused to go down, but it was enough for the judges to make up their minds: Riley was their winner, on points. A report in the *Wisbech Standard* described the duel as a 'grand scrap … in which the boxing skill on the part of Riley triumphed over the heavy wallops of Seekings the mixer'.

Two and a half years later the two men were to meet again, but not in the boxing ring. In August 1941 the pair found themselves in Egypt at an RAF station at Kabrit, some 90 or so miles east of Cairo. Surprised to recognize his old opponent, Riley demanded to know, 'What the hell are you doing here?'

'I've joined this outfit too!' came the response.

And so Seekings, a private from the Cambridgeshire Regiment, and Pat Riley, a sergeant from the Coldstream Guards, were to fight together as freshly recruited members of L Detachment – the first men of the SAS.

Chapter 1

FEN FIGHTER

Albert Reginald Seekings was born on 19 March 1920. He would grow up to be known as Reg, perhaps partially to avoid confusion as his father was also named Albert, but more likely out of respect for his late uncle Reginald, who had been killed in the Great War.

Although the cathedral city of Ely lay just a mile or so to the west, Seekings was delivered in a far less grand setting, at Quanea Farm. His birthplace was one of a series of agricultural smallholdings located either side of Quanea Drove, a narrow back road that led into the heart of Middle Fen. On a summer's day with the Ship of the Fens, as the cathedral is known, towering above the surrounding fields, it is an idyllic scene. In the grey days of winter, however, that extraordinary feat of ancient artisanship looms over a landscape that is no longer lush and alive but often shrouded in freezing fog. There is a bleakness about the dormant fields, flanked by icy dykes, that tests both mind and body.

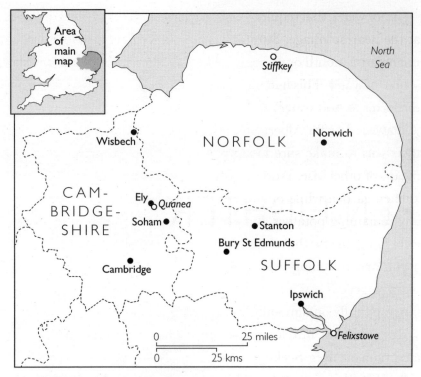

Home territory: the East of England where the Seekings brothers
were born and raised.

It was a basic two-up, two-down cottage that served as home
to Seekings' parents at the time of his birth. Albert was a farm
worker and Reg's mother, Annie, came from a similar background.
Life was tough and lacked the basic comforts that most folk in
nearby Ely enjoyed. There was no electricity out in the Fens; oil
lamps were used. On those raw nights when a cruel easterly wind
whipped across the fields, a well-stoked fire in the main family
room of a cottage offered the best resistance to the cold. Other
methods brought about varying degrees of success. Applying
goose fat to the skin was said to provide an additional layer of
protection, but more often cottage dwellers simply chose to pull
on layers of clothing and hunker down in bed once their evening
meal was finished.

As for water, that required taking a horse and cart to the standpipe at the nearest village, Stuntney. There, a 400-gallon tank, which might last a month or more, was filled. Guttering provided another source of water. This had to be boiled before use and was known by the locals as 'soft water'.

Pay was low for Albert Seekings and his like, who needed to use their wits to make sure food was on the table through legitimate means or otherwise. Workers would nurture and harvest their own kitchen garden while often adding to supplies through 'gleaning': any remaining potatoes, onions, and other vegetables in the fields were fair game for the taking after a crop was 'in'. Some men owned a gun and poaching was common, with pheasant and rabbit the main targets. It was a necessary method of survival, but it was also fun, especially on a moonlit weekend night.

Into such an unrelenting, impoverished and, at times, brutal environment, Reg Seekings was born. The deaths of three of his sisters before their first birthdays – Doris in 1919, Martha in 1924 and Ena a couple of years later – underlined the harsh reality of life in the Fens.

Prospects for progression for land workers were slim and so, in August 1920, Albert, with his wife and five-month-old son, emigrated, boarding the SS *Grampian* in Liverpool bound for Quebec, in search of new possibilities. Albert's elder brothers, Robert and John, were already in Canada, in Winnipeg, and while neither had yet found fortune they had both made fresh lives for themselves. Albert wanted something similar for his family, but it failed to work out. Annie could not deal with the seasonal weather extremes and returned with Reg to Liverpool from Montreal on the SS *Vedic* the following May. Unsurprisingly, she made her way back to the shadow of Ely Cathedral and Middle Fen, moving in with her mother Susan, who had remarried. Also close by was Annie's older sister Emma Pearce, who had just given birth to a second son, Stan. He and Reg were to become almost inseparable in their formative years; best pals as well as relatives.

Albert remained in North America to earn his fare and returned alone to Plymouth via New York in January 1922. Once more he turned to the farmlands of Quanea and the vicinity. In more than one sense, the Seekings were back where they started.

There was an addition to the family the following February with the birth of a second son, Robert William. By 1927 the Seekings were a family of five with daughter Evelyn becoming Albert and Annie's third and final child. Evelyn was barely the weight of a bag of sugar on her arrival. Amid fears that she may not survive long, she was baptized immediately and named after the midwife who delivered her at the women's infirmary block at Ely's workhouse. Happily she survived, unlike Albert and Annie's three previous daughters.

All three children went to Stuntney School, which meant lengthy daily walks across dykes and fields, which were always exposed to the elements of each season. Not that Reg and Robert – known as Bob-Robert and later Bob – minded the exercise. They were both tough, outdoor lads shaped by their immediate surrounds.

Bob showed a greater aptitude than his brother for learning, in particular mental arithmetic. It was a skill that would serve him well in later life when totting up the odds of his accumulator bets on the horses. A bright soul, who became politically minded, Bob was offered the chance to go to grammar school but was told that would put too much strain on the family's finances.

For those who wanted to learn, Stuntney School offered more than just a pragmatic grasp of numbers and spelling. Teachers such as Mr Walker shone a light on a wider world beyond the everyday sights and sounds of horses pulling reaper-binders across the fields and the smell of 120 sows at Dunstalls Farm, which lay across the road from the classrooms. Bob never forgot being taught about faraway places with exotic names. Some of which he would find himself visiting soon enough, not that he had any inkling of what was to come as he sat listening attentively in lessons.

The biggest influence on both boys were their parents, although Annie and Albert were very different in character. The couple married in 1917 when Annie was nineteen and more than seven years younger than Albert, who had been seriously wounded in action earlier that year at Passchendaele, the third battle of Ypres. A professional soldier from 1911 with the Bedfordshire Regiment, he lay alone in no man's land for three days until he was rescued. So severe were his shrapnel wounds that a large part of his rib cage was cut away. Bob would later tell his own sons, 'You could put your fist inside the hole in his back.' But for Albert, more painful than any of the lingering physical effects of the war was the loss of his younger brother Reginald, a private in the Yorkshire Regiment. He was nineteen years old when he was killed at the Somme.

Given all he had seen and experienced, Albert would rarely discuss the war, but there was one aspect of soldiering that he passed down to his sons: the concept of 'duty'. Reg and Bob grew up understanding that the battlefield was no place for cowardice. 'I was most afraid of being afraid,' Reg would say later in life when reflecting on his motivations in the field. 'Afraid of not being able to face people, face my father. He was a good soldier and I couldn't have faced him as a coward.'

Albert wasn't a demonstrative man but always stood his own ground. If sufficiently provoked he could more than handle himself with his bare fists – something else he would pass on to his sons. But by and large he was a quiet man, who when opportunity presented would while away spare hours in his garden, invariably whistling tunelessly to himself.

By contrast, Annie was a hot-tempered individual. Friendly and jolly for the most part, she was also forthright and opinionated and rarely ceded the last word in an argument. She also hated losing – even a game of cards with the family. On one occasion her young grandson Kerry suspected she was cheating and Annie responded in fiery fashion by chucking away her cards. There was also a Christmas when the Ludo board was hurled into the fire in a fit of pique as the game turned against her. An attitude of win-at-any-cost was there for Reg and Bob to see, and Annie was the assertive figure in the Seekings household.

Reg certainly inherited some of his mother's personality traits. Like her, the red mist could descend in a flash. On one occasion the brothers were sparring in the garden and the younger sibling caught the elder one with a handy punch. Reg's instincts kicked in and he hit back with a blow so powerful it sent Bob crashing through a fence and hedge. On another occasion, he knocked down a farm shire horse that bit him.

If Reg had brute force to call upon, Bob was more athletic and had a passion for sport. A cricket fanatic, he was also a useful left-hand boxer with boundless stamina, a quality that saw him shine as a middle- and long-distance runner, who could lick Reg when it came to races around the path and droves. At 5 feet 10 inches tall, he was the slightly shorter of the two and had hazel eyes as opposed to Reg's, which were murky blue in colour. Bob's thick mop of hair was darker and he possessed a strong, square jaw with a noticeable cleft.

Reg knew he wanted more from life than simply to labour on the land, and yearned to have his own farm. But on leaving school aged fourteen, his reluctance to join his father in working for a local farmer almost had serious consequences for the family. The farmer broached the subject of the strapping young school-leaver coming to work for him with Albert, who replied that his boy had no desire to follow in his footsteps. The tricky conversation ended with the farmer informing his employee that he would no longer have a house if Reg didn't come and work for him, forcing Albert to plead with his son to back down and avoid the family being evicted. Reg had no choice. He'd set off each morning with his 'docky', a chunk of bread with the corner cut out and in which a lump of butter and cheese would be inserted. The food would be consumed along with a flask of cold tea at lunchtime. It wasn't the life he imagined for himself. Nor was he about to accept it. Those endless hours grafting through all four seasons allowed him to plot possible escape routes.

One plan to alter his circumstances revolved around his boxing ambitions. By his late teens, Reg was using much of his spare time to train hard and develop his skills at the local amateur boxing club, which met on a weekday evening in a gym above the stables of The Club, a local pub and functions facility in the centre of Ely. Around the same time he began to fight in public. This could mean a bout on a Saturday night card at the Corn Exchange on Ely marketplace, or around the county in towns such as Huntingdon, Wisbech or Chatteris. The latter was home to Reg's boxing idol of the time, Eric Boon. The fighter nicknamed 'The Fen Tiger' was a nationally known figure, registering well over a hundred bouts and taking the British lightweight belt in 1938 (such was his status that Boon's title defence against Arthur Danahar in February 1939 was broadcast live in cinemas and also televised by the BBC).

It was no wonder that Seekings gravitated towards Boon, including making a 30-mile round trip on his bike to train at Boon's gym in Chatteris. Reg and his cousin – and ringside corner man – Stan Pearce would head across the Fens together. Stan would eventually get a motorbike, which made things a little easier, for him at least. He would transport the boxing prospect, bicycle and all, over to Chatteris and make Reg cycle home to build up his fitness.

Aside from the boxing ring, the Territorial Army offered a life away from the fenland fields. The younger Seekings brother, Bob, signed up in Ely on 13 February 1938. It was his fifteenth birthday but he forged the papers to appear two years older. It was not to be the last time that one of the Seekings boys would play fast and loose with official documents.

Reg's official Pay Book confirms that he volunteered to serve in the Territorial Army on 20 January 1939. His local unit was the Cambridgeshire Regiment – and within it he and Bob were assigned to B Company of the 1st Battalion. The Cambridgeshires had the uncommon but not unique distinction of being entirely 'Territorial Army', composed of non-professional citizen-soldiers. Conventional structure saw regular infantry regiments embrace battalions of part-timers under their wing within their formal composition. But the Cambridgeshires wore their own cap badge, had other uniform distinctions and proudly referenced their first battle honour – 'South Africa 1900-1901' – on the Regimental Colour (their distinctive flag). Previously there had been historical connections with the neighbouring Suffolk Regiment and this continued in terms of documentation, but in other matters such as recruiting, training and future deployments, the Cambridgeshires retained autonomy. The ranks were formed of local lads, and Reg and Bob were very much men of their home county regiment.

For Reg, joining up meant that he also had the opportunity to box – and have a shot at a title. Early February saw him in action in Bury St Edmunds at the 54th Divisional Championships, in which the best boxers from the East Anglian infantry division squared up.

Seekings was fit and ready, having scrapped with Riley a week earlier in that thunderous toe-to-toe in Wisbech. The Quanea boxer had also fought in early January in front of a home crowd at Ely Corn Exchange. On a typically packed programme, he'd suffered a narrow loss on points, despite landing a couple of trademark heavy punches. But it was a different story in Bury St Edmunds, where his big-hitting style saw Private Hugman (Suffolk Regiment) knocked out in the semi-finals of the light heavyweights. Initially, it had been a difficult fight against a gangly opponent. The Suffolk man had found his target early on with a forceful left hand. Between rounds, Reg's corner man told him he had to slip beyond that long reach and dangerous left. 'So I went out and for the first time saw the left hand coming and bang-bang, I nipped under and he went out like a light.'

In the final, Seekings was up against a lance corporal called Jeffreys from the Hertfordshire Regiment. After refreshing himself with a pre-fight nap, Reg received advice from his father: 'Go out there and box him a bit and work out if you can get him by points or if you'll need a knockout.' His rival was fresher, having had the benefit of a bye – an automatic advance without competing – at the semi-final stage. But a determined Seekings 'caught him with a good one-two' and Jeffreys was defeated, saved from a knockout only by the gong. Reg was overjoyed at his success. He would step into the ring on several more occasions, but that night in Bury St Edmunds proved to be the highlight of his boxing career.

As winter gave way to spring there were other developments, near and far, that had a greater impact on Reg and Bob's lives. The 15th of March saw the German Army march unopposed into Czechoslovakia; two days later Neville Chamberlain, the British prime minister, questioned Adolf Hitler's future intentions. With war brewing and closer to home, B Company, comprising four officers and sixty-eight other ranks, had their new drill hall on Barton Road, Ely, opened by Major General Luckock in mid-May. The *Ely Weekly Guardian* published a picture of a 'spacious building' in which 'a staff instructor resides on the premises'.

Elementary and then more progressive foot drill helped give the Seekings brothers and other new faces a sense of discipline and order. Similarly, as the men learned to march together, they quickly grew to understand what it was like to be part of a cohesive unit. The evening training after work also included a study period in which they were taught a wide range of subjects: how to assemble their webbing (the straps and gear used to carry all their equipment), rank structure (badge recognition) and regimental history. The drill hall was used for 'dry' weapon training; in other words, how to become familiar and proficient with the rifle and – importantly – do so in a safe manner, before progressing. Later, Reg and Bob became masters of the tried and trusted Lewis gun and then the much newer Bren light machine gun, which had only just entered service with the Territorial Army. They were constantly drilled in how to hold, aim, adjust sights, load/unload and make safe their weapons. Bob would never forget the eighteen stoppage drills that could be applied to overcome any potential firing issues on the range with the Lewis gun.

Only when the non-commissioned officers (NCOs) in charge of training were confident that each soldier had attained the necessary skills in the lecture room could they progress to firing live in an outdoor setting on training weekends. In addition to range work, these weekend sessions would be invaluable in terms of gaining experience, and gave officers and men the opportunity to hone the many infantry skills at individual, section, platoon and company level. Tactical movement, battle drills, map and compass work, communication and hand signals were among the many basic essentials required to weld together an effective fighting unit, whatever the rank.

The annual camp was an opportunity each summer for Territorial battalions to harness all their sub-units in one location for two weeks of coordinated training. Yet, in spring 1939 it was decided that the Cambridgeshire Regiment should expand into two battalions, with the newly established one having its headquarters in the Isle of Ely. So, in late July of that year Reg and Bob headed off for a fortnight under canvas at Dibgate Camp in Kent as potential soldiers of the 2nd Battalion, commanded by Major E. T. L. Baker.

Regimental archives record that there were 1500 regiment

Lining up for the camera at the Cambridgeshire Regiment's annual camp in 1939. Reg (left) cuts an assured figure, while (right) Bob's poise is striking for a sixteen-year-old.

members present in the second week. An official camp photograph captures the differing moods of those attending. Many are caught with a nervous smile on their faces; others appear surly, while some look downright uninterested. Reg and Bob reflect none of the above. The black-and-white picture has both staring at the camera with what appears to be unblinking assurance and almost a hint of defiance. There is a mix of dress with some men still in civvies, but Reg, on the extreme right-hand end of the second back row, is noticeably smart.

The apparent poise of Bob – twelfth along from the left in the first row of those standing – is also unmistakable. The way he seemed to carry himself is all the more remarkable given that he was still only sixteen, having slipped the net for minimum-age admission a year and a half earlier. His confident bearing, shoulders back with strong jaw to the fore, suggests that he was far from overwhelmed by being among hundreds of older men during his time at Dibgate.

As well as drill and skill-at-arms work, the days would also have been used for familiarization with communications systems and low-level tactics. Like all of the recruits, the Seekings brothers were on a steep learning curve. But the likelihood is that they would have emerged from camp with an increased status among peers and superiors. Fit through sporting endeavours and hardened by the rigours of their outdoor working life, their potential would not have been missed by officers who used the fortnight to scrutinize recent recruits. What would also have been evident in both brothers from an early stage is that they were not the types to let down their mates, a quality their father Albert always reminded them of.

The Kent camp concluded, and the Seekings returned to the farm for the summer harvest on the Fens. It was the last one they would experience for a long while; their time on the land was about to come to a sudden if not unexpected end. On 1 September 1939, Germany invaded Poland and two days later Chamberlain gave a radio address in which he announced that Britain was at war. The Territorial Army was immediately mobilized into full-time service and on 1 November both battalions of the Cambridgeshire Regiment were heading for Norfolk. It had taken five years or so since he had left school, but at last Reg had found his escape path.

As for Bob, he had been told by his father that he could get him out of the forces on account of his young age. Bob was having none of it: 'I want to go.' Albert Seekings accepted the situation but made one thing clear on their departure. 'I shall never be able to give you much, I suppose, in material wealth,' he said to his two boys. 'But there's one thing I have given you and that's a name for honesty and hard work. Both of them are hard to come by, easy to lose and once you've lost them, you'll never get 'em back. So, treasure them.'

Albert had one final thing to say before seeing his sons off to war. 'Never darken my door if you're dishonest.' Reg would never forget those words, even if he might not always adhere to them.

Chapter 2

COMMANDOS

Once the frisson of heading off to war had waned, Reg's early experiences as a soldier offered him few thrills. He had grown used to the regular adrenalin rush provided by boxing in front of packed houses, but there was little excitement for him during the winter of 1939–40. An arctic chill had descended on Britain and few spots were icier than north Norfolk where the 2nd Battalion of the Cambridgeshire Regiment were based. From January onwards, Reg and Bob were camped in the small coastal village of Stiffkey. There were cross-country runs to boost fitness and a rifle range was established at a disused gravel pit so that shooting skills could be worked on. But the freezing conditions were never far away. At one point, the snow was so heavy that the soldiers had to help keep transport networks operational. Reg never forgot the bitter cold of that lingering winter.

In spring 1940 the Germans launched their invasion of the Low Countries. Between 10 May and 22 June, Hitler's forces seized control of Luxemburg, the Netherlands, Belgium and – finally – France. The mass evacuation of the British Expeditionary Force from Dunkirk also took place in the days either side of the end of May. It was against this backdrop that Reg attempted to make moves of his own. He applied for various special service duties, but initially got nowhere. One day, word went around his company that volunteers were required for a new parachutist unit. Immediately, Reg expressed a strong interest and asked for his name to be put forward. However, a few days later he heard from an adjutant that the appropriate paperwork had not been submitted. Frustrated and bemused, Reg decided to take a risk. He slipped into a deserted office and found the lists not only undelivered but also not filled in. 'There was nobody under parachutists and nobody under sea raiders,' he said. 'So I put my name down under parachutist, put [the list] in an envelope and delivered it to the adjutant.'

The higher powers were fuming when they found out what he had done. 'My company commander threatened to put me inside for meddling with official documents,' he recalled. But there were no lasting repercussions and soon afterwards Seekings travelled 10 miles south to Melton Constable for a medical in which his quest to find a new unit met with another hitch. At 14 stone, Reg was deemed too heavy to train as a parachutist. 'You'll hardly get through a three-foot hole,' the medical officer told him. Quick as a flash, Seekings responded: 'Well, put me down for sea raiders then.' Perhaps more of a concern for the young private was that he had a lazy right eye. The condition was to become more evident in later life as the eye often wept, but, importantly, it did not get in the way of him passing his medical with flying colours in 1940.

When Reg joined up with the sea raiders in high summer, they had formally become known as the Commandos, a new force that had the backing of Winston Churchill. The prime minister, who took over from Chamberlain in May 1940, insisted that Britain should retain an offensive state of mind. To that end, he wanted specially trained forces that could attack the coastlines of those countries conquered by the Nazis in their spring offensive. Churchill called for 'troops of the hunter class who can develop a reign of terror'. The PM tasked his Chiefs of Staff accordingly and, within a few months, across the United Kingdom a string of Commando units with respective strengths of 500 were busy preparing for action.

The seaside town of Felixstowe in Suffolk was the base for 7 Commando, the unit to which Reg was posted. Initially, he had been the only man from the Cambridgeshire Regiment to meet with a captain recruiting for the special service unit. 'No chance of getting any more like yourself?' the officer asked Seekings. 'You look a likely looking lad. Can't you get any mates?' The young private offered a confident response, reeling off the names of half a dozen lads for the captain to see. They were all duly accepted and among the additions were Bob Seekings and Eric Musk. Eric hailed from Soham, some five miles to the east of where the brothers were born. Reg and Bob both thought a lot of 'Musky'. If the Seekings boys liked someone they would be termed a 'good bloke' and Musk was a level above that in their opinion. Reg labelled him a 'bloody good chap' – and he was. Musky barely ever uttered a cross word and was a popular lad.

Eric had been just three months old when his father Robert died of Spanish Flu in the winter of 1918. But Robert's wife Florence made sure she gave her son Eric and daughter Marjorie a stable family environment. The three of them moved in with her sister Hannah, who was married to Jack Heyhoe. Florence always set a fine example, working hard as a general store assistant in Soham, and Jack, a farm worker, became a father figure to Eric.

Musk grew up to become a talented and level-headed young man. He got a job in his early teens working for the electricity board, but it was on the football field that he made his name in

Cambridgeshire. Stories about his prowess on the pitch would often appear in local papers through the mid-to-late 1930s. There was even talk of a potential trial with a top Scottish club. The athletic six-footer packed a powerful shot and, post-match, shook hands with an iron grip. Musky was as solid as they come, reliable and always kept an eye out for his mates. You couldn't ask for a better person to cover your back, as Bob would later find out.

The three Fen lads spent August to late autumn with 7 Commando on the coast in Suffolk. Specialist training alongside plenty of fitness work made for long days. By November, the unit and 4 Commando were part of No.3 Special Service Battalion posted to Girvan, on the Scottish coast and some 50-odd miles to the south-west of Glasgow. The men went to the Isle of Arran from where Eric sent home a postcard of Beinn Bharrain, but there was little time for relaxing in the final weeks of 1940. The commandos were hard at it, fine-tuning their skills and undertaking exercises integral to their anticipated use. These included perfecting coastal landings while facing a simulated attack from shoreline positions.

By this point, 7 Commando had trained for months and were desperate to be unleashed. Their frustration increased in the middle of December when a proposed assault on Pantellaria in the Strait of Sicily was postponed. The situation worsened as other jobs were lined up and then called off. 'We'd had a gutful,' said Reg. 'Cancellation, cancellation – we'd had enough.' The mood became so bad one day that the first Director of Combined Operations, Sir Roger Keyes, was forced to address the men from the bridge of HMS *Glengyle*, a ship that 7 Commando troops got to know very well from the start of 1941. Some individuals seemed ready to mutiny and a large-framed sergeant-major was forced to call for a degree of order. 'Give the old bastard a chance, give him a hearing,' urged the senior figure. At last, the highly decorated Keyes started to deliver his message. 'You remind me of a bright sword rusting in the highlands of Scotland,' he told the fed-up commandos. Reg was fuming as he listened, but years later would look back and laugh at the incident: 'He could talk, the old so-and-so.'

Keyes promised the frustrated group that the next time they sailed that it would be for action – and 'he kept to his word there,' added Reg. Late on the final day of January 1941, a year and a quarter after they had left the Fens for north Norfolk, the Seekings boys finally departed the British Isles. They sailed from the Isle of Arran as part of Force Z, under the command of Lieutenant Colonel Robert Laycock. The formation contained men mainly from 7, 8 and 11 Commando; their destination was North Africa and the Desert War.

The constant peril of enemy presence throughout the Mediterranean Sea meant the journey to Egypt was undertaken via the much longer Cape route. The five-week voyage was only broken up with some much-needed shore leave at Cape Town on 19–20 February. The ships were met by South Africans in cars, some of whom were happy to take soldiers back to their homes. It was a slice of warmth and normality that Bob Seekings particularly appreciated. Collected by a retired South African doctor and his wife, Bob was treated to a meal that was a significant upgrade from the endless stews and buckets of tea served from the *Glengyle*'s galley. He struck up an instant rapport with the South African couple, who treated him as one of their own for those few hours. Bob, who had turned eighteen a few days earlier while at sea, never forgot that glimpse of genuine care. His youth, charm and situation also impressed the couple, who would send postal orders for months until contact was finally lost.

The *Glengyle* dropped anchor in the Suez Canal on 7 March and within twenty-four hours Force Z was renamed Layforce with all references to commando units discontinued as a security measure. Consequently, 7 Commando became A Battalion and on 11 March the unit advanced to camp at Geneifa, just inland from the Great Bitter Lake. The first days and weeks on African soil saw the men attempt to get acclimatized to a terrain and climate that could hardly have been further removed from the west coast of Scotland. Searing heat was one thing the men had to get used to – a private died of heatstroke – and then there were the sandstorms. On 14 March, Layforce witnessed a blizzard of dust and dirt whipped up by the wind. 'Sand was everywhere and inches deep,' chronicled A Battalion's War Diary. Such storms could last for hours and spell disaster for any individual unfortunate enough to be caught out in one. Men also learned to give their boots a firm shake and thorough search first thing each morning. One never knew what creature might find comfort in a warm boot through the chilly nights. Snakes and spiders were common in the desert but not as prevalent or routinely irritating as the flies. They seemed to be everywhere.

Around this time a photo of the Seekings brothers and Musk was taken. The image captured them squeezed together on a bench in their tropical kit and steel-studded ammo boots, field service caps wedged jauntily on each right ear and cigarettes lodged between their fingers (Victory V, an Indian smoke, was a common brand among Allied troops). Musk, the single stripe of a lance corporal on his sleeve, was the only one with a smile on his face. Sat to his left – not quite shoulder to shoulder, more like under a wing – was Bob, four and a half years his junior. Eric's seniority perhaps emphasized the younger man's callow looks. Whether it is the exposure of the photograph or not, the teenager also appears whiter in skin colour than the other two, giving an impression of innocence. And then there was Reg. Fists almost bunched, as befitted a boxer, legs set wide apart and broad shoulders angled slightly forward. His expression was neutral; seemingly he felt no necessity to find a smile.

Reg was more than ready for action; all he required was the opportunity. The first month or so in Egypt had presented a

Reg Seekings, Eric Musk and Bob Seekings (l to r) during their Layforce
days in the first half of 1941.

familiar story to the men of Layforce; an operation was planned
– and cancelled. It was all the more galling as General Erwin
Rommel masterminded major German gains, having arrived in
North Africa in mid-February 1941. The Axis powers' surge across
Cyrenaica (the eastern region of Libya) began on 24 March and,
aside from the besieged port of Tobruk, forced the Allies back to
the Egyptian border.

It was into this alarming picture that Layforce finally got a chance to have its first crack at the enemy. Either side of midnight on 19–20 April, A Battalion was chosen to attempt a hit-and-run raid on the recently fallen coastal town of Bardia. The objective was to disrupt the enemy's lines of communication, destroying transport, materials and supplies. It was just the sort of offensive that Reg had been yearning for, but it turned out to be something of a damp squib for him. After unopposed landings, there were some relatively small-scale successes with one detachment blasting a bridge and another setting fire to a supply dump of tyres. Also, the breeches on four seemingly out-of-service naval guns were destroyed. However, tragedy occurred within one section when, in the darkness, an officer was shot and mortally wounded. He had failed to offer the agreed recognition signal, having been challenged by a commando sentry. From another detachment, sixty-seven men ended up being left behind in the re-embarkation process and the Italians subsequently claimed their capture.

Otherwise, there was little or no suggestion of enemy presence in and around Bardia. The only near contact came after a sub-section spotted a couple of motorcycles on patrol leaving the town and proceeded to hurl grenades that detonated too late. In the same incident, one commando took aim with his Tommy gun, but without success. The battalion's official record of the raid detailed that the encounter led to 'two slight casualties' – one of whom may have been Reg, who had returned from Bardia with a thigh wound. 'Exactly how it happened, I don't know,' he'd say many years after the event. But the wound became infected, resulting in a hospital stay that left him disheartened and increasingly irritable.

• ● •

Bardia was hardly a showstopping display from Layforce, but at least the unit had been deployed in the sort of operation for which it had been trained. The next time A Battalion was called on, they found themselves embroiled in a desperate fighting withdrawal instead of carrying out an amphibious assault. Crete was the scene in late May and Reg was absent, still hospitalized in Egypt. He may have cut his leg in Bardia, but the Greek island was where Bob and Eric fully cut their teeth. In fact, the pair would end up headline news back in Cambridgeshire.

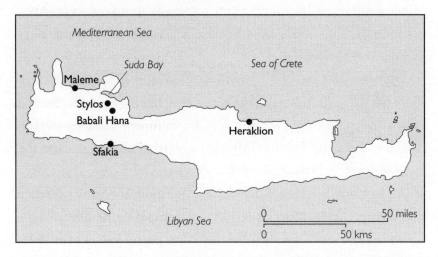

May 1941, Crete: the scene of Layforce's fighting withdrawal – and from where Bob Seekings and Eric Musk escaped.

The Battle of Crete began in earnest on 20 May when the Germans launched the largest-scale airborne invasion that had ever been seen. The skies around the north of the island were full of paratroopers, along with gliders bringing in assault troops. By the next day the enemy had seized control of Maleme Airfield, paving the way for substantial reinforcements to be flown in.

Layforce was ordered to support the Allies' objectives on Crete, arriving in time to take part in one of the most gruelling and dramatic hand-to-hand battles of the war. An advance party from A Battalion reached the island on 24 May, followed two nights later by the remainder from the unit, along with D Battalion. Their transport had barely dropped anchor at Suda Bay on the north-west coast when it became clear that the commandos were going to be used in a rearguard action. Crete was already all but lost, and the Allies' aims had changed from holding the island to evacuating as many as possible of its drained and fatigued troops. Layforce was tasked with playing a key role in covering the withdrawal to Sfakia on the south coast. The route to the town was only around 30 miles, but mountainous and exposed countryside added to the challenge facing the commandos.

Eighteen-year-old Bob experienced a baptism of fire through the days of 27–28 May when he was fully introduced to the realities of war. As part of the defensive line, he witnessed close-up the fate of fellow Fenman Private William Green, who hailed from the town of March, around 20 miles from Ely. Green also came from an agricultural background; his father looked after horses, a role a notch or two above most farm workers. With such common ground, it's unsurprising that he and Bob were together – along with Musk – when the trio sought cover from the latest in a seemingly never-ending series of air attacks made by Stuka dive-bombers and feared Messerschmitt fighters. Years later Bob told his three sons how he, Musk and Green had leapt into the nearest slit trench as they were being strafed. They landed in a jumble, but Bob quickly realized that something was dripping on him. It was blood belonging to Green. His mate had fallen on top of him after being shot in the head. Astonishingly given the severity of his wound, Green was still alive. A medic attended and was similarly surprised that Green had not been killed. Musk and Bob were advised to leave their comrade and re-join the fighting withdrawal, which they did.

Official lists initially categorized Green as 'Missing, believed

Prisoner of War'. This was later amended to 'Presumed Died of Wounds'. It is possible that he never left the slit trench and that either locals or Germans buried him there in a remote Crete corner. Green's name is among those of nearly 3,000 Allied soldiers at the Athens Memorial, commemorating those with no known grave. He died aged twenty-one years old.

Not long after dawn on 28 May, Bob was involved in a fierce fight as the Germans sought to break the defensive line near the village of Stylos, a few miles south-east of Suda. Layforce HQ's War Diary outlined that Major Ken Wylie, second-in-command of A Battalion, led his men 'in conjunction with some New Zealanders' in a successful counterattack. It was a source of pride to Bob that he stood side by side with the Maoris, helping to drive off the enemy from an advantageous hillside position.

Those efforts bought valuable time for the Allied forces trudging southwards and also allowed for preparations for further Layforce resistance a few miles down the road at Babali Hani. The rural hilly outpost, among the olive groves, saw Laycock's men pounded with mortar bombs as well as targeted by snipers. That night, they were relieved of their rearguard responsibilities as orders came for them to take up defensive positions in the vicinity of the evacuation area. Bob and Eric stayed together, making it to Sfakia where the Royal Navy ferried beleaguered troops to safety. In total, 18,000 were evacuated across four nights from 28 May but, as late arrivals on the island, Layforce was set to be the last fighting force to leave. When Major-General Weston gave orders for surrender to take effect from 1 June, hundreds of commandos were still on Crete. Bob and Eric were among those left stranded – but they were not ready to accept defeat.

● ● ●

Back in Egypt, it had been a depressing and evermore anxious time for Reg. Initially he was frustrated by the 'poisoned bloody leg' that kept him in hospital while his brother and mates embarked on the mission. But Seekings' mood darkened significantly after he was discharged and returned to Geneifa depot where news filtered through of the 'Cretan business', as he termed it. With each passing day, Reg heard more of what had unfolded on the island and his concerns about Bob grew. The gloomiest of thoughts went through his mind. 'I was even so desperate I was planning to desert and walk back to England. I'm not kidding, I was so fed up,' he said. The blackest thoughts of all surrounded how he might explain everything to his parents if ever he were to return home without Bob. Day after day, Reg's responsibility as big brother hung over him, accompanied by the gnawing agony of not knowing.

The miserable brooding came to a head one morning after inflammatory words from a corporal in the Horse Guards regiment. 'Ah poor Seekings, you're never going to see your brother again,' came the taunt. Reg reacted instantly with his fists. 'By Jesus, he never said that again to anybody.' The tactless corporal was 'hit so bloody hard I think he still feels it'. The angry reaction was understandable, but Seekings still received fatigues duties as a punishment for his breach of discipline. Now he had to deal with drudgery along with fears for his brother's safety. But one day when he was busying himself with a sack of tent pegs, he glanced up and saw a familiar figure walking across the desert. 'Musky! Christ, where Musky was, I knew Bob would be. So I told them what they could do with their bloody tent pegs and sure enough, Bob was there, just behind him.'

The sheer relief and joy he felt at seeing his brother and good friend again was tempered by their condition. Eric's usual sportsman's frame was diminished – he had lost 2 stone in weight. Bob was also thinner and nursing a head injury. Both were showing obvious signs of exhaustion, but they were able to proudly share their great escape tale with Reg. Barely had the Allies' 1 June surrender been confirmed on Crete when men began to consider alternatives to life in a prisoner of war camp. Some made for the hills, while others viewed the sea as their best chance of escape. Landing craft used in the evacuation process had been left bobbing just off the beaches of Sfakia, and it was in one of those that a thirty-plus party, including Bob and Eric, made a break for it.

Towing a whaler – a large rowing boat – the craft successfully cleared the bay under a helpful shroud of mist. The plan was to voyage across the Mediterranean and Libyan Sea before landing on friendly shores in North Africa. But only a few of the 180 miles or so had been covered when serious problems began. First, the petrol ran out, leaving the men to drift on a becalmed sea. A shortage of supplies soon became a major issue. The food situation deteriorated to such an extent that Bob resorted to eating toothpaste from his personal pack. At a similar stage it was decided that a group of eight would be sent off in the whaler to double the chances of the escapees being spotted by any passing Royal Navy vessel. Bob was one of those selected, but just before embarking he was knocked out when a splinter-screen (a shield to block shell fragments) came down, smacking into his head. The resulting concussion meant he was not fit to be part of the whaler sub-section. Eric had also been chosen to go on the rowing boat, but Bob asked for his friend to remain with him. The head injury turned out to be a stroke of good fortune for them both. Those that departed on the smaller boat did not return, while the landing craft was eventually spotted and picked up by a Royal Navy ship more than a week after they had fled from Sfakia.

The following month, Bob and Eric's story became the talk of the Fens. 'Ten Days in Open Boat: Little Water, No Food. Soham and Prickwillow Men's Escape from Huns. Amazing Adventures.'

Three headlines, no less, at the top of a page-leading article in 25 July's *Cambridgeshire Times*. Before its publication, Bob and Eric had been in hospital recovering from all they had suffered on Crete and at sea. During the convalescence period both men wrote home to let their families know what they had been up to, without being able to give full details because of security reasons. Bob informed his parents that 'You have the luckiest son in the world.' His upbeat letter went on to explain that he'd had 'plenty of adventure and I will tell you all about it when I get home.'

FRIDAY.   The Cambridgeshire Times   JULY 25, 1941.

TEN DAYS IN OPEN BOAT : LITTLE WATER, NO FOOD.

Soham and Prickwillow Men's Escape from Huns.

AMAZING ADVENTURES.

After drifting for 10 days in an open boat, with no food and very little water, two local men serving with the Middle East Forces have made good their escape from the hands of the Germans.

One of them is 18-year-old Pte. R. W. (Bob) Seekings, son of Mr. and Mrs. A. Seekings, of White House, Ely-road, Prickwillow. The other is Pte. Eric Musk, 23-year-old son of Mrs R. Musk, Millcroft,

"You have the luckiest son in the world," said Pte. Seekings.

Eric Musk lost 2 stones in 10 days.

recovery when their letters were written.

Making headlines in *The Cambridgeshire Times*: news of Bob Seekings' and Eric Musk's amazing escape from enemy clutches reaches the Fens.

But it would be a few more years before any such conversations took place.

Chapter 3

KABRIT ROUGHNECKS

The relief that Seekings felt on seeing his brother return from Crete was in contrast to other news he received later that month. Layforce was to be disbanded. Given its significantly reduced manpower and lack of impact in the North African and Mediterranean theatres, this was unlikely to have come as a major shock to Reg or his fellow commandos at the sprawling Geneifa depot. However, the break-up probably only added to the exasperation he felt during his early times in the desert. By midsummer, the irascibility that occasionally led to him venting with his fists was in danger of being replaced by an enduring bitterness.

Reorganization plans from General Headquarters in Cairo detailed a series of alternative options for the disbanded personnel from A, B and D Battalions (at the time, C Battalion was garrisoned in Cyprus after an operation against the Vichy French at Litani River). One choice allowed men to re-join their original unit or

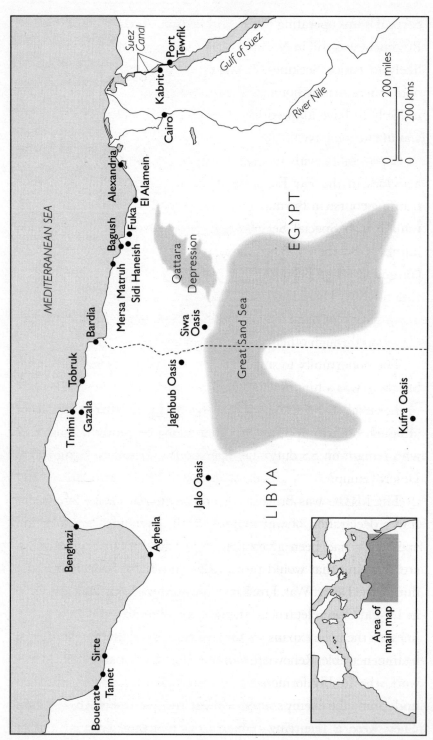

SAS operations in North Africa, November 1941 to September 1942.

corps if it was operating in the Middle East. As the Cambridgeshire Regiment was still in Norfolk in the middle of 1941, this was hardly likely to entice Seekings. Neither would he have considered the option of returning home on compassionate grounds; his father was unlikely to have allowed him over the threshold even if Reg had wanted to come back.

A possibility with more appeal was to volunteer for guerrilla activities in the Far East, which would be preceded by a short training course in Burma. The men were also informed they could remain in a Special Service unit, provided there were sufficient numbers. But there was no guarantee of this, given that 600 Layforce commandos had been lost in Crete plus 120 killed or wounded at Litani River. There had been additional casualties, too, in Tobruk; and a sixty-plus band left behind in Bardia, not to mention further depletion through other causes such as sickness.

The opportunity to stay on came with precious few certainties, but there was a hint of what might be on offer for those who chose to stick it out in North Africa. They were notified that 'It is possible, although no firm decision can be made at present, that personnel who remain on SS duty may later be formed into a Long Range Desert Group.'

The LRDG was Brigadier Ralph Bagnold's special force. After Italy's declaration of war in June 1940, Bagnold – a soldier and explorer – had been given the green light by General Wavell to create a unit that would prove to be invaluable in so many ways during the Desert War. From mid-September of that year, travelling in 1.5-ton Chevrolet trucks, the LRDG began to slip behind enemy lines via the huge expanse of the desert territory that was thought to be impenetrable. Renowned for their navigation and reconnaissance work, the freshly formed detachment's covert journeys saw them undermine the enemy's supply route along the North African coast. They were a recurring menace, destroying aircraft and petrol dumps, as well as engaging in other sabotage initiatives.

Perhaps it was the stories of the LRDG's success that persuaded Seekings not to bother with the Far East mission. Maybe he just felt that North Africa was where the action was and that it was worth sticking around. Either way, in the high summer of 1941 Seekings was among the throng assembled in a large tent at Geneifa where a recently promoted captain outlined plans for a new Special Service unit. This was the quietly spoken David Stirling, whose pitch for a dynamic new force, capable of behind-the-lines warfare, was sufficiently powerful to prompt Seekings to join a line of would-be recruits. Seekings was struck by the Scotsman's intensity. 'He knew what he was up to,' he said. 'You were looking for men that you thought were better than the present ones you were serving under. And he certainly gave us that impression.'

Stirling explained that his new unit was to be dropped into enemy territory to target aerodromes and landing grounds. The work was to be carried out by small raiding parties and might include arrival by parachute. This had been one of Stirling's key selling points weeks earlier when he had persuaded Middle East Headquarters in Cairo to let him establish a detachment of up to six officers and sixty other ranks. The chance to pursue his own longstanding parachutist aspirations was also a reason why Seekings was ready to throw his lot in with the nascent formation. In the first half of 1940, a rise in weight to around 14 stone had stopped him. However, months in the desert on army rations meant that his physique was no longer a hindrance. Instead it was all down to whether he could convince Stirling of his suitability.

The soldier in front of Seekings was asked why he wanted to become a parachutist. 'I'll try anything once,' came the response, but Stirling was clearly unimpressed by the man's flippant attitude. 'Yes, and if you don't bloody well like it, you'll just drop it. I don't want people like you.' The man was promptly dismissed. Now it was

Reg's turn. Thinking on his feet, Seekings outlined that becoming a parachutist had been a long-held ambition. But that alone didn't seem to be enough to convince Stirling. 'I told him I was an amateur champion boxer and did a lot of cycling and running,' he added.

Interview over and the Fenman had passed. 'I was one of thirteen selected from there,' he said. 'We were the first people, apart from a detachment of Guards at Geneifa.' Seekings became a founder member of the newly formed unit that was to be known as L Detachment of the Special Air Service Brigade. Reg once asked his CO about the name and received an enigmatic response, 'You're part of something that doesn't exist!'

The L Detachment title had been supplied by Colonel Dudley Clarke, an innovative and influential figure in charge of military deception in North Africa. Clarke wanted the enemy and its vast network of spies and informants in Cairo and beyond to believe the British were readying a large-scale airborne threat, involving both parachutists and gliders (a K Detachment was already charged with helping to create such an illusion). Stirling's volunteers fitted into Clarke's bigger-picture plans; an actual unit, part of whose remit was to launch surprise attacks from the skies on the supply lines of Rommel's Afrika Korps.

● ● ●

In August, L Detachment began to assemble at Kabrit, located on a headland at the southern end of the Great Bitter Lake. Close by was an RAF aerodrome, as was the naval base HMS *Saunders*.

Kabrit was a far from welcoming place; it was predominantly desert terrain made all the more inhospitable by an invasive wind that often whipped in from the adjacent water, and such was the strength of the summer sun that Seekings' coppery hair tones lightened to almost blond. Yet in other ways it was a landscape that wasn't so far removed from the Fens; Reg was used to wide open space and challenging, changeable weather. Those long, labour-intensive days in the fields had shaped him as a lad. They had taught him to be adaptable and hardened his resilience.

While the conditions could be tolerated, the camp, if it could be called such, was a let-down. On arrival, Reg found only a stores marquee and a couple of other tents. It was hardly an inspiring start, and familiar feelings of disillusion and disappointment from his commando days started to resurface. These intensified when he was part of a group handed picks and shovels and told to put up a tent. This had not been in Stirling's sales pitch: they had been promised no fatigue duties, no guard duties. The tent was duly dumped and the frustrated men headed off to a nearby naval canteen to enjoy some liquid refreshment instead.

More beer was consumed on their return and it was not long before an officer in a kilt emerged to complain about the noise. The officer was told to 'bugger off' before being offered a drink. The hospitality was accepted but the officer later returned with a sergeant to put the dissenters on a charge.

The next morning they found themselves up in front of Sergeant-Major Yates, who demanded to know who had insulted the officer. He outlined that the guilty individual was to be punished and the rest let off the hook – and it was Seekings who stepped forward. 'I elected to be spokesman and told him if that was their attitude, return us back to Geneifa depot. If that was the type of men they wanted in this unit – who'd split on their own mates – then it was time we buggered off. We didn't want to know anything about them.'

Seekings' brazen approach was a gamble but his point had been made. He and the others were told to step outside while the officers considered how to deal with the group. Eventually the dissenters were called back in, instructed to mend their ways and to put the tent up, which eventually they did. But the episode had demonstrated to those who had witnessed it that Seekings was a man of conviction, character and leadership skills – qualities that would serve him well in the SAS.

• ● •

L Detachment, comprising Layforce remnants, contained plenty of men Seekings already knew and he described it as 'a gang of roughnecks'. Stirling concurred: to him they were a 'band of vagabonds'. More than a dozen were from the 7 Commando formation in which Seekings had served. His pal Lance Corporal Bill Kendall, a Yorkshireman who joined the Royal Tank Corps in his mid-teens, had been successful in the selection process. Then there was Phillips who, according to Seekings, lacked in stature and 'wanted to fight every big man he came across, because he thought they were laughing at his size'. As for Austin, he was known for getting excitable when taking a drink. With a couple inside him, 'he always ripped his shirt bit by bit and poured the odd pint over his head,' recalled Reg.

Also among the volunteers from 7 Commando was Hawkins, a typical Cockney in Seekings' eyes. 'On leave he was usually found playing the drums in some cabaret with a trilby hat stuck on the back of his head.' He once came across Hawkins clad in his greatcoat on a blazing hot Cairo day and asked him what the idea was. The private, originally from the West Kent Regiment, opened his coat to reveal he hadn't another stitch on him as somehow the locals had made off with all his other clothing.

Kaufman was another Londoner to switch from the same commando unit. He ended up as the canteen manager, helping L Detatchment's sparse home at Kabrit become better furnished. 'Everything had to be pinched,' said Seekings. 'This is where Kaufman came in. He was very good at scrounging and I used to help him very often do deals; pinch a truck, go off and do a bit of black marketeering to get stuff. We just had to do it, we had nobody helping us.'

Right from the start, Stirling's unit had to use its wits and initiative to get itself up and running. A nearby New Zealanders' camp provided particularly rich pickings for night-time excursions. 'That's where we pinched a lot of our stuff from. We did a raid or two and came back with tents and whatnot and suddenly the place started to blossom. We built a brick canteen – the bricks and stuff were pinched from the Air Force. Eventually we got a marquee up where we could put a bar in; managed to do a bit of fiddling and get a few beers down there occasionally.'

In those early days, the men tended to gravitate towards others from their old commando units: it made sense to stick close to those you knew. However, Seekings also came across familiar faces from 8 (Guards) Commando and 11 (Scottish) Commando, two other formations that had been fertile recruitment grounds. A few days after he arrived, Pat Riley – his old Fenland boxing opponent – jumped off a truck. Riley had come to Kabrit after a spell at the besieged garrison of Tobruk. Another impressive figure who had also been in Tobruk was Jim Almonds. The sergeant had not been long with L Detachment before Seekings noted his proficiency working with wood and his 'deadly accuracy in throwing a small axe'.

Reg was also quick to recognize an officer whose giant frame had been conspicuous a few weeks earlier in Geneifa. There the officer had stuck out not just because of his 6-foot-plus broad physique, but also his attire. The man's shorts were remarkable for their extra length, as were his shirt sleeves, which were worn half tucked-up. 'He was one of the scruffiest officers I'd ever seen,' said Seekings. His name was Robert Blair Mayne – 'Paddy' Mayne – and, at the time, aged twenty-six, had already proven himself in terms of brain and brawn.

Born to the east of Belfast in the town of Newtownards, Mayne was a top-class rugby international, having played as a second row forward for both Ireland and the British Lions prior to the war. He was also an accomplished heavyweight boxer and possessed an academic background having studied law at Queen's University, Belfast, before practising as a solicitor. The outbreak of war cut short Mayne's rugby days and put his legal career on hold as he volunteered for 11 Commando and excelled in the operation at Litani River in June 1941.

It was there that commanding officer Lieutenant Colonel Dick Pedder had been killed. He was succeeded by Geoffrey Keyes, whom Mayne did not hold in the same regard, and before the end of that month the Irishman had both left the commandos and fallen ill with malaria. Through the recuperation period he had his eye on the military mission in the Far East that other Layforce troops had signed up for. But Stirling's persuasive powers resulted in a

Paddy Mayne and friend. The Northern Irishman soon became a hugely-admired figure within L Detachment – although Seekings' initial impression was that he was 'one of the scruffiest officers I'd ever seen'.

change of plan, which is how Mayne came to find himself at Kabrit, heading up L Detachment's 2 Troop that included Seekings.

'He was a great one for the physical side of things, but he was still a bit of a loner, very quiet,' recalled Reg of his early dealings with a man he would come to know extremely well. 'He was so big and huge that people didn't take it on to argue the toss with him. We got along with Paddy. At that stage the only thing that impressed you, really, was his size.'

Seekings saw a good deal more of Mayne than he did of Stirling. In those formative stages, Stirling was often in Cairo taking part in what he described as a 'running battle with Middle East HQ'. He was heavily involved in canvassing for supplies and support, by necessity tapping into extensive social and military connections (his father was a brigadier-general, while his family's ancestral roots had lain for centuries at the Keir House estate in Perthshire) as he sought to establish the new unit. 'He was busy trying to get official blessing; trying to scrounge stuff for us, get us on the map,' said Seekings.

Stirling's absences meant training was left in the hands of his deputy, Lieutenant Jock Lewes. The men could not have had a better instructor. Lewes had been a prime target for Stirling when he was forming the unit. Early in the summer of 1941, he had already carried out parachute jumps, an experimental venture that Stirling joined and in which he suffered injuries requiring hospitalization. Plus, Lewes had proved his mettle in Tobruk, regularly displaying ingenuity and drive when leading his commando section in raids, including at night. The port city might have been under siege, but Lewes still went on the attack with men who didn't think twice about following him.

Lewes' professionalism, intelligence and high standards pushed the new recruits to their limits. So much so that late one night, with everyone else snoring away under canvas, a desperate thought flashed across Reg's mind: 'I'm never going to make it.'

Chapter 4

JAM NOT YAMS

Jock Lewes' early parachute training required men to leap from trucks as they rolled across the sands; a practice not found in any manual, nor one that comes with any recommendation. Indeed, for the recently assembled L Detachment, it was fraught with peril and a constant source of injury. Lewes led from the front – or rather the back. The Welsh Guards officer stood at the rear of the truck and jumped before executing a precision backward roll on landing. This was initially at 15 miles per hour; later it was replicated at speeds of 20 and 25 miles per hour. On each occasion, Lewes would jump and complete his back roll. Others were less inclined to follow suit, seeking alternative exit strategies. Reg was among those who had somehow managed to stay on their feet after departing from the truck, much to their instructor's irritation. 'Drive at 30 miles an hour,' Lewes told the driver. 'I'll guarantee they'll do backward rolls.'

As the truck began to go through the gears, Seekings stood at the tailboard, face opposite to the direction of travel. 'The driver was in his glory. It wasn't 30 miles per hour – he was putting his foot down and laughing like hell.' The would-be parachutist knew if he stepped out, his feet would be whipped from underneath him and he'd be forced into a backwards roll. It was a far from appetizing prospect and in a split second another idea presented itself. Hurling himself over the side, he succeeded only in taking a couple of giant strides before plummeting headfirst into the sand. 'I ploughed the bloody desert up with my face. I was in a hell of a state – the last time I tried to be clever.'

Others ended up with bumps, bruises, scrapes or worse, including troop leader Paddy Mayne. 'Paddy jumped out and you could hear his head hit the deck and thud, half a mile away,' said Seekings.

That the officers and other ranks all undertook the often dangerous and risk-laden training was, in no small degree, down to Lewes. He was not just to the fore in the drills but also set an extraordinarily high technical example of what was required. The men couldn't fail to recognize that in Lewes, who rowed in the 1936 Boat Race for Oxford University, they were being led by a supremely fit and extremely intelligent soldier.

The foundations for their admiration of Lewes were laid in the early days at Kabrit following a confrontation in the mess. Lewes summoned the men there after some had applied to 'Return to Unit' as a result of resentment at the routine of digging and filling in of holes, alongside guard duties. Seekings was among those who sought an RTU. 'To hell with this … we want to go back to our unit,' was his mindset then. As Lewes faced up to the men, he made no attempt to conceal his contempt. In fact, he let them have it: 'You're just bloody yellow – that's how I feel at the moment.' He told them the yellow streak across their backs extended a yard wide before throwing down a gauntlet: 'Prove me wrong!'

Given that some of his audience could turn violent at the slightest provocation, it is hardly surprising that the speech triggered uproar. 'It's a wonder he didn't get killed,' thought Seekings. And yet Lewes' assessment, as he'd doubtless calculated in advance, had the desired effect: the men accepted his challenge.

As part of the mess-room dressing-down at Kabrit, Lewes made it clear he would always be involved in the training process. 'I'll do anything that you do, you do anything that I do.' The message struck a chord. 'When you had a man setting the example, what else could you do, but do it?' said Seekings.

In the days and weeks to come, Lewes turned L Detachment – including all of those who had been ready to jack it in – into a crack force. He designed a programme that kept Seekings, at least, occupied almost around the clock. It was as inventive as it was rigorous, as detailed as it was varied. And it was taxing, designed to weed out those who couldn't cut it at the elite level Lewes knew

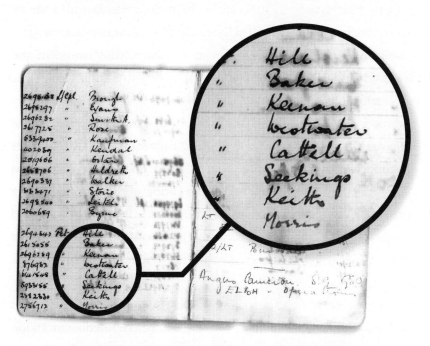

A page from Jock Lewes' original notebook listing some of the very first men of the SAS. Seekings' name is third from bottom.

would be required if the new unit was to land a succession of meaningful blows square on the enemy's nose.

Among the challenges was one that Seekings likened to Kim's Game, the memory test featured in Rudyard Kipling's novel, *Kim*. 'You put so many objects on a table, look at 'em for so long, then leave and come back later on and number them off,' he said. 'You'd gradually step it up; so they'd want to know the make and name – and step up the number of things. We did a lot of that because it was agreed we could take no notes, everything had got to be held in our head. We couldn't write down map reference numbers and all that sort of stuff, so it was memory training. We had a hell of a lot.'

Even the marches, of which there were many, called upon the men to use their wits as well as their feet. The lengthy treks – of 10, 20 or even 30 miles – were focused on more than simply pushing forward fitness levels. Navigational skills were essential if L Detachment were to succeed in the desert, which was a life-or-death environment in itself. Under Lewes' meticulous tutelage the men familiarized themselves with maritime navigation techniques and learned to read the stars at night.

Testing was commonplace with notepads and pencils handed out to help Lewes assess those who were up to standard, or otherwise. Seekings marvelled at the response. 'To see some of the toughest and most unruly men in the army – even if they were deadbeat – keeping their exercise book up to date for Jock Lewes' weekly inspection, it didn't seem true.'

However, this was an aspect that caused concern for Seekings. Indeed, it haunted him in the small hours because of his dyslexia (although, at that time, there was limited recognition of the condition). The extra time he required to complete his paperwork meant he had to work long into the night at the expense of much-needed rest. 'Sleeping, I was a bit worse off than the others,' he said. 'Physically I didn't worry about anybody, but it was the writing, the mental side of it; I thought I was never going to make it. Everybody else was asleep and I'd be struggling away with my notes.'

Yet it could be argued that his dyslexia fuelled as well as frustrated him. Here was the opportunity to prove to others, and also himself, that reading and writing problems were not going to restrict or define him. In his mind, this was a battle he had to win because of the size of the prize at stake. 'I desperately wanted to be a parachutist,' he said. And in the same never-say-die spirit of his boxing days, the only way he'd stop was if they had to haul him off the canvas.

If Reg's struggle with his notes was a private one, his resentment towards the food, or lack of it, was evident to all. Seekings suffered from a ravenous hunger that was never sated. And one dinnertime a blameless orderly ended up with a face full of jam roll as a result.

Marching had left the men lean and 'fit as hell' according to Reg, who was always ready to 'eat a donkey'. Invariably there would be a less-than-filling portion of tinned sausages or herrings in his mess tin at dinner. Seekings had his suspicions that the ascetic Lewes may have had something to do with that.

'The food was terrible and his idea was if you wanted to be a parachutist you'd go through hell to be one. It was just as simple as that. So it was bloody-mindedness all the way through. There was nothing more annoying; you'd been out all night – you'd perhaps covered 40 miles, going like the clappers of hell over the desert – and you came in, absolutely buggered, to a dry bit of bread for your breakfast.'

Seekings became fed up with an endless supply of yams when all he wanted was a bit of jam. He articulated his craving one morning over a less-than-filling breakfast that followed a long night's exertions and was told jam would be part of the afternoon 'tiffin'. Tiffin duly arrived sans jam and Reg's grumbles caught the ear of officer Bill Fraser, who told him he would get some jam that night in a roll which was being prepared for dessert.

'Come dinner time we got our swill, then went up to get jam roll,' said Seekings. 'They had a poor little orderly there – I always feel ashamed of this – and not only did he give me a small bit, but he gave me the end of the bloody roll. There wasn't a bit of jam and I just picked it off the plate and stuffed it straight in his face. Poor little bugger, it wasn't his fault. But I was frustrated, waiting for my jam all this time and that's all I got! So Fraser quickly took me across to the cookhouse and said, "Give this man a meal!" I was going berserk.'

Seekings' suspicion that Lewes was behind the inadequate meals was probably down to the officer's strict controlling of water consumption. As they worked in the desert, men were only allowed to take on water when given permission and often the activities Lewes set had to be completed without once reaching for a bottle. The iron discipline that Lewes required was born of necessity. 'What you'd got to train your mind to do was carry the water and leave the damned stuff alone,' said Seekings. 'Otherwise the whole effect was lost. One old chap joined us and did everything fine, but couldn't do without his water. On one trip I caught him with a length of tubing, pinching the water. Naturally he had to be out.'

Lewes also called in a seemingly never-ending line of experts to help instil an all-important edge. Architects and builders addressed the men on how to identify the structural weak point of a bridge; specialist targets such as railways and even oil rigs were given consideration. Doctors were brought in to offer training 'right up to amputation', said Seekings. 'There was nothing slap happy. Jock was fantastic at organizing all this stuff.'

Lewes combined a splash of genius with an everyday wisdom, exemplified by how he simulated night conditions. This took the form of individuals being blindfolded in daylight hours before tackling tasks posed by Lewes. This enabled him, along with instructors, to identify and then eliminate errors that otherwise might have gone unseen and uncorrected in the dead of night.

'This is the way Jock Lewes carried out his training; this is what made him so damned good,' said Seekings. 'He was a stickler for detail and downright common sense. He kept it plain and simple, the basics. Get the basics and then it all falls into place. But he made them hard, everything was hard. As he told us, the aim should be in training to make it as hard as humanly possible so that when you got on the real job, you found it easy. That built up confidence. And as he said: "The confident man will win".'

Lewes also used those formative weeks in Kabrit to solve an important operational challenge. He created a lightweight, easily portable bomb that would both blow up and catch fire at the same time. It was exactly what was required by parachutists arriving in the dead of night to target the Axis airfields and landing grounds of North Africa.

'He wanted fire and eventually he got it,' said Seekings, who had become accustomed to the almost daily sound of Lewes, off on his own, experimenting close to the camp. The men were having a beer at the time of the Eureka moment. A succession of bangs was suddenly replaced by a jubilant cry: 'I've got it, I've got it!'

En masse, the men forgot their drinks – for once – and hurried to find Lewes in a rare state of elation. His experiments with plane wings scrounged from the RAF, drums of petrol and a formula combining thermite, plastic and oil had at last created a device capable of wreaking havoc on the enemy. 'He was going nuts,' said Seekings. 'That's the only time I've seen him get excited. Apparently he'd had two or three goes before he'd started shouting. Each one – bang!' The assembled men were treated to further demonstrations as the 'Lewes bomb' was officially born. It was to prove a crucial weapon in L Detachment's armoury.

• ● •

On a cold mid-October morning, Seekings shivered in the moments before his maiden parachute jump. But it was not only the dawn chill that caused a quiver as he sat on the floor of the Bristol Bombay, a troop transport aircraft designed for use in the Middle East and India. It was impossible for Reg and his fellow jumpers to banish the thoughts of the two comrades who had plunged to their deaths the previous day. A problem with the Bombay's static line and the respective hooks belonging to Ken Warburton and Joe Duffy had resulted in neither man's chute opening. The exercise was immediately abandoned with an initial rumour flying round that Seekings was one of the two to die. Word reached Pat Riley, triggering a whirl of thoughts. He had swapped chutes with Seekings, having been handed one carrying the number 13. It was not until the two men saw each other later on that Riley realized his superstitions had not resulted in a friend's death.

What happened to Warburton and Duffy left the unit shocked and saddened, but Stirling and Lewes ensured there was no time to brood. The fault was addressed and resolved and everyone was asked to jump the next morning. And as he waited for the dispatcher to send him and his fellow 'stick' (aircraft load) members on their way, Seekings was all too aware of the tense faces around him. He knew the wire and the anchor points had been reinforced but was far from alone in paying close attention to his final checks, shackling himself on to a big U-bolt. Double-checks and treble-checks were carried out. 'We made damned sure it was secure.'

Despite the concerns, every man in L Detachment kept the faith and leapt into the skies. 'We didn't have one failure,' said Seekings. 'This thing we were very proud of in L Detachment. We never had a refusal in jumping.' The unified response to adversity underlined the strength and togetherness within a group that had only been together for a couple of months.

Several volunteers had failed to make it through to that point,

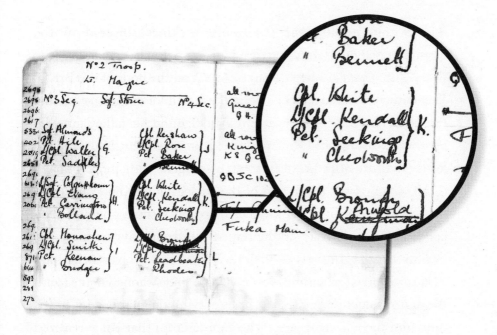

Details of L Detachment's 'No.2 Troop', commanded in the autumn of 1941 by Paddy Mayne. Seekings is in 'K' patrol, part of 'No.4 Sec'.

mainly because they were unable to reach the standards required in training. But all of those who jumped on that highly charged October morning were motivated and tightly knit. What they badly wanted next was an opportunity to prove themselves to everyone else, not least the doubters at Middle East Headquarters.

That chance came with the 'Cairo March', a few days after the dawn drop. Stirling had made a bet with an RAF group captain that his unit, comprised of several small groups, could arrive undetected at Allied base Heliopolis, elude its defence force and 'destroy' aircraft by affixing stickers rather than Lewes bombs. The 'attack' would serve as the ideal dummy run for what lay ahead for the detachment.

The men set off on an approximate 100-mile march across the desert, which was mostly carried out at night to avoid RAF spotter planes. More difficult for the men, as they lay up in the daytime, was coping with the intense heat while limiting water consumption. Each man carried four bottles and Lewes' famous water discipline had been tested to the maximum by the time L Detachment arrived at Heliopolis during the fourth night of the exercise. The raiders had little difficulty in beating the airfield's security measures and sticking labels onto planes before ghosting away to ensure Stirling collected on his wager.

However, towards the end of that march, thirst had begun to play tricks on Seekings. He fought to suppress visions of a refreshing cocktail. 'All I could see on the last day on that trip was a big John Collins dancing in front of my eyes.' The extreme limits that the men were forced to endure were reflected in another memory from the dummy operation. 'Chaps, at the end, filling their water bottles time and again, just to have the satisfaction of seeing the water gurgle out into the sand.'

But L Detachment had displayed its durability and proved itself adept at stealth. Also apparent was the attachment that each man had for the unit. It had not always been the case. Seekings recalled a couple of times, when he and others had been given time off, that they 'went down and created hell in Suez' with barely a thought given to the consequences. 'We were just a gang of rough-necks, who were rough and tough,' said Seekings. 'We just took our fun where we could find it.' Day by day that devil-may-care outlook began to change, replaced by a growing sense of pride in the unit they had joined just months earlier.

This was reflected in the response generated by Stirling's call for suggestions for a cap-badge. Around a dozen or so designs were considered before a 'winged dagger' was approved. Lewes designed separate wings that incorporated a parachute and a motto also emerged: 'Who Dares Wins'.

The men, who by now had completed their training and passed out, were given a choice ahead of their first operation. 'We were given the option of wearing the wings on our sleeves immediately and wearing the cap badge,' said Seekings. 'Or to wait until we came back and wear the wings on our breasts.'

On the face of it, such a decision might have appeared worthy of a coin flip, minimal in its significance. As things turned out, it was anything but. The men agreed on the second option. And by the time Seekings was able to sew those wings on to his breast, their value had risen more than he could ever have imagined.

Chapter 5

A BLOODY BAPTISM

It was 16 November and Reg Seekings was enjoying one of the finest 'slap-up' meals he had ever tasted. His food was served in the officers' mess at Maaten Bagush – between Mersa Matruh and Alexandria, in Egypt – where the British forces had established a huge transit camp not far from the Mediterranean shore. In a few hours Seekings was to jump into the darkness and land more than 100 miles behind the lines as part of L Detachment's maiden operation. As he savoured each mouthful washed down by a welcome beer, a number of thoughts occurred – but one stayed with him. He would look back on the meal as 'rather like the "Last Request",' in the tradition of a condemned man sitting down to good food one final time.

Months earlier, as part of his initial submission to Middle East Headquarters, Stirling had included a plan to support General Auchinleck's upcoming offensive against the German–Italian military alliance. Stirling's proposal was for five 'sticks' (aircraft loads) of parachutists to raid airfields at Tmimi and Gazala on the northern coast of Cyrenaica, east Libya. The men were to be dropped into the desert on a moonless evening, lay up through the following day and then exploit the element of surprise the next night when they would target fighter planes and bombers. The subsequent development of the lightweight Lewes bomb (ready to be activated by a series of differing 'time pencil' detonators) was to give L Detachment exactly what it required to carry out such audacious attacks.

The main elements of Stirling's plan were still in place when his unit arrived at Bagush ahead of Operation Squatter, which was scheduled for the hours prior to the Eighth Army's major 18 November offensive codenamed Crusader. (The Eighth Army, comprised of British and Commonwealth formations, was established in September 1941 and was the main Allied force in North Africa for much of the Desert War.) The SAS men were placed under armed escort and not permitted to speak to anyone beyond their own unit. Having eaten, they were allowed a trip to the canteen where Seekings made a single purchase, a sealed tin of Craven "A" cigarettes, 'for which I was very grateful later'. Once again, they had been accompanied by an escort and the canteen cleared of all other personnel. 'All this made us feel very important,' wrote Seekings. 'Whether it built up or lowered our morale, it's hard to say. I think the general idea was, "OK, we are going to die. So what the hell." Any rate, that's the way the conversation ran.'

The mood was not helped by a grim weather forecast for the evening ahead. Predicted high wind speeds made an already risky night-time parachute jump an even more perilous assignment. A postponement was discussed but given how often disappointment had already beset the Commandos, and that the timing of L Detachment's raid was aligned with the wider Crusader offensive, Stirling was opposed to a delay. So were the men. They stood squarely behind Stirling, showing their support for his stance at a meeting in which he and Lewes addressed them. 'Everybody wanted to jump,' Seekings recalled.

Darkness fell and the men paraded by the five Bombay planes that were to fly them west across the desert. Chutes were fitted and checks carried out, activities which invariably involved an individual with an Indian Army background whom Seekings understood to be the unit's 'welfare officer'. The man had acquired a dubious moniker. 'His main interest seemed to be the checking of jockstraps,' claimed Seekings. 'If you was wearing one, it didn't seem to matter whether your harness fitted or not! Naturally, he was nicknamed "Jock Strap"! It always raised a laugh and eased the tension.'

Earlier that evening, the stick in which Seekings was attached had been given a briefing by Sergeant Ford from the RAF's No.216 Squadron. 'A grand fellow', according to Seekings, Ford was the designated pilot of the Bombay parked alongside an attentive audience. 'He told us he would get "well upstairs" and try and glide in on target with engines cut.' Seekings was due to depart at 19:40 hours in the final plane as one of an eleven-strong section whose target was an airfield at Tmimi. The number one objective for the stick – led by Paddy Mayne – was Messerschmitt Bf 109's, the renowned Luftwaffe fighter plane.

As he waited for the other Bombays to take off, Seekings was left to his own thoughts. The action as a paratrooper he had long yearned for was finally about to happen; an exhilarating prospect and the fulfilment of a long-held dream. Yet there was also a powerful feeling of uncertainty. For all their extensive training and meticulous preparations, he and his pals were heading into the unknown. 'It was a queer sensation seeing them roar away into the darkness, to leave us wondering if we should ever see them again.'

At last, it was time for Mayne's section to depart. The plane in front, under the command of Lieutenant Bonington, had been delayed so it was not until 20:20 hours that Ford had Mayne's section in the air. They had embarked with encouraging words from the ground crew ringing in their ears. 'Give the Jerry hell,' was the chief message as the RAF men shook their hands and wished them luck.

A journey of around two and a half hours initially saw them head out over the Mediterranean before turning south-west and back towards land. Taking up much of the fuselage was an enormous petrol tank installed to extend the aircraft's range. Seekings found the fumes 'terrific'. He would remain forever sensitive to similar smells – something that would benefit him on more than one occasion in the future. But that night the fuel wafts only added to his discomfort in the extremely cramped conditions. Clad in tan overalls on top of standard issue shirt and shorts of a similar colour, he felt freezing. Just yards away was a wide-open door space, the source of a bitterly cold draught and a constant reminder of what lay just around the corner for the plane's passengers. The prospect of facing the enemy suddenly felt very real when searchlights preceded bursts of ground fire. 'Here and there we saw some flak, some rather close.' For the first time in his life, Seekings was experiencing what it was like to come under attack.

Then there was the wind. The worrying forecasts about its strength had proved accurate but there was to be no turning back at the eleventh hour. As Ford took the plane down through thick, low cloud and ever nearer the drop zone, a red light signalled and the men checked each other's kits before hooking up: in sixty seconds' time Seekings would find out exactly how forceful that wind had become. Months of training were about to kick in, yet nevertheless he experienced 'a funny sensation'. With the eleven men packing the space by the door, it hit him that he was about to infiltrate enemy country.

Once his chute had opened without a hitch, Seekings was aware of his comrades in close proximity as they descended. But that sense of reassurance was swiftly dismissed by a series of 'bangs and flashes' from below. The cause became a subject for later debate. It was suggested that the blasts emanated from separately dropped equipment containers carrying Lewes bombs, detonators, weapons and other supplies, which exploded as they thumped to the ground. Corporal 'Geordie' White (Royal Scots) took a different view. He landed revolver in hand having somehow removed it from under his overalls as he dropped. Seekings was also convinced that he was being shot at and subsequently heard how there were gun emplacements in the vicinity, 'which proved to my satisfaction it was gunfire'.

Either way, the fireworks were unsettling for the parachutists. But Seekings soon had more pressing concerns: fierce winds of 30 miles an hour and upwards caught hold of him just as he was nearing the ground. He crashed down a split second later and felt himself being dragged – face upwards, legs floundering like a stricken insect – across the desert at an alarming speed.

The entrenching tool that was attached to his backside was caught on the lift-web of the chute; he was trapped, unable to shake himself free. 'I struggled and struggled and I'd just about given up.' Confronted by the very worst of thoughts, Seekings' fighting instincts helped him summon strength for another effort to extricate himself. This time he managed to flip over on to his front but the wind was still pulling him around like a helpless rag doll.

At one point he ripped through a large thorn bush headfirst, which stripped off swathes of skin. His face was badly lacerated and damage to his eyes left him fearing for his sight. 'It was murder.' And yet the searing pain he experienced may just have been what saved him. As the blood poured, his internal fire raged and he tapped into a fresh pool of strength that at last enabled him to break free.

Seekings had become detached from the rest of Mayne's section, many of whom had experienced their own troubles on landing.

Reg sat for a while to recover and gather his thoughts. His face, hands and fingers were a bloody mess but the most important thing was that he could still see. With his breath back, he put the entrenching tool to good use and buried his chute. 'After I finished, I could hear someone else busy – it was Kendall.' Unfortunately, his pal was in a worrying state, restricted by a suspected broken ankle. 'We then followed our tracks until we picked up everyone or they picked us up.'

Regrouping had proved comparatively easy but the same could not be said of finding their equipment. Several containers were missing, although a couple of Thompson submachine guns were located, as was a pack containing blankets and food. It was a pretty slim haul with which to proceed, plus the section's manpower was about to be reduced. Along with Kendall's ankle problem, Doug Arnold had sustained a serious knee injury, giving rise to a tough call. 'Much against everybody's will it was decided to leave them and pick them up on the return journey,' explained Seekings. 'So we shook hands knowing it was a poor chance of ever seeing them again.[1] Then we marched and we were behind time, so we had to push along pretty fast.'

With dawn drawing nearer, the depleted and exhausted section came to a dried-out riverbed known as a wadi. Satisfied that they were in the target zone, Mayne's men stopped for some much-needed sleep. But their rest was interrupted not long after daybreak by the sound of aircraft. Italian Ghibli reconnaissance planes were in the skies, alerted by the events of the night. 'This worried us a bit – we thought that something had gone wrong,' remembered Seekings, who had hidden in the bushes that populated the channel-like area. But their anxieties about the enemy were soon to be replaced by

---

1 Kendall and Arnold fell into Italian hands the day after jumping and became prisoners of war. Both escaped in 1943 and returned to the SAS.

a further intervention by the elements; only it was not high winds returning. This time, black clouds gathered and merged; the men had landed in the eye of a monumental storm.

As the hours passed and dusk drew in, the rainfall became ever heavier to the point where Seekings and his comrades were endangered by a flash flood. 'All of a sudden the water was rushing down and next thing we were chest high in water. What was a dry desert was a raging torrent.'

Mayne's leadership qualities shone through as he urged his men onto nearby high ground. There they huddled together and tried to shelter from rain so heavy that it battered their heads if they so much as peeked out from beneath shared blankets. Mayne also advised them to take the merest sips from their flask of rum. 'For God's sake don't guzzle it,' he said, knowing full well that anyone who did so risked falling into a sleep from which they might never awaken. 'I've never been so cold in my life,' said Seekings, who offered around cigarettes from his tin of Craven "A" to help boost morale.

The rain had eased by the morning when it soon became clear that any hopes of fulfilling their objectives had gone. The equipment they had collected on landing had been washed away or rendered useless by the torrents. All that remained was the odd grenade and the men's personal weapons; not nearly enough to mount a raid on an aerodrome. And, as Seekings observed during the long, saturated hours of the previous night, there was another reason why an attempt to reach the target seemed a hopeless pursuit: the enemy now knew they were there. 'At Z hour the 'drome was lit up with flares, etc, and it seemed pretty obvious that the game was up. Jerry had got wind of us.'

Yet there was one man in the party who was reluctant to give up: Mayne. He spoke of going in on his own to try and destroy at least one plane and it was a while before he was persuaded to change

The returnees from Operation Squatter. Seekings is pictured fifth from the right, back row; Stirling (sunglasses) is in the centre.

his mind. 'You couldn't knock an aircraft out with a grenade,' said Seekings. 'Or you might if you got into the cockpit, but what chance did you have of getting into a bloody cockpit on your own … and in daylight too?'

Instead, it was decided that the nine men should withdraw to a pre-arranged rendezvous point (RV) where the LRDG had been tasked with picking them up. The long march through sodden red mud proved challenging and, in keeping with everything else that had unfolded, was not without incident. Seekings had an uncomfortable encounter, in more ways than one, after diving for cover as reconnaissance planes passed overhead. 'Unfortunately, I picked a bush with a damn great snake in. I don't know which frightened me the most – plane or snake. Still, I was able to kill the snake.'

He probably wished he'd taken the dead reptile with him as a potential meal because soon the men were starving hungry and relying on muddy pools of water to ease their thirst. Seekings later recalled that 'it was then we started to bless the storm'. Proper rest was also not an option. 'It was too cold to sleep for more than a few minutes at a time.' The men's injuries were also worsening, making each mile a painful one. Seekings began to lose track of time; was it the third day of marching? As he trudged on, a bitter wind lashing his weary body, there was one thing he was certain of: he was in a pretty poor shape, as were others around him such as Corporal Dave Kershaw, who was nursing a broken arm. But Mayne succeeded in keeping them on the right path, both literally and figuratively. This was underlined deep into their march when it was agreed that they had come upon a set of tracks from another L Detachment section, which appeared to be heading in a different direction to the one Mayne's men were taking. After already walking for days and nights, a wrong call at that stage would have had serious consequences. 'Thank God we had in Paddy a fine leader who could make a decision and stick to it,' Seekings wrote. 'We kept to our course.'

Mayne's judgement was vindicated early that evening when Seekings' sharp eyes spotted one of the lights set up by the LRDG to help guide in the returnees. Not everyone agreed with him. 'They reckoned it was a star. I said, "But bloody stars move!" Eventually I got Paddy's backing.'

Confirmation came just after dawn on 20 November with the identification in the distance of the LRDG's signal fire. Relief swept through the small band, who suddenly discovered a new lease of life. However, through the very last steps of the gruelling trek, Mayne's composure and clear thinking once again were to the fore. As a truck travelled towards them, he ordered his section to take up an 'extended line and to fight it out if it was Jerry'. It wasn't long though before the long beards of a New Zealand patrol from the LRDG became apparent; at last, the march was over. His Craven "A"'s long since smoked, Seekings gratefully accepted a cigarette from a Kiwi. 'They were good; didn't even bother to speak until they had given us cigarettes and we had them pulling well.'

Seekings was one of just twenty-one SAS men who returned from the fifty-five that boarded the five Bombays on the evening of 16 November. Most of the twenty-one, including Seekings, feature in a photograph taken shortly after they had reached the rendezvous. It is an intriguing study and at the centre is Stirling, towering over everyone, sunglasses on and hands on hips. Although it is a group picture, two men in particular appear to be somewhat isolated. Mayne is just behind and to the left of Stirling, facing away from the unit's commanding officer (CO). Also on the back row and fifth from the right is Seekings. Although the image is grainy, he seems detached from those around him; his focus is solely on the camera. With cap comforter pushed back on his head, Seekings' expression – maybe due to sheer exhaustion – is impenetrable, giving no indication of the extraordinary events he'd lived through in the previous four days or so.

Of those who didn't make it back to the RV, four died or were lost at the drop zones and one further man suffered fatal injuries after the plane carrying Bonington's stick came under fire, forcing it down in the desert. Many others were captured or injured – both, in some instances. 'You felt bloody sorry about it and terribly disappointed,' said Seekings. 'Not so much at losing the men, in a sense, but that we achieved nothing.'

It was true that not a single Lewes bomb had found its way onto an enemy aircraft. Also, the already-small unit's manpower had been reduced by more than half. No wonder that Stirling – among others – regarded Squatter as 'a complete failure'. However, as all the returnees reflected upon an unsuccessful operation, a glimmer of hope emerged in terms of a lesson learnt that would lead to a fresh dynamic. Stirling realized that the risky business of parachuting, especially night jumps, was not the only way to get in behind the enemy's lines: if the desert experts from the LRDG could successfully pick up his unit from an operation, then surely they could also drop the men off beforehand?

Stirling raised the subject with Seekings as they scoured the desert for stragglers. The pair had headed out together from the RV and found a high point where they spent much of a day passing binoculars back and forth. It proved a fruitless exercise, but Seekings listened intently as Stirling outlined his admiration for the LRDG. 'Why, I don't see any sense in parachuting in when this is so much simpler and far, far more efficient,' exclaimed Stirling. 'This will be the ideal thing; if we can get these people to ferry us up, we can walk in whether it's 10, 20, 50 miles.'

Seekings was buoyed by Stirling's vision. The dreams of success harboured by those who flew from Bagush airfield days earlier, were still attainable. While Seekings' verdict on the operation was that it had indeed 'achieved nothing', he also recognized that it had not all been for nothing. 'We didn't have any success against the enemy but it put within our grasp the means of attacking – and attacking in a sure manner.'

Gone were the hit-and-miss vagaries and variations that could occur with parachuting in at night. Instead, L Detachment was about to ride the desert in partnership with the equally innovative and determined men of the LRDG. 'It perhaps wasn't so glamorous but we weren't glamour boys,' assessed Seekings. 'We wanted to do a job.'

Chapter 6

TARGET TAMET

On 1 December 1941, Stirling saw fit to give Seekings his first promotion. Reg rose to acting corporal, as confirmed in his Soldier's Service and Pay Book. Stirling may well have been impressed by the young soldier's overall demeanour during the long hours the pair spent together gazing into the desert for stragglers after the failure of Squatter. But Seekings' upgraded rank probably stemmed, as much as anything, from the number of men that died or were injured or captured in the SAS's first operation. The losses meant that Stirling needed to reorganize to keep alive his severely depleted unit. He also required results – and fast – to prevent the naysayers in Cairo from attempting to disband L Detachment. Which explained why its remnants swiftly found themselves back in transit in early December. Stirling had hatched fresh plans and once more his men were bound for the desert wilderness, heading to a new forward operating base at Jalo Oasis.

The first leg of the journey involved a flight to Bagush, part of which brought back a few unwanted memories for Seekings as another sandstorm whipped up to make for an uncomfortable descent into the airfield. He took reassurance that his old friend Sergeant Ford was again in the cockpit and in due course the plane made it down safely. Further scrapes of a different type unfolded over the following hours as members of the travelling party sought to kill time ahead of flying south-west the next day. After a few beers had been consumed, a raid on the RAF officers' mess resulted in two men stealing VAT 69 whisky and bringing it back to L Detachment's tent.

The plot thickened when the squadron leader paid a visit to his overnight guests. The man – 'a grand chap with a big black handlebar moustache' – had also consumed a fair few drinks and introduced himself as 'Pussy Arse Pete'. He began to offer around his whisky … which was none other than VAT 69. L Detachment realized it was the well-oiled squadron leader they had robbed, unbeknownst to him at that stage.

A comical situation began to get out of hand when boisterous SAS man Arthur Warburton set off back to the mess, ready to regale those there with details of the whisky theft and bluntly ask the officers 'what the heck they was going to do about it?' At this point Seekings decided he needed to step in. Rushing to the mess, he got there just as Warburton was preparing to spill the beans. 'I had to hit poor old Warburton,' was Reg's recollection of how he snuffed out a potential storm in a whisky glass.

That was not quite the end of it though. Jock Lewes got wind of what had occurred and was in no mood for brushing the matter under any carpets. The following morning the SAS training officer let rip at his men, peppering them with insults. According to Seekings, 'He was more than disgusted. As far as he was concerned, we were "delinquent idiots" and "blackguard criminals".' The irony was, despite all efforts to ensure otherwise, Pussy Arse Pete did find out about the pilfering of his VAT 69. But Seekings recalled how he was 'the only man who seemed to take it OK'. Proof that the squadron leader was indeed 'a grand chap'.[2]

In delivering his verdict on their behaviour and character, Lewes also outlined how the men were about to have the opportunity to show him otherwise. Later that day they flew on to Jalo, a newly acquired Eighth Army supply outpost from where a series of operations in partnership with the LRDG were to be launched.

Jalo was a fortress oasis that had been captured from the Italians by Brigadier Denys Reid's E-Force. It was by no means a picture postcard location – as other oases in the region were – but it was ideally situated for mobile raiders. To the north and north-west, ranging from around 150 miles away to more than double that distance, lay a meandering line of Axis airfields and landing grounds dotted around the Gulf of Sirte which could be accessed – and hopefully penetrated – with the assistance of the LRDG. In December it was agreed that the SAS were to disrupt Rommel's lengthening lines of communication by targeting aerodromes, depots and supply dumps. This would help pave the way for a fresh Eighth Army offensive scheduled for the same area.

It was early morning on 8 December when a convoy of five Ford trucks set out for Sirte, located deep inside enemy country in Tripolitania, western Libya. Seekings, with not much more than his toothbrush in terms of personal comforts, was on the job. A journey of around 350 miles gave him a first opportunity to take in an alien landscape that he would later grow to love. Operation

---

2   Other writers have linked this story to the countdown to Operation Squatter. Seekings' handwritten account documents how he recalled it taking place prior to L Detachment travelling to Jalo Oasis ahead of the second operation. His reference to Warburton supports Seekings' chronology of events as Warburton's name does not appear in the five sticks listed for the first operation (November 16–17). Also, Bob Lilley's account (most likely completed in the decade postwar) aligns with Seekings' recollection on the timing of the incident.

Squatter had revealed the desert in its most deadly light, when only survival mattered. But the first couple of days of travelling on a truck piled high with fuel, ammunition, food and water allowed Seekings to scan the extraordinary expanse and absorb it. Banks of dunes aside, all the eye could see was mile after mile of sand, stones and rocks.

Some of those stones were sharp enough to puncture a truck's tyres; some of the sand was so treacherous a vehicle could sink without warning. When that happened, invariably the men had to pile off and use steel sand channels to help get it mobilized again. The fluctuating terrain was another factor. Smooth progress at 50 miles per hour could be disrupted in less time than it took to strike a match. However, the SAS's companions from a Rhodesian S Patrol of the LRDG were ingenious at managing travel in the highly demanding conditions. They were also adept at using the sun and the stars to plot a course across ground without even the clue of a camel track to provide a steer. Not least, the LRDG were good company around the campfire in the evenings.

The relaxed nature of the first few days in transit changed abruptly one lunchtime. A Ghibli had spotted the convoy. The silence of the desert was shattered by the sound of gunfire as those on the ground took aim skywards. The Ghibli replied by dropping two bombs – both of which missed their target – before heading off to safety.

The travelling contingent swiftly sought cover in a patch of scrub a few miles away, aware that the brief confrontation was unlikely to be the end of the matter. Sure enough, a small party of Italian aircraft were soon buzzing up above in the skies. Not for the last time, Seekings understood what it was like to be a hunted man. The sustained rat-a-tat-tat crackle of machine guns was all the men could hear for what felt like ages as the planes flew back and forth, strafing the area. Eventually silence returned with the aircrafts' ammunition spent and the raiding party emerged from their hiding places, breathing a collective sigh of relief. This time they were unscathed, but they also understood their presence was no longer a secret from the enemy.

Despite no longer possessing the element of surprise – a key asset for any raider – the convoy still had a trump card in the shape of LRDG navigator Mike Sadler. The twenty-one-year-old Englishman, who had moved to Rhodesia in his mid-to-late teens, was to become renowned for delivering the SAS to their targets. The first time he did so was guiding in Stirling's party to within striking distance of Sirte. It was at that point Stirling chose to split the group. He was to hit Sirte, while Paddy Mayne was detached in a six-strong section, including Seekings, to proceed a few miles west in search of the landing ground at Tamet. The others under Mayne's command were Sergeant Edward MacDonald (Cameron Highlanders) and parachutists Tom Chesworth (Coldstream Guards), A. T. Hawkins (Royal West Kent Regiment) and Harold White (Royal Army Service Corps). The last-named boasted impressive pre-war sporting credentials. White had been a very promising footballer, playing for West Bromwich Albion in 1938–39.

The LRDG, soon to become known as the 'Libyan Desert Taxi Service' by their roguish passengers, continued with their support and not just with transport to and from the target. One of the patrol ventured off on a recce, leaving Mayne's party to lie up in a nearby wadi. The exercise proved worthwhile as the LRDG man eventually returned with positive news. 'He had seen a lot of fighter aircraft land farther on,' Seekings recalled. 'So we decided that should be our target.'

As the afternoon of 14 December turned to early evening, the raiders closed in to within a handful of miles of their objective. A couple of trucks weaved their way around salt marshes and between low-level dunes before Mayne's sub-section jumped off at 18:30 hours to cover the remaining distance by foot. After darkness had fallen and they had been walking for half an hour or so, Seekings' strong sense of a particular smell kicked in. It was octane – no doubt in his mind. 'I hated the smell and could smell it for miles.' He tried to share his suspicions with his sergeant, who chose to ignore him. In his written reflections, Seekings does not name the sergeant, but is highly likely to be referring to Edward MacDonald, a man whose 'coolness and steadiness' later that night resulted in him being decorated with a Distinguished Conduct Medal. Perhaps the sergeant did not believe Reg possessed such a keen nose for aircraft fuel or maybe there was a deeper clash of personalities between the two. After all, Seekings was not everyone's cup of tea, nor was he the type to swear quietly under his breath if he could curse over it. Either way, the party pushed on without Seekings' hunch being followed up.

With the long march continuing and a winter desert night enveloping them, the raiders became 'browned off', according to Seekings, who heard talk about turning back. But he knew, surely as they all did, that L Detachment simply could not afford another fruitless assignment. A result was required to ensure its future. Scanning through the darkness, something caught his eye – a marker of some sort. A closer inspection revealed a concrete post that he was convinced indicated the end of a runway, but once again his theory ended up falling on deaf ears, adding to his earlier frustration. However, it was not long before Mayne's marauders all but bumped into a couple of Italian troops. The close encounter indicated they were deep inside the aerodrome and, shortly afterwards, sight of an occupied building confirmed the same.

Mayne decided that he, MacDonald, Chesworth and Hawkins would investigate. At the same time, the Irishman told Seekings and Chalky White to 'have a shufti' at a smaller hut nearby.

'Chalky and I crept up to our objective,' Reg recalled. 'We must have been fifty yards away when hell broke loose. Paddy and co had just walked up to the door [of the larger hut], kicked it open and opened fire on the inmates.'

Adding to the mayhem, the building that Seekings and White were stalking suddenly burst into life. Fixed lines of tracer fire forced the L Detachment duo to 'jump or crawl' to avoid being cut down. An adrenalin-fuelled dash saw the pair reach the hut just as an Italian was beetling along in the opposite direction on all fours. The bizarre sight amused Seekings. 'I have never seen anyone move so fast!'

It was to be a brief distraction. Mayne and his team had shot up the larger building before reconvening with Seekings and White. Their exertions were far from over, however. Seekings still had a bee in his bonnet about aircraft being nearby and shared his thoughts with the patrol's officer. 'So we retraced our footsteps and at last I spotted a plane – it was the CR.42 [an Italian single-seat fighter].' Mayne's reaction was to set about demolishing the plane – by hand! 'I thought Paddy had gone mad as he dived in the cockpit. He ripped the dashboard clean out; how he done it, I shall never know. I don't think any of us had ever been so excited before. Our first aircraft; I'm afraid none of us acted the true Englishman.'

The SAS were finally on the scoreboard and more was to come. Similar to the dummy operation at the RAF aerodrome of Heliopolis a couple of months earlier, the men ran amok among unguarded aircraft. This time, though, they were not merely slapping harmless labels onto their targets. Feverishly, they rushed to plant their Lewes bombs, activating the time-fuses that would allow them to complete their work before exiting the scene. 'It was one plane after another,' explained Seekings. 'All fighters and dive-bombers, petrol and bomb dumps until we were nearly out of bombs.'

There was one other important consideration for the raiders:

it was imperative they allowed sufficient time to get back to the rendezvous point to escape before daylight returned. However, Mayne and Seekings were not prepared to leave until every last bomb had been deployed, so they took what remained and set off on their own in search of yet more planes. 'We found another four, the last being a Stuka for which we had no bomb. Paddy went at the cockpit. I was underneath trying to find the petrol cock, thinking to drain some off and set fire to it that way. While I was searching, Paddy joined me saying he couldn't find the undercarriage release gear. In our excitement, he had forgotten the Stuka had a fixed undercarriage for which I was thankful, being under it at the time!'

Still hell-bent on destruction, Seekings climbed into the Stuka's cockpit and tried to rip out the dashboard. He'd been inspired by Mayne's furious antics with the CR.42 earlier, but despite his best efforts, the Stuka's dash was not for budging. 'I couldn't shift it, so I smashed it with my revolver.' Not quite as satisfying as Mayne's eye-popping display of brute force. And indeed, the whole episode would have wound up badly for Seekings were it not for an intervention by the giant from County Down. Somehow Seekings managed to get caught on his own lanyard (seemingly a cause of endless irritation) while jumping down from the Stuka. Much to his relief, Mayne had his back. 'I was helpless until Paddy came and got me free.' At last, the pair concluded it was time to steal away and get in position to witness the anticipated explosive scenes.

Whether through sheer exhaustion after hours on the go, bravado, or a sign of their composure, Mayne and Seekings stopped for a smoke on reaching the edge of the drome. Settling into a bush, they took a break to 'watch the fun'. But before their fag break could be finished, they realized unwanted company was on its way – a group of Italians were heading straight for them.

On the move again, it was not long before their hunters became distracted by other events. 'We hadn't gone 50 yards when up went the first plane. We stopped to look, but as one went up near us we had to run for it. After a while we felt fairly safe and stopped for another look. What a sight; planes exploding and burning all over. Then, the petrol and bomb dumps went off with a terrific roar.'

The LRDG patrol members waiting at the rendezvous were also jubilant: it was a firework display like no other and they had a grandstand seat. They began flashing a light at regular intervals to help the raiders home in on the collection point. However, the enemy also began to signal in similar fashion, which confused Mayne and Seekings, who had packed away their compass. For a while they wandered off course until eventually resorting to plan B: whistles. 'We blew ours, to be answered nearby – much to our relief.'

It was after 01:00 hours when at last they spotted the friendly faces of the LRDG and their trucks. At that point, Seekings' number one priority was to source a badly needed drink. 'I was gasping. We had no water with us and Paddy had set a cracking pace.' It wasn't long before the LRDG's Sergeant Jackson offered him one of the large water bottles the Rhodesians used. A grateful Seekings took a 'long, big drink from it'. Far too late he realized that it wasn't water he'd just guzzled, but neat rum. 'In minutes I was three parts to the wind. I staggered to my truck and went to sleep in spite of the rough going.'

The difficult travelling conditions made for slow progress and the situation wasn't helped when, after around half a dozen miles, the steering went on one of the trucks. The fitter was called and Seekings awoke to the sound of hammering and swearing. The delay was unsettling, but there was no sign of any pursuers. It backed up what had been apparent hours earlier during the raid: the enemy simply did not expect the British Army to turn up in their own backyard and had been utterly unprepared for any such eventuality.

When the Tamet team was finally underway again, it was

down to Mike Sadler to plot the path back out into the deep desert where Holliman was transporting Stirling and the others. They had largely been out of luck at Sirte but the illuminations from further west informed them that Mayne's section had very definitely introduced themselves to the Axis.

Stirling's crew were first back to the rendezvous and decided on an appropriate greeting when Mayne's raiders returned. Sure enough, late on the morning of 15 December – and a full week after the convoy had set forth from Jalo – the desert skies were blasted with round after triumphant round. The voluble reception party was almost too much for the weary Seekings. 'They started to fire everything. God, we nearly died of shock. We thought they had mistaken us for enemy, but luckily they were firing into the air to give us a royal welcome.'

After more than two years at war in which his pent-up frustration had often driven him to distraction, Seekings had tangible success to savour. The SAS War Diary's report on the operation states that fourteen aircraft had bombs placed on them; a further ten had their dashboards damaged. Blowing up the petrol dump was another significant win that was listed on the record.

Travelling back across the desert to Jalo, Seekings had time to process a blur of events. Once the initial elation had given way to deeper reflection, he must have enjoyed a significant confidence surge. Earlier in the year he had returned from the Layforce raid on Bardia with nothing to show for it apart from a minor injury that became infected. Then, in November, he had endured the wretched experience that was Operation Squatter. But at Tamet it had turned out to be third time lucky. Mayne's section had taken a momentous step in delivering on the original template that saw L Detachment assembling at Kabrit less than four months earlier. And, in what would have been his father Albert's assessment, Seekings had also done his duty. On top of that, he had proved himself to himself. He knew that if called on for similar action in the future, he wouldn't hesitate. Which was fortunate, because Seekings' feet had barely hit the ground in Jalo before he was back on a truck, celebrating the Christmas of 1941 on route for the Gulf of Sirte once more.

Chapter 7

FOES TO FRIENDS

J ohnny Cooper had an easy-going charm and an engaging smile. He also possessed guts in abundance.

Born and raised in Leicester, Cooper had moved to Bradford to work in the wool trade when war broke out. Initial efforts to enlist proved unsuccessful on account of his age – he had barely turned seventeen – but undeterred, he still found a way in. A couple of half-crowns dropped into a recruiting sergeant's hands helped him join the Scots Guards. It was an example of the initiative that would serve Cooper well in a military career that would prove long and glowing. In the war years he rose from private to captain; during those times he also became best pals with fellow SAS Original Reg Seekings.

On the face of it, the two men had little in common. Indeed, their respective characters seemed 'so different' to Mike Sadler, who first came across them during the Sirte-Tamet operation in mid-December 1941. The ace navigator's take on Seekings was that he was 'a bit rough and ready'; the type of individual who 'sounded tough' and was also 'quite difficult to get to know'. It was a different story with Cooper, possessor of a kindly face and an evident warmth. 'Johnny was a more sociable kind of chap,' Sadler said. 'Quite a smart, educated chap.'

That Seekings and Cooper didn't get on in the early days of L Detachment was hardly surprising given the lack of common ground between them. 'When John and I first met, we hated each other's guts,' said Seekings. 'I was the country yokel, he was the public schoolboy,' a description that is not entirely accurate. Seekings was a long way removed from any farm-hand stereotype and Cooper, while well-spoken and more worldly – he had been mountaineering in Chamonix just prior to the war – attended a grammar school where, by his own admission, his education was 'hardly a resounding success'.

Seekings' resentment towards his fellow private came to a head after the ill-fated first job. The remnants of L Detachment were on their way back to Kabrit via the oasis at Jarabub where they had been transported by the LRDG's R1 Patrol. Cold and exhausted, their mood was not helped by the vast number of flies that populated the place – 'more than I've ever seen before or since', Seekings later remarked.

Thoughts turned to settling down for some much-needed sleep as the beleaguered bunch drew a couple of blankets each. Seekings temporarily left his bedding and went off for a chat elsewhere. On returning, the red mist descended as he discovered his blankets had gone. 'Naturally, I went round and was checking the number of blankets everybody had got and woe betide the bastard that had extra.'

'Go and bloody well lay down,' was Cooper's response when the blanket probe arrived at his makeshift bed. It was all that was needed to tip Seekings over the edge. 'You get on your feet, you bastard, and I'll knock your bloody block off – big, bloody mouth. I've had enough of you.' Perhaps wisely, Cooper chose to remain where he was and no blows were traded. Even so, the mutual antipathy was evident again just before Christmas.

For the first time, the duo were bound for an operation as part of the same section. Seekings and Cooper – still a teenager at the time – found themselves on a truck heading for a swift return to Sirte and Tamet. Neither did much to disguise a mutual loathing as the hours in transit crawled by. 'We weren't happy, I'm telling you,' said Seekings. 'We didn't speak, we looked daggers at each other all the way up.'

And yet the pair were soon to discover that when it mattered most they shared a crucial similarity: neither shirked from the high-adrenalin moments that came during action. In fact, both appeared to relish them. Differences in class and education soon held little relevance as past petty issues were swept aside. 'They liked doing ops,' said Sadler. 'I think that was the thing that drew them together.'

Their first raid alongside each other was intended to be on the airfield at Sirte, under the command of David Stirling. Seekings' success in the first Tamet operation had clearly been noted. He was now going into action alongside the CO in a five-strong party that also included Sergeant Jimmy Brough and Lance Corporal Charlie Cattell. Meanwhile, Mayne was to have a second crack at Tamet. And, in almost a repeat performance of the events of almost a fortnight earlier, his patrol laid lethal Lewes bombs on twenty-seven aircraft, as well as taking out two trailers laden with spare parts for planes. In addition, petrol dumps were blown up. All in all, it was another stunning night's work for Mayne's party.

Stirling's group was considerably less successful in fulfilling its objectives. Working in partnership with the S1 Patrol of the LRDG, they were held up after dropping off Mayne's party by a procession of German trucks and heavy armour heading down the coastal road towards Rommel's new front at Agheila, some 200 miles to the east. It was a while before the SAS could move to within a handful of miles of Sirte where lines of enemy vehicles were camped either side of the road. However, time was ticking..

The last couple of miles were completed easily enough on foot. But there were soon fresh challenges that put paid to plans of explosives being planted on aircraft at Sirte that night. First, the section encountered a newly erected perimeter fence; then their progress was checked at a roadblock, with Seekings recalling that they 'came up against sentries'. It wasn't long before the alarm was raised and the airfield was bathed in floodlight. There was nothing else for it; they had to make a swift return to the awaiting LRDG personnel, who themselves were parked up in close proximity to the Germans.

Not that the raiders had any intention of departing the scene without leaving a calling card. Axis troops received the rudest of early-hours awakenings as the SAS party let fly along the coastal road. Enemy transport spread over miles came under fire from Thompson submachine guns and Bofors guns. Official reports stated that trucks were blown up and explosives took out a couple of large lorries. The final scorecard didn't come anywhere close to matching the feats of Mayne's crew at Tamet, but the departure from Sirte was stirring stuff nonetheless. It was concluded in near-theatrical style with the LRDG trucks heading off road and vanishing into the desert just as dawn was breaking.

Seekings and Cooper's respective accounts are intriguing in their differences. In Seekings mind it had been merely 'a bit of action' – certainly not on a similar scale to his earlier exploits with Mayne. Cooper recalled the incident in a far more vivid manner. He wrote about 'shooting up enemy traffic on the road which we left behind us in a total confusion of blazing vehicles'. What was not in doubt, however, was the change in how they viewed one another from that night onwards. As a shared experience, it proved transformative. 'He'd got guts, I'd got guts and we just clicked,' said Seekings.

As daylight returned, two Messerschmitts circled in the skies, doubtless sent out to hunt down the behind-the-lines fighters. On this occasion, the party on the ground went undetected and the chat turned to the previous evening's activities. 'John spoke – and Jimmy Brough,' said Seekings. 'We got talking about that night; it was quite exciting and what-not. Then John turned round to me and said: "What are you doing when you're on leave?"' From barely being able to stomach the sight of one another, Seekings and Cooper were trading tales and planning to spend a few rare days of downtime together. It was a serious 180-degree about-face from both parties.

Cairo beckoned, but before they could get there the SAS was to be dealt a setback of enormous proportions.

A couple of days after the Sirte-Tamet party set off, Jock Lewes and Bill Fraser embarked with their respective sticks to attack an airfield at Nofilia, plus another known as 'Marble Arch'. Nofilia turned out to be a disappointment – forty-plus Stukas flew out before Lewes and his men could touch them. There was nothing for it but to make the RV with Morris' T2 Patrol of the LRDG.

Next stop was the arranged collection point with Fraser's team, but the small convoy never got there. Mid-morning, with the close of 1941 just hours away, the trucks were targeted first by a German fighter plane and then Stukas. The aerial onslaught went on for several hours. At the end there was one casualty – Jock Lewes. The man whose trailblazing training had created a unit of such potential had been killed by the Messerschmitt's deadly fire.

Lewes' loss hit hard within the tight-knit L Detachment. It was felt from top to bottom, triggering a flurry of concerns to accompany the very keenly felt sadness. 'This was a severe blow to us, very severe because there's no doubt Jock was outstanding. He was going to be very difficult to replace,' said Seekings, who also noted the impact Lewes' death had on Stirling. 'He was very cut up. A debate was going on whether it was really worth it all to carry on and he spoke to us about it – Brough, Cooper, myself. My idea was that we have something to fight for, to get our own back and we owed it to Jock to see that the thing was a success. He had done so much. It was decided then that we would get back to base and start to recruit and train people to do the job.'

Stirling wasted little time at Kabrit before moving on to Middle East Headquarters. As well as talks about bolstering personnel, he had plans to lead another operation within weeks.

Seekings, Cooper and others were also in Cairo, taking that much-needed leave. Let off the leash with plenty of cash in their pockets, there was no way this was going to be a quiet drink.

Mike Sadler described Egypt's capital city as 'Full of ideas and fun. And masses and masses of people everywhere – it was pretty fast-paced.' He also noted that a hand hanging out of a streetcar window on a hot day in Cairo was an invitation for any passing chancer to try to steal a wristwatch.

Certainly it was all the livelier for the SAS putting in an appearance between ops. Their new white berets drew plenty of attention – of the wrong sort. The desert returnees were made the subject of relentless mickey-taking by the hordes of other troops cramming the bars. No shrinking violets, the men responded in predictable fashion with scraps breaking out all over the place. Stirling returned to base to find a pile of charge sheets detailing the fights his men had become embroiled in. The white beret got the blame for the bother and was replaced by a less ostentatious blue forage cap.

Foes-turned-friends Cooper and Seekings were photographed at the time wearing the short-lived white beret. In battledress, Cooper's open and friendly outlook is captured on camera; smiling, he has thrown his left arm around his new mate's shoulder. Seekings' facial expression is in keeping with many other such snaps. It gives next to nothing away, while a cigarette burns between the fingers of his left hand. But the alliance forged through the dark hours on the edge of Sirte seemed just as strong in the social whirl of Cairo. Indeed, when he was once asked about what made the dynamic between him and Cooper work, Seekings explained: 'Whenever we put in anywhere, things used to liven up.'

Cooper, who had taken part in stage productions in his school days, was far from shy. He would happily jump on a bar table and start belting out a version of 'I Love a Lassie'. Such high spirits had implications, but Seekings invariably stood up for his mate and on one occasion handed out a hiding to some Glaswegian artillerymen after they had mocked Cooper's good-natured antics.

There were many layers to a friendship that matured to be as lengthy as it was effective. Cooper, the younger by more than two years, was struck by the burlier man's strength of character and apparent lack of fear: 'I would never let myself down in front of him … I think that was the relationship.'

For his part, Seekings instinctively knew that Cooper was someone who had his back. 'We didn't have to worry about whether we had got support from one another – it was automatic it was there,' said Seekings. 'We didn't argue the toss about whether there was something to be done or not, if one or the other suggested it. We said, "Right, let's go, let's get on with it". And where we went, it seemed to be that things just developed.'

The photograph also shows one other very important aspect:

Cooper (left) and Seekings' friendship began on an operation in late 1941 and was consolidated during subsequent leave. Note the short-lived white berets!

both men had their breast wings. Prior to Operation Squatter the men had agreed not to wear the Jock Lewes design on their arm but wait until they had been in action, after which they could be sewn on the chest. 'It was a good move, because it had an added value then … all our mates that we'd we lost, chaps who never got the chance to wear it,' said Seekings. 'So I think it was a very good decision; it worked out fine … built up tremendous pride. Most of us were youngsters, the great majority were twenty-year-olds. Coming back off your first job like that and wearing your wings up on your chest and the old cap-badge was a good feeling.'

The wings were both dark and light blue with a white parachute in the middle. The sense of having earned the right to wear them was powerful for Seekings. It must have felt like an endorsement, at least within the small band that were awarded them off the back of those initial airfield raids.

But the presentation of his wings triggered another strong emotion within Seekings: a dread that he might suffer the shame of an RTU – being returned to unit. 'That fear was with everybody,' he said. 'It was made absolutely clear that if a man was returned it was because he couldn't make it, in disgrace for not making the grade. Not failing in training, that's to be expected. I'm talking about being RTU-ed after you'd been accepted into the unit.'

Given his exploits in the previous couple of months, Seekings had little cause for concern on that score, and not just because the unit was depleted in terms of trained personnel. By that stage, his reputation within the group was high thanks to his durability and determination on Squatter, his daring at Tamet and the dawn of that double-act with Cooper at Sirte.

That Stirling had switched Seekings to his own sub-section from Mayne's was a strong indicator in itself. Neither would the CO have missed how well Seekings and Cooper seemed to work together on the Sirte trip. They were athletic, courageous and decisive – just the type of self-governing individuals Stirling had in mind at the inception of L Detachment. That they were unafraid to speak up for themselves was not a problem either. In fact, Stirling encouraged the creation of an egalitarian atmosphere that accommodated creative thinking from the ranks. Discussion among the men and the sharing of ideas was fine. 'It wasn't a case of officer and NCOs – we were mates,' was Seekings' opinion on the prevailing culture. 'We were in this together and one idea was as good as another. We depended upon each other.'

Unsurprisingly, Stirling selected Seekings and Cooper to join him for the very first operation of 1942. Brough and Cattell, both of whom had been at Sirte post-Christmas, were again on the job. But this was to be an expanded team, including operatives from the Special Boat Section. Stirling no longer just had eyes for aerodromes and landing grounds. Now he was ready to take aim at a port.

Chapter 8

BOUERAT BANDITS

D etermined, dependable and focused, Reg Seekings was not the
sort of soldier to be caught with his pants down. Apart from one
notable occasion, that is. The unlikely scenario played out during
an incident-packed operation in the second half of January 1942.
Seekings was among a party of SAS raiders bound for Bouerat, a port
to the west of Sirte. The intention was to wipe out enemy shipping
and supplies, and disrupt lines of communication. For the journey,
there was a change of LRDG personnel. This time, the 'para-shites'
– as they were jokingly labelled by their unconventional chauffeurs
– were to be ferried by G1 Patrol, led by Captain Anthony Hunter.

The trip's early stages were straightforward but, as the group
drew closer to Sirte, a break in radio silence protocols alerted
the enemy to their presence. Indeed, the following morning the
travelling contingent had not long been on the move when a bomber
circled and pounded the location of their overnight camp.

A day later, Seekings experienced a much closer shave. The
trucks were concealed in Wadi Tamet after a perilous dawn

descent and breakfast had only just been consumed when a Ghibli skimmed over the edge of the escarpment. 'We sat and prayed they hadn't seen us, but no such luck,' said Seekings. 'It banked steeply and came for us. The rocks I was sitting by suddenly became small as peas.' Seekings knew he was a marked man. Those within the Ghibli had him lined up, along with Johnny Cooper and Charlie Cattell. The trio swiftly sought better cover with a dash for a shallow cave. It offered only marginally better protection, however, as their tormentor continued his attack. 'Time and again, the rear gunner had a go at us,' noted Seekings.

The tension on the ground was tremendous; being singled out in such a manner tested mental fortitude to the limits. 'It was this feeling of individuality that was the tough thing to handle,' said Seekings. 'When you're with a small party, when aircraft came in to attack, they weren't attacking a bulk regiment of thousands of men, it was you as an individual – they were gunning for you. And that got very personal.'

Eventually the Ghibli departed, ammunition seemingly exhausted, and the three men opted to move, conscious that their ordeal was unlikely to be over. They ran down the valley before landing on another small bolthole. It was then that Seekings also decided on a change of underwear; perhaps understandably given the stressful circumstances. However, Reg's rationale for delving into his escape pack for fresh pants and vest was more calculated. 'So as to lighten my load a bit in case of a long march, I thought I would have a change, forecasting that they would come back as soon as I was stripped. Sure enough they did, bombing and strafing all likely places.' He found himself 'very cold and uncomfortable' until the threat from the skies moved on, at which point Seekings, Cooper and Cattell felt it safe to go in search of their truck.

Other men from the patrol were also gathering and it soon became evident that three LRDG personnel were missing. A search began but by 19:00 hours it was called off; the operation could not be compromised by further delay, even though one of the missing men was the wireless operator, whose absence would be keenly felt. According to Seekings, the wireless operator was 'the most important man with us this trip as – due to the changing frontline – Cairo was going to send us any important targets that our recce planes saw'.

With the moon large and due to set late, the reduced party resumed their journey, which became hindered by mechanical breakdowns. But despite transport frustrations, there was much for Seekings to admire about the LRDG's masterful circumnavigation of the Sand Sea. Their vast knowledge of the desert and methods of managing its many challenges became clearer with each trip. He recognized that these skilled and resilient soldiers were 'damned good'. They had to be; not just to operate, but to survive in the most exacting of conditions. And as well as offering the best taxi service in the Western Desert, there were other benefits that came with aligning with the LRDG. Their ration scale was different to the rest of the army. 'We were well fed,' recalled Seekings. Along with such perks as tinned fruit were the renowned LRDG 'sundowners', a rum tot accompanied by lime juice and water. It was a refreshing tonic after long days in the heat.

Much of the outward journey was carried out under the cover of darkness. It was the depth of winter and while the desert would often be baked by a bright sun from mid-morning, temperatures plummeted during the evening. Seekings swiftly realized he would need every item of available clothing – 'heavy battledress, overcoat, balaclava, gloves, mitts' – to combat the freezing winds that cut through all but the thickest layers at night.

On and on they travelled until, much to Seekings' relief, they laid up in sand dunes 'not far from the Bouerat track, which ran east and west'. On the night of 23 January, six days after they had pulled out of Jalo, the SAS prepared to infiltrate their coastal target. Two men from the Special Boat Section, bringing along a Folbot (a collapsible canoe), joined Stirling's party on the solitary truck that was to travel towards the target area. The SBS pair were to paddle out into the harbour and attach explosives to enemy shipping. However, that plan was soon in tatters, not unlike the Folbot, which broke as a result of the overburdened truck juddering on its route into the port.

With Bouerat finally within walking distance, Stirling split the SAS men up into teams and included Seekings in his own. Stealthily the small parties zoned in on the small town with most heading for the waterfront. Unlike at Sirte, this time there were no suspicious sentries. In fact, the place could hardly have been quieter and, infuriatingly, it was discovered that there was no shipping at all on the water.

The raiders aimed to keep footfall light and they used the moonless night to move undetected around the harbour. To find suitable spots for their Lewes bombs, they crept in and around the unguarded warehouses that surrounded the water's edge. The buildings seemed mainly to serve as food dumps, with rations piled high. Bombs were duly placed on the crates, as well as on machinery items.

Seekings was also on the hunt for soft-skinned vehicles to destroy, in particular mobile petrol tanks or bowsers. Despite the gloom, his eyes were drawn to some mysterious shapes he could just about make out not far from a roadside. Bingo. A closer inspection revealed 'a nice line of bowsers'. While not the enemy ships Stirling had hoped to wipe out, blasting the huge petrol carriers offered more than just a decent consolation.

Bombs were soon attached, a task that was interrupted by a couple of small incidents. The first served as a mildly amusing distraction. Seekings and Stirling were working away when they bumped into

Sergeant Dave Kershaw. 'The CO took a dim view and severely ticked him off for picking our truck,' Seekings reflected. 'Poor old Dave, he never did get over it!' The second incident, perhaps triggered by the first, was a little more concerning. A driver inside one of the bowsers awoke and started to shout, threatening to draw unwelcome attention to the raiders' activities. 'Go to bloody sleep,' an English voice responded from the shadows. Now it was time for the Bouerat bandits to clear out …

Before Stirling's small group reached the relative safety of the RV, a bizarre scenario unfolded. Making their way out of town, they clocked sentries following them. The pursuit continued with those in front going as 'quickly as we could without giving the game away' before the dicey situation took a fresh twist at a barbed wire perimeter fence. As the SAS men began to climb, a sentry called out to them. Seekings was ready to bring the matter to a fiery conclusion – 'I very nearly gave them a burst.' But before reaching for the trigger, he realized the sentries showed little sign of wanting to engage in a shootout. Quite the opposite, in fact. 'They seemed friendly and wanted to help us get over the wire.' It was a strange turn of events, indeed. But perhaps the sentries felt so far removed from danger, given the frontline was several hundred miles away, that it somehow failed to dawn on them that a patrol of men tackling a perimeter fence in the dead of night might just have been up to no good. If that was the case, their perspective was surely changed minutes later by a series of huge explosions and raging fires in the immediate vicinity. SAS bombs had taken out eighteen petrol bowsers and four food dumps around Bouerat – but the night's activities were not yet at an end.

Back at the RV it was established that the SBS duo, accompanied by L Detachment Original Corporal Rose, were still to return. The glow of a light a little further up the road piqued the interest of the hit-and-run crew. 'We all went to investigate and look out for the missing men,' documented Seekings. Instead, they discovered an enemy wireless truck and unleashed just about everything at their disposal. Tommy guns, revolvers and grenades all contributed as the truck was turned into a complete mess within moments.

Seekings paused to fit a new magazine on to his Tommy. But as he did so, a further burst of fire rang out followed by a yell from one of his comrades. Seekings turned to find an Italian running straight for him and his Tommy cracked back into action. 'I gave him a long burst that must have almost cut him in two. He dropped almost at my feet, kicking and calling for his mother.' For a split second, as the Italian died in front of him, Seekings experienced a flash of sorrow for the fallen man. However, the thought was soon replaced by another: 'He would have done the same to me.'

Later, the cold crept into Seekings as the truck rumbled back to the sand dunes. But not much more than thirty-six hours later, he would form part of a small group revisiting the Bouerat locale to head to an arranged secondary RV where it was hoped the three absentees would show up. Of course, this was not all that Stirling intended to do on the return trip. He planned to mosey up the coastal road to see if he could 'find anything to destroy'.

In preparation, Seekings decided to give his guns a thorough cleanse while shooting the occasional anxious glance skywards at the Axis recce planes buzzing overhead. As the day unfolded, the wind whipped up, resulting in a sandstorm. 'It solved one problem. The aircraft couldn't see us, but it was very uncomfortable. I was thinking about my guns. A Tommy, in particular, is hard to keep clean in the sand.' But that diligence in ensuring his weapons were ready was to pay off when darkness fell.

Conditions remained unpleasant as eleven men – eight from the SAS and three from the LRDG – left the hideout. Stirling had decided Seekings and Cooper should be on the wings, Tommys at the ready in case the party ran into roadblocks resulting from their previous activity in the area. 'Also in that position we could quickly slide off and use a knife if necessary,' noted Seekings.

First port of call was the prearranged collection point to pick up the Folbot pair and Rose. That passed off without a hitch and the group switched to the main coastal road north of Bouerat to look for some action. The intention was to sabotage passing transport by lobbing bombs with time-fuses attached, but such a haphazard approach met with limited success. Firstly, the grim weather meant there was hardly any traffic on the road. Also, as Seekings admitted, 'We proved very poor pitchers'. Instead, a decision was made simply to flag down passing trucks. 'If they refused to stop, then we were going to open fire.'

The would-be highwaymen of North Africa hung around for hours with only themselves for company. It was only when they moved on that the night began to liven up. Not far down the road a large truck was spotted, which soon had a Lewes bomb fixed to it. 'As Captain Hunter had never seen the effect of one of our bombs, it was decided to give him a ringside seat.' Unfortunately for Seekings, he almost ended up the fall guy of the intended show – along with Stirling. When the anticipated explosion failed to materialize, the pair decided to creep back to the truck to see what the problem was. 'Just as the CO picked up the bomb, off went the time-pencil. Although we had ten seconds to spare, I'm afraid we dropped the damn thing and dived across the road to cover. The bomb went off with a terrific bang!'

Amid the confusion, the cab door of the truck flew open and out came a small Italian wearing one boot. Seekings took aim at the tiny, hop-along figure but missed as it was 'about the first time' in his life that he had used a Tommy gun from the shoulder. The petrified Italian begged to be spared. Dropping to the ground and throwing his arms around Seekings' knees, the man called on 'all the saints for mercy'.

The half-dressed man's wild fear increased further as other SAS men joined a scene that Seekings would reflect on with amusement. 'I don't think one of us was under six feet and, with all our extra clothing and beards, it's a wonder we didn't scare him to death.' Ever the opportunists, the raiding party asked the scared-stiff individual if he had any cigarettes. Once it was established that he had, the Italian was allowed to return to his truck to fetch the fags. While he did so, another bomb was surreptitiously placed on the truck – this time with a ten-second fuse. The SAS made a dash for it just as the Italian vehicle blew up.

That was just the start of the night's activities. They were not long back on their own truck when the run for home was disrupted … ambush! Cooper was the first to identify the threat, spotting flashes of light in front of them as shots fizzed through the night sky. He was also the first to respond, quickly jumping into action on the Ford's mounted Vickers K, a rapid-fire machine gun designed for aircraft use.

Seekings, alongside his friend, began to see shadowy figures jumping up from their positions to launch an attack in earnest. The SAS party was in a tight spot with limited options. Seekings, poised with the Tommy gun he had cleaned so attentively amid the previous day's sandstorm, and Cooper quickly realized they would have to fight their way out. 'We shouted at the driver to drive straight at them,' noted Seekings in a written account.

The LRDG man at the wheel was Archie 'Flash' Gibson, who without hesitation sent the truck hurtling down an incline, straight towards their assailants. Presented with point-blank range targets, Cooper and Seekings were relentless as the hostilities drew to a furious climax. 'The air was thick with tracer and exploding bombs,' according to Seekings.

Somehow the truck smashed through the eye of the ambush. That was some feat given the odds seemed stacked against the patrol. Perhaps even more amazingly, the raiding party emerged on the other side without taking a single hit. 'Luckily for us, they must have been bad troops,' was Seekings' verdict. The ambushers had not got away so lightly. The LRDG report noted, 'No casualties were sustained though it seems certain some were inflicted on the enemy.' Gibson's daring driving was a major contributory factor to the outcome. As were the guns of Cooper and Seekings.

With dawn drawing closer, Gibson kept his foot down and his truck was still travelling at a fair lick when Stirling's fighters bounced past a fort. The party tensed in preparation of fresh skirmishing but had no further interruptions before finally winding up back at the dunes hide-out.

The following hours were spent preparing for the long haul back to Jalo, which was to commence that night. Petrol supplies were deemed insufficient to get every truck back. 'We had to blow up two at least,' recorded Seekings, 'including the truck we had done both trips in. It nearly broke Flash Gibson's heart.'

Gibson was a popular man on that hard trek back and not just because of his recent daring driving. He had a stash of a local brand of cigarettes and handed out one a day to those who rode with him. 'And did they taste good,' was Seekings' observation. But the cigarette perk was just about the only thing to look forward to as by this point they had run short of water and food.

As the trucks journeyed across the sands, another problem was about to present itself – one that the dog-tired travellers knew nothing about. Away to the east, Axis armoured forces were back on the front foot thanks to a counterattack launched on 21 January. Stirling's party had been without wireless operators since the air assault on them at Wadi Tamet and consequently had no idea of the enemy advance. However, that changed one night when Hunter managed to pick up the BBC news on his receiver. 'What a shock we got to hear the Eighth Army was retreating at a terrific speed and how we cursed our missing wireless operators,' wrote Seekings. 'We had a big headache now. Was Jalo still in our hands? If it wasn't, we were in very serious trouble as fuel, food and water were nearly finished.' On drawing close to Jalo, Stirling made the decision that only he, Seekings, Cooper and a driver would proceed to the oasis to ascertain if the LRDG had pulled out. First appearances were worrying. There was not a soul around, not even the locals. Seekings entered the fort feeling 'very trigger happy'.

It was desolate inside but there was some good news. The LRDG had left much-needed supplies behind. Seekings began to drink some milk before he was interrupted by the sound of an approaching truck. Immediately, he readied for a firefight, but a potentially disastrous outcome was averted at the last moment. 'Johnny and I had just got down behind our Vickers when a LRDG truck drove around the corner. At the very last second we recognized each other. I think all our party felt a bit weak at the knees for a few minutes. The patrol that had just driven up had been cleaning up and keeping an eye open for us. We had arrived just in time as this was their last day.'

The rush of adrenalin from that near-confrontation was the last Reg was to experience on that particular mission. There had been sustained strafing in Wadi Tamet; the cool-as-you-like stroll through night-time Bouerat; Lewes bombs lighting up the petrol carriers; close-quarters encounters with the opposition and the blazing-guns getaway after almost falling prey to an ambush. Seekings had much to process as the LRDG and SAS men abandoned Jalo and headed for Jarabub. There he hoped to find food, drink and a good night's rest, not to mention some fresh underwear.

Chapter 9

A PRETTY PICTURE

avid Stirling had not long returned from the Bouerat mission
when he commandeered a Ford V8 utility car in Cairo.
Christened the 'Blitz Buggy', the grey vehicle with its German sign
on the bonnet gave the SAS commander an additional mobility
that he relished. In the spring of 1942, he used the car for various
meetings and pow-wows that invariably ended up as high-jinx road
adventures. Life was rarely dull with Stirling at the wheel, and
Seekings and Cooper were regularly along for the ride.

One of Seekings' first trips in the Blitz Buggy was to Tobruk,
which was still in the Allies' hands at that point. Not long after
the visit had concluded, the vehicle was back on the road, hurtling
out of town, when Reg noticed a checkpoint apparently blocking
the way. Stirling, unconcerned about anything – or anybody –
in his path continued to career towards the sand-filled oil drums
attended by a sentry. In the back seat, Seekings hunkered down
and prepared himself for an almighty crash. However, after a few
moments in which there was no impact, he risked a glance and to

his astonishment the checkpoint, oil drums and all, were receding in the distance. 'I don't know if we sprouted wings and went over the top,' reflected Seekings. 'I think I died for a few moments.' Cooper, sat in the front seat, endured similar anxiety through the hair-raising caper and made his feelings known. But Stirling responded in typically languid manner, informing him there was another option: he could always 'get out and walk'.

Seekings and Cooper began to be recognized as Stirling's unofficial bodyguards as they accompanied him on a series of excursions. The trust within the trio swelled yet further and, despite the uncertain state of the Desert War after Rommel's offensive early in 1942, there was still plenty of laughter and levity surrounding the Blitz Buggy outings. On one occasion, the three men set off to visit the Scots Guards on the Gazala-Bir Hakeim frontline. Nearing their destination, they needed to navigate their way through a minefield that was being inspected by a corporal from the Royal Engineers (RE). Stirling drove up in the Blitz Buggy – its German markings obvious to anyone – and asked the sapper to show him the route through. On being asked for identification, Stirling's advice was not to be 'a bloody fool' and hurry up with the appropriate instructions. In the face of such chutzpah, the RE man duly complied. As the vehicle pulled off, Stirling asked, 'What would you do, corporal, if we are German?' The man's shocked expression amused Seekings. 'I'll never forget the look on his face as we drove away.'

A similar incident unfolded on a trip to Battle HQ when Stirling became embroiled in a row with a military policeman, or 'Redcap'. Once again the Scotsman was without his papers. 'Show him yours, Reggie,' he instructed Seekings, who pulled out his pay book. But the Redcap was not satisfied and demanded his identification number, which, 'for some unaccountable reason', Reg had forgotten. In the end, the SAS men took a 'to-hell-with-you' attitude and the Blitz Buggy carried on towards its destination, General Ritchie's caravan. The Redcap, fuming at being ignored, dashed after them while Seekings offered a running commentary from the back of the vehicle. Stirling had parked up at Ritchie's headquarters when their out-of-puff pursuer caught up. As the man gasped for air, Stirling asked sweetly, 'Did you want me, corporal?' and strode into Ritchie's caravan. Finally, when the Redcap had sufficient wind in his lungs, he turned to Seekings and Cooper and informed them that, 'You can't do this.' 'Sorry chum, it's done,' came the response.

It is easy to imagine how Stirling's manner, which mixed audacity with levity, would have rubbed off on those who served under him. Seekings had just turned twenty-two and his unconventional alliance with his commander would have topped up an already plentiful pool of self-belief. It would also have further strengthened his loyalty to this most unusual unit.

By this point, Seekings was starting to find himself closer to the Eighth Army's top echelons, albeit not yet in direct contact with them. As the first months of 1942 played out, he was even privy to crunch talks about the future of the SAS – specifically, regarding its primacy ahead of other Allied special forces operating in the Middle East theatre. He later reflected that the Middle East Commando were 'trying to copy us', hence Stirling's desire to make his frustrations known to Ritchie. 'I remember the CO telling Johnny and I that he wasn't having any more of it and, after he had seen the general, either the SAS would be all-powerful in the Middle East and other special units receive our OK before going on ops – or that we should be finished,' documented Seekings, who underlined the 'or' for emphasis. Not for the first time, Stirling's powers of persuasion won the day. He came out from the meeting with a thumbs-up that signalled victory to his two confidantes.

The following morning, however, the trio were engaged in a battle for survival of a different kind as the Blitz Buggy made its way back to Cairo. Seekings was in the back as usual, sat with some fresh eggs that had been procured during their overnight stop. His job was to safeguard the precious cargo but soon he had more dangerous shells on his mind. The Blitz Buggy had drawn the attention of a cluster of Italian fighter planes, who were preparing to attack. Seekings glanced up in dread: 'Shells started to burst over our heads. To my horror I saw five or six Macchi 202 fighters diving at us with guns blazing, two even coming under the telephone wires.' Yet the car was not the sitting duck the pilots might have assumed. Stirling's customary foot-to-the-floor, flat-out driving style came to the rescue. 'That saved us,' was the verdict of the back-seat passenger. Mind you, he was less impressed with the driver and Cooper's priorities once they had made their escape. 'All the CO and Johnny seemed to be worried about was the eggs on the back seat, [and] had I broken any?'

The air attack took place around the time the Afrika Korps made their push from Tmimi in late May 1942. Rommel was once more on the offensive, pushing east towards the objective of seizing Egypt and the Suez Canal – an outcome, if it materialized, that would spell disaster for the Allies in the Western Desert campaign. An associated and immediate concern was the future of Malta. Considered a vital base in both the Middle East and Mediterranean theatres, the island found itself under heavy and regular airstrikes from November 1941 onwards. Losing mastery of its skies would not only mean that enemy convoys could sail to Libya with reduced interference, but it would also become practically impossible for Allied ships to resupply the island.

The Governor of Malta, Lieutenant-General Sir William Dobie, sent a series of telegrams outlining an increasingly grave position. Even on siege rations, general supplies would only last until June.

The War Office informed General Auchinleck in Cairo that Malta was 'the dominant factor in the Middle East and the Mediterranean at that time'. It had to be relieved, and swiftly. Therefore, in the moonless period of mid-June 1942, a convoy of ships was to attempt to get crucial supplies to Malta. And the SAS, itself restocked largely thanks to a sizeable intake of Free French[3] parachutists, was tasked with playing an important part in the action.

Stirling came up with a big-vision plan in which teams of his men were to be launched in a series of coordinated night raids on Axis aerodromes across Cyrenaica and Crete. Stirling reached out to the SBS for support and also called on the Special Interrogation Group (SIG), a small, relatively new unit in the British Army that included German-speaking Jews.

The objective was for enemy planes to be grounded temporarily, thus facilitating a smoother passage to Malta for the large convoy carrying essential supplies. Midnight on 13 June was scheduled for the synchronized SAS assaults and, for the first time, Seekings was going on operation as a paid-up lance sergeant, three chevrons on his right sleeve. The previous month he had still been a corporal in a party travelling to Benghazi for an intended hit on the major port. Unfortunately for Seekings, he was unable to take his place in the 21 May raid after being injured in the preparations when a detonator exploded, impairing the use of a hand. His frustration mirrored that of the small raiding party whose night-time attempt to blast shipping had failed to come to fruition.

The hand healed sufficiently for Seekings to be among Stirling's men when they set off from Siwa on 8 June. The oasis, with warm, clean pools bubbling away and trees yielding dates considered to be among the finest in Egypt, was more of a desert idyll than Jalo, their previous forward operating base. But it was further to the east,

---

3   The Free French were led by General Charles de Gaulle and their forces aligned with the Allies to fight against the Axis powers.

which meant an even longer cross-desert trek for Seekings, who was bound for the drome at Benina, 10 miles inland from Benghazi. He had worked flat out prior to departure, organizing supplies for the unit's biggest undertaking since Operation Squatter. This time he knew less than usual about what lay ahead, although he had heard Stirling issuing a directive to the men about 'attacking with determination'. It was not until the long journey north-west that Seekings discovered from Stirling exactly what was at stake. Malta's perilous position meant that the cause was more important than individual safety. 'His instruction was that if I was the only one left, "You carry on till you're dead". Simple as that. Previously it had always been, you save yourself.' It was a do-or-die mission and the men were all to operate with live bombs.

The SAS who were targeting air bases in Libya were conveyed by the tried and trusted method of LRDG transport. G2 Patrol officer Robin Gurdon's trucks included Stirling, Seekings and Cooper, and also a four-man group headed up by Paddy Mayne. Unsurprisingly, there was a competitive aspect to relations between Stirling and Mayne, especially on operations. Both were focused on the main objectives, but a personal rivalry added an extra edge. Mayne's extraordinary personal 'bag' of destroyed aircraft meant he was well clear in that particular head-to-head going into mid-June's Operation 10 (Mayne's raid was recorded as TEN (A) and Stirling's as TEN (B) in the official SAS War Diary).

Gurdon dropped off Stirling's team on an escarpment, far lusher and greener than the desert environment that they were accustomed to, close to Benghazi. The final stage of their journey was to be completed on foot and it proved to be a long march for the three men, who laid up at last in a hideout on a cliff face overlooking Benina. They were awoken by a searing sun that made life ever more uncomfortable as the day unfolded. 'It was like a furnace,' observed Seekings. 'But we had a good view of the hangars and the work going on.' A further advantage was that three months earlier they had broken into Benina and so had a sound knowledge of the site. On their second day of observation, a Messerschmitt Bf 109 air test helped to pass the time. Seekings was impressed: 'Could that pilot fly!'

With darkness approaching, it was time to move in. The initial descent was not entirely straightforward as they clambered and sometimes slid their way down steep, rocky slopes. Once on the level, it was with ease that they slipped onto the airfield and made their way towards its hangars. They had not long arrived, however, when an air raid alarm began to blare across Benina in response to an RAF bombing assault on nearby Benghazi. The shadowy and sleepy airfield was transformed, much to the discomfort of the small group that had just broken in. 'It wasn't nice,' mused Seekings. 'We had to wait in the middle of an enemy drome until things got quiet.'

The timing of the RAF activity had displeased Stirling, whose subsequent mood was not helped by what he felt was Seekings' leaden footsteps. The officer delivered an unusual and lengthy admonishment that reflected his Perthshire country-estate background. 'I had a terrific lecture on deer stalking from the CO,' recalled Seekings. 'Apparently, I wasn't moving quietly enough for him.' Not long afterwards he feared another ticking off when, seeking to quench his thirst, he turned on a tap. At the same time a sentry was spotted, so dealing with that became the priority, sparing him further admonishment.

When midnight struck, they pressed the time-pencils on their respective twenty bombs and set about dotting them all over the enemy stronghold, starting with a string of dumps. Once the first safety pins were pulled, thirty minutes remained for them to make good their exit – there was no time to lose. Next to be targeted were hangars and workshops – and what a discovery they turned out to be for the invaders. 'They were full of aircraft and tools – 109, 110 and JU 52s,' wrote Seekings in his account of the raid. Each man got busy placing their bombs, but while at work in the last hangar they heard the sound of guards marching nearby. 'I flew through the hangar door to a row of crated engines outside; I didn't want to get trapped.' Stirling clambered into an empty oil drum and did so 'with a hell of a clatter'. Seekings couldn't help but reflect on the earlier reprimand he'd received. 'I thought him a hell of a fine deer stalker!'

The majority of the Germans proceeded towards an adjacent hangar in which there was a guardroom, but Seekings was still lying low when he spotted Stirling peering round a door. 'The CO, in a voice of thunder it seemed to me, said, "Where the bloody hell are you? Pack up playing the fool!"' Seekings emerged from his hiding place and quietly pointed out that a sentry was still near. Stealthily, they made their way down the crates of aircraft engines, until their supply of bombs was almost exhausted. As they came to the end of the line, Seekings saw that the patrolling sentry was almost upon them. Had they been rumbled? He signalled to Stirling and Cooper to freeze and aimed his Tommy gun at the enemy. Seekings watched his enemy load his own weapon and readied himself for a shoot-out. But he needn't have worried. 'Somehow or other the sentry hadn't spotted us and about turned and marched away.'

The trio quietly made their way to the next-door hangar, which housed the guardroom. Inside were a number of enemy soldiers, including an officer sat at a table. 'Johnny and I covered, while the CO opened the door and heaved in the grenades. I didn't see anything but I heard the scream of horror from the Jerry officer as he saw the CO.'

Barely had the guardroom exploded before the Lewes bombs all over the drome started to go off. Aircraft, buildings and machinery were blasted and flames soared as Stirling, Seekings and Cooper sprinted into the night and back up the escarpment. Once away from the immediate danger, they paused to catch their breath and take stock of the destruction their work had brought about. 'It was a pretty picture,' assessed Seekings.

They had stopped to view proceedings from the vicinity of an enemy gun emplacement; it was too good an opportunity to miss. 'It seemed deserted, so we stuck a bomb up the breech.' Next, they began to make their way towards the assigned RV. Or, as Seekings put it: 'The agony started.'

The excitement, exertions and stress of the night began to catch up with the patrol by the time dawn drew close. Stirling was hit by a severe migraine, which was not helped by the fact they had no water. Indeed, all three of them were parched and desperate for a drink. Cooper spoke up, recalling that there was a well in the escarpment. 'It meant going out of our way but we decided that thirst would get us down long before we reached the RV if we didn't do something,' wrote Seekings. So they struck out in what they desperately hoped was the right direction.

As daylight returned, certain features became recognizable and, after what seemed an age, the weary walkers wound up at the well, which did not bring immediate relief. There was a lid across the top, secured by a lock that Stirling and Cooper struggled to undo. It was all too much for Seekings. 'Here we were dying of thirst and they were still acting the gentlemen. With "Rip the bloody thing off!", I tore off the lid.'

Brute force made the breakthrough but ingenuity was required to get their bottles deep enough down the well to access the water. First he whipped from his waist a length of cord that he had wrapped round himself before leaving camp ('What made me do it I don't know; I had never done it before or since'). Next, he requisitioned Stirling's tie, worn throughout the raid, and a knotty problem was solved. Two water bottles were lowered, filled and given to the others. 'After a very long time the CO came up for wind and said,

"Some, Reg?" About time, I thought. But alas they had hardly left me enough to wet my lips.'

Many refills later, the men resumed the slog back to the LRDG trucks and came across a group of Senussi tribespeople who were camped in the area. Seekings was keen to requisition food from the nomads and began to barter with the locals. The process took too long for Stirling, who 'pulled a damn great roll of notes from his pocket', leading to prices soaring for the goods under discussion. However, the bartering soon ceased when Seekings' suspicions were sufficiently raised by a couple of tribesmen sneaking towards an enemy fort that lay over the hill. It was time to get away.

With the sun fully up, the long march to the RV became increasingly difficult but a Senussi in a lone tent they encountered proved to be more accommodating than the camp inhabitants. He offered shelter away from the burning rays and gave the soldiers milk. Energy levels remained low, however. 'It got so bad I didn't think we would make it,' wrote Seekings. 'The CO sat down and told Johnny and I to go on. We sat down and talked it over – we were all done up. Then came the thought of Paddy and his party; that done it, we all staggered on.'

• ● •

Both patrols made it to the RV and Stirling discovered that his had enjoyed more success than Mayne's. The other group had found the satellite airfield at Berka to be well guarded and were not helped either by RAF flares lighting it up (the RAF were bombing Benghazi harbour). Mayne's four-man team was challenged by vigilant sentries and dealt with them with grenades, while a bomb was thrown into an aircraft for good measure. But the element of surprise had gone and the objective switched to the avoidance of capture or worse. For hours, enemy trucks scoured the area in search of the quartet – one of whom, Corporal Warburton, did not return.

It did not take long back at the rendezvous for Stirling and Mayne's old rivalry to resurface. The SAS commander could not help an element of glee creeping in as he described the Benina demolition job. 'You wouldn't like to take a look at the debris?' he invited Mayne. The Irishman accepted the offer, and then raised the stakes with a counter-proposal. 'If we got hold of a car we could drive right into Benghazi and shoot up some stuff along the road.' He had no intention of listening to Stirling's triumphalism all the way back to Siwa without having another crack at the enemy.

And so, the seeds were sown for a shoot-'em-up that was high risk even by L Detachment's standards. Stirling persuaded Gurdon to loan him an LRDG truck for the trip, which began early evening. He sat next to Mayne, who took the wheel, while Seekings, Cooper, Bob Lilley and Jimmy Storie were in the back. There was one further passenger, a middle-aged German by the name of Karl Kahane. He had been plucked by Stirling from the Special Interrogation Group – and had previously been a sergeant-major in the Germany army. In those days Kahane held his British counterparts in low regard; events around the corner were about to change his mind.

The operation began in mildly comical circumstances as the wagon stopped by a fort where a quick win was identified: the cutting of telephone wires. But this was not as simple as anticipated. 'Nobody could climb the pole,' Seekings recalled. 'I managed to hold Johnny above my head, but what a job he had to cut them. We thought a small pair of ordinary pliers would do, but what a job.' The incident was a portent of what was to follow.

Shortly after passing Benina's burnt-out hangars, in the distance a red light straight ahead slowly came into view. Mayne was forced to bring the vehicle to a halt at an Italian-manned roadblock. Given what had unfolded on the Libyan airfields nights earlier, the Axis forces were on high alert.

A guard approached the truck and was confronted by the wagon's unkempt and unshaven occupants. It was for such moments that Kahane was on the firm. '*Tedeschi*,' he called out – the Italian for 'Germans'. But if Stirling's party had hoped this would see them waved on their way, they were in for a nasty surprise: the Italian shouted for support. 'Out of the pill box on the other side of the road came running German soldiers – one was a RSM [regimental sergeant-major], Karl told me later,' wrote Seekings. 'Two on each side of the road held us covered; one with a stick grenade stood by the roadblock.'

The sergeant-major asked for the appropriate password and Kahane responded with an outdated one, leading to an argument between the two men. Kahane mounted a strong defence of his error, brusquely explaining that the party had been in the desert for a special mission, hence they were using a captured British truck and were not clued up on the latest password. It was then that Mayne took the initiative. 'Paddy gently drew his pistol and laid it on the seat,' Seekings recalled. An increasingly stressful situation had now come to a head. Slowly, the German started to back off and the vehicle moved on. Seekings was on the edge of his seat, eyes firmly fixed on the guard with the grenade. 'We were carrying plenty of touchy bombs; I meant to get him if trouble started.' Somehow the stand-off concluded without a bullet being fired.

Closing in on the outskirts of Benghazi, the truck soon encountered another checkpoint. This time it was the beefy Fenlander who tried his hand at essential Italian for desert raiders. '*Tedeschi*', hollered Seekings, while swinging into sight his Vickers machine gun. The Italian guards parted and the vehicle sped on.

If word had not already got out, plenty of Benghazi-dwellers were soon to find out for themselves about the lethal threat heading into their midst. The SAS swiftly set about sprinkling bombs across petrol and ammunition dumps before they discovered what appeared to be a rest house. Several trucks were parked outside, which Cooper and Seekings raked with Vickers fire. Mayne was readying for the getaway when Seekings spotted Italian troops running into the road. 'I called to Paddy to pull up and sent burst after burst into them and a good burst or two right down the road.'

Once more the SAS had dealt the enemy a series of unexpected and deadly blows. But, in Seekings' words, 'the balloon was up properly now' and the party of seven required some magic behind the wheel from Mayne to get out of town. Leaving via their entry route was no longer an option so the Irishman improvised with a spot of off-road motoring. His objective was to beat the pursuing German transport to a wadi crossing from where escape would be possible. To reach it first, Mayne would have to master treacherous ground conditions at night. Seekings was in awe of the officer's many attributes as the cross-country chase unfolded. 'What a drive. In spite of his great strength it must have given Paddy hell. The Jerry, two or three miles across from us, were racing to cut us off. It was touch and go but we made it first.'

The enemy racers gave up their search, but the night's excitement was still not at an end. The vehicle had barely made it up the escarpment when a couple of cracking noises from the back gained the attention of Lilley and Seekings. 'At first it didn't strike us what it was, then I smelt it,' wrote Seekings. The bumpy terrain had activated the time-pencil on a Lewes bomb.

Seekings and Lilley roared out a warning. Mayne jumped on the brakes and a split second later everyone bailed out, with Seekings rolling over the side and briefly getting caught up on a rack. He and Lilley dashed for their lives – 'Believe me Jesse Owens never did run like it!' – and they had barely got clear when the truck was blown to smithereens. 'It knocked Bob down and flung me yards.'

The pair, in fact all of the party, had survived by the skin of their teeth, yet in next to no time, Cooper and Seekings were able to find humour in their latest near-death experience. Kahane was almost at a loss for words at their happy-go-lucky reaction. 'You must be men of steel to laugh at things like this,' said the veteran German. 'I'm too old.' Kahane went on to tell Seekings how experiences of the previous hours had totally changed his views of the British. 'He was convinced for the first time that we would win the war. The Germans, he said, would not laugh in the face of such danger as we had.'

For the next couple of days or so the SAS soldiers were harboured by friendly Senussi before being collected by the ever-reliable LRDG. What had begun as little more than a sightseeing trip but became a seemingly never-ending sequence of adrenaline-packed encounters was finally at an end. During the return trip to Siwa, Stirling was reacquainted with the Blitz Buggy, which had had a mishap with a mine on the outbound journey. The wagon lived to fight another day, somewhat ironic given the fate of the Chevrolet that Stirling's party borrowed from the LRDG for their spur-of-the-moment Benghazi jaunt.

Aside from the success at Benina in which Seekings played a major part, the SAS's raids had scored significant hits on aircraft at Berka Main aerodrome and across Cretan airfields. But there had also been serious setbacks. On Crete an enemy ambush led to the death of one man from the Free French patrol, while three others were caught. Casualties and capture were also the outcomes at Martuba and Derna; the planned attack on the latter airbase was wrecked by treachery. Herbert Brueckner, another ex-German soldier who had aligned with the SIG, betrayed the raiders to enemy guards.

Consequently, fourteen of the party did not return from the two airfields.

As for Malta, a couple of ships packed with crucial supplies managed to get through. Not only did the island survive through June, but for the entire war. Seekings was left in no doubt as to the size of the SAS's role in preventing it from falling. 'We grounded all the aircraft ... we got the supplies through. We certainly saved Malta.'

Chapter 10

JEEPERS

By the start of July 1942, the to and fro of the Desert War had swung further in the enemy's favour. The Eighth Army had fallen back to El Alamein after its withdrawal from Gazala was made necessary by the Axis's latest offensive, which began on 26 May. Rommel swiftly followed up his success by masterminding others, including moving his men further east to take the vital port of Tobruk on 21 June. General Auchinleck's depleted force was unable to prevent the enemy from advancing into Egypt and closing to within 75 miles of Alexandria.

The seemingly relentless surge resulted in drastic measures. Defences were hastily erected to protect the approaches to Alexandria and Cairo, official papers were burned and a contingency plan drawn up for potential relocation of the General Headquarters of Middle East Command. However, Churchill was insistent that Egypt must be held. Its Suez Canal was such a vital shipping corridor, not least to the Middle East oilfields.

Against such a backdrop, the SAS were called into action. The targets were familiar ones: airfields and the enemy's supply lines, which were now longer and under more strain as a consequence of their advance. The LRDG were again instrumental regarding transport duties. But this time the tactics had changed: Stirling's men were to establish a desert hideout from where they could strike relentlessly with a series of night-time attacks throughout July and beyond. This informal base was to be located a sufficiently safe distance south of the by-now Axis-controlled Mersa Matruh, just over 100 miles to the west of El Alamein.

To reach its destination, the party moved through the southernmost positions of the Eighth Army's line, which extended 35 miles from Alamein down to the Qattara Depression, a huge area of marshes, mud and dry lakes. Stirling and Mayne took with them many of the usual faces, British and French, but one regular was to miss out: Seekings. He had been sent to a Royal Electrical and Mechanical Engineers' (REME) workshop near Heliopolis on the north-east outskirts of Cairo.

Stirling wanted the SAS to become a self-contained entity that was no longer reliant on the LRDG and had successfully lobbied for extra transport, obtaining a fleet of 3-ton trucks and a draft of Willys jeeps. The latter were gamechangers. These four-wheel drive vehicles were lightweight, tough and versatile and had arrived from America at just the right time for the SAS. But for desert duties they needed essential modification work, which is where Seekings came into his own.

He was despatched to Cairo by Stirling in order to obtain the necessary supplies. The process began with a convivial meeting with the quartermaster general who issued Seekings with a letter to smooth the path. 'I played hell with a lot of colonels in ordnance depots, going along and demanding this, demanding that. "Who the hell are you coming here? Get out! I'll have you for insubordination!" And I'd just flash this letter,' chuckled Seekings. It wasn't long before he'd ticked off the items on his wish list including Vickers K machine guns, magazines for the guns, sun compasses, windscreens from Hurricane fighters ('to give us a bit of cover') and two spare wheels for each vehicle.

Stirling also wanted him to watch over the work and iron out teething problems; the weight of the mounted guns had initially led to broken springs. Seekings also ended up having a major say in the jeeps' camouflaging. He had been unconvinced by the REME's initial attempts, explaining how their efforts failed to reflect the vivid colours of the desert. 'Do it yourself!' came the terse response from the Irish major who commanded the workshop.

While admitting he was no skilled tradesman, Seekings 'had ideas', as he put it. He had also seen the LRDG's 'very gaudy' camouflage patterns and set about putting knowledge of them to good use. He showed his work – full of pastel colours – to the major, who immediately 'laughed his bloody head off'. The man scoffed that the jeep could be seen from England, never mind the frontline. 'For Christ's sake, it's like something from a fairground.'

Soon afterwards, the major revised his opinions on the colour palette of pinks, blues, greens and yellows when the jeep was taken to a nearby firing range. Seekings parked his creation not far from an embankment behind the range. He and the major then walked 100 yards away before turning back to face the vehicle. 'I can't believe it!' exclaimed the Irishman. 'I can hardly see the thing. If I didn't know it was there, I'd miss it.'

That wasn't the only shock the officer received that day. Seekings was keen to check the newly consolidated springs in the jeep to see if they could now stand up to the burden of the gun mounts. His plan was to speed towards a trench, jump across the gap and land as high up the opposite embankment as possible. 'You'd better get off, sir,' he advised the major, who was sat at the back, legs dangling

over the side. 'Oh, I'll be all right,' came the reply. Words he came
to regret.

Seekings gave the jeep a long lead-up, gradually increasing the
speed until it was well beyond the 60 miles-per-hour mark. 'That
was the only way you could jump anything.' The vehicle was just
about flat out by the time it reached the trench, whistling over it
before crashing down towards the top on the other side. Seekings
quickly glanced over his shoulder – his passenger was no longer
in the back. 'I think he'd just hit the deck as I turned round and
looked. He was a huge chap, lean, raw-boned; absolutely white.
From his armpit, down his arm, it had taken all the skin off. What
a bloody mess. Jeez, that must have been giving him hell.' Seekings
offered the officer an apology. 'No, it's all right, it's all right,' came
the reply. 'But I know you're mad now. Is there any more like you?'

From then on Seekings received 'wonderful service' from the
major and the REME workshop team. 'No arguments. They went
to town and we really built up those jeeps.' The vehicles were soon
on their way to the desert rendezvous. 'We sent batches of them out.
They'd come down, pick 'em up and take them up there.'

Meanwhile, Stirling and Mayne enjoyed plenty of success as the
SAS took out yet more enemy aircraft and vehicles. On one hand,
Seekings was frustrated not to have been involved but on the other
he knew his time was being spent wisely. 'I was happy we were
getting some work done and I could see what was coming out of it.'
And it wouldn't be long before he was back in the thick of the action
at the spearhead of a flotilla of jeeps carrying out an SAS raid that
was to become famous.

• ● •

The North African aerodromes and landing grounds under Axis
control were on high alert throughout the spring and summer of

1942, so often had Stirling's patrols turned up to wreak havoc. Security was stepped up or modified to try and thwart the raiders. Initially a single sentry was detailed to protect each plane through the dark hours, then guard patrols were increased. Beefed-up perimeter defences were also installed around airbases.

But Stirling devised an attack for 26 July that the Axis forces could surely not have anticipated. Instead of three- or four-man sub-sections undergoing lengthy walks to bases before littering their bombs, the SAS commander hatched a plan to deploy his new toys in a full-on attack. A fresh consignment of the heavily weaponized jeeps had arrived at the desert hideout of Bir el Quseir, and Stirling intended to storm Sidi Haneish airfield with them. Intel outlined how the base, near Fuka, was stuffed full of German aircraft. The jeeps[4] were to penetrate the perimeter and, in a box formation, proceed down the airfield blazing outwards with a mix of deadly fire at the static planes. The formation would swing round and continue unleashing on the same targets before splitting up to escape. It was a bold and dangerous plan that required lengthy rehearsals, staged deep in the desert the night before. The timing for the specific movements was to be orchestrated by coloured Very lights (illuminating flares discharged from a specially designed pistol), fired by Stirling.

Just before sundown the vehicles, loaded with ammunition, left the RV. Stirling had Seekings and Cooper with him – they would lead the massed jeeps onto the airfield. Either side of his vehicle were columns headed by Mayne and George Jellicoe; the latter had recently joined the SAS from the Special Boat Section. Mike Sadler, by now part of the SAS rather than the LRDG, was assigned with guiding the party in, using his finely honed skills.

---

4   Different accounts record the number of jeeps used as between fifteen and twenty.

Also on navigation duties was Cooper. A quarter moon offered a little assistance with visibility as night fell, but passing clouds meant that at times it was just about pitch black.

The journey into the target was far from straightforward and was halted by a steady series of punctures as the jeeps travelled across rough ground. With the convoy drawing closer to the coast, it also passed an area that revealed all the signs of a recent battle – fire-ravaged vehicles and fallen soldiers.

Hours spent in transit meant that time was slipping away if the group was to fulfil its goal. The jeeps paused and Stirling asked Sadler about their latest position. 'Mike, where is this bloody airfield?' enquired the SAS commander. The navigator estimated that Sidi Haneish was about a mile dead ahead and confirmation arrived with his words still fresh on the air. 'At that minute the airfield lit up,' Sadler recalled. 'It was right across the front of us – we had absolutely hit it in the middle. From my point of view, it was a very gratifying piece of navigation. The landing lights came on just for a minute or so and a Heinkel came in and landed. The lights were switched out again almost immediately.'

There was no time for congratulations, however. While Sadler sped off to man the south-east corner of the base as a rescue point should any of the party 'come unstuck', the rest of the jeeps announced their arrival at the perimeter with a deafening broadside from the Vickers K machine guns. After the initial torrent of fire, a green Very light conveyed the message that the jeeps were to line up in formation with Stirling's vehicle to the fore. In the following minutes the columns moved forward steadily, unleashing a withering onslaught on the mass of bombers, fighter and transport planes that were parked up, many at unmissable range even in darkness.

'You had two lines, one parallel to each other but both firing outwards so they weren't firing at each other and they drove round in a box formation,' explained Sadler. 'How well they did so in the dark I'm not quite sure, but of course it lit up fairly soon.'

Indeed, it was not long before an orangey-red glow illuminated the airfield, which became enveloped by acrid smoke. Plane after plane exploded into flames as the barrage from sixty-plus guns inflicted massive damage. Such was the scorching heat emanating from the burning aircraft frames that it singed the hair of the raiders as they drove past.

The base's ground defences began to respond. A mortar shell landed worryingly close to the formation, while a persistent Breda gun also targeted the raiders. Amid the resistance, Stirling's jeep took a hit and instantly came to a halt. Seekings was asked to investigate, with Stirling demanding to know what the problem was. 'Well, don't get out and look, but we haven't got an engine,' came the retort from the man on the ground. Help was at hand and the vehicle's occupants cadged a lift with Captain Sandy Scratchley. However, lifeless in the back of the jeep was its rear gunner John Robson, who had been shot in the head. Cooper gently moved the fallen man before taking possession of his gun.

All around, the Vickers Ks kept on adding to the ever-rising tally of destroyed aircraft, but there was still time for one final flourish before the SAS took their leave. Mayne spotted an undamaged plane that was just too tempting to pass up. Jumping from his jeep, he applied a Lewes bomb in the tried and tested manner. Yet another aircraft for him to notch up. But on this occasion it was primarily the lethal Vickers Ks that accounted for the vast majority of the wrecked planes scattered all over a site that only fifteen minutes earlier had lit up for the incoming Heinkel. 'I think we decided they had fired off 27,000 rounds of ammunition,' Sadler reflected many years later. 'Armour-piercing, inflammable and explosive bullets alternately; a sort of soup of different kinds of charges. The chaps with the machine guns had all got a full load of those and they fired off that many on the airfield – a tremendous piece of firepower.'

Sadler was in the last jeep to head south. Hidden away in a corner of the airfield, he had hung around for ages. By the time he was moving, the Germans were already up and about. Dawn had broken but the desert was shrouded in an early morning mist, which proved helpful for Sadler as he endured 'quite an alarming experience'. Peering through the foggy conditions he noticed a party of Germans ahead of him. 'They were parked in the early-morning light having a quick cup of tea and I drove through from the rear. They didn't particularly set great stall by me, and I didn't wait to bother them.'

Late that afternoon, having initially sought cover to avoid the retaliatory threat from the skies, the jeeps started to return to the hideout. Mayne, who was with those first back, was asked how many planes the raiders had got. 'Forty maybe,' came his response. 'I doubt that we'll be claiming more than thirty, you couldn't really count them properly.'[5] It was indeed a difficult one to weigh up, given the absolute bedlam of that action-packed quarter of an hour.

Soon after the jeep raid, Stirling was called back to Middle East Command's General GHQ. In a formal meeting he discovered the SAS was now required for a major offensive on Benghazi, a significant port for the enemy's supply purposes. He was to be given additional personnel that would see him mobilizing a force comprised of more than 200 men. The attack, slated for mid-September, was part of a grand scheme that would also attempt to wrest back control of Tobruk and Jalo. If everything worked out well, it would divert the attention of the enemy away from the

---

5   In his memoir, *Born of the Desert*, SAS medical officer Malcolm Pleydell wrote: 'We claimed twenty-five aircraft destroyed, but I was told later that our reconnaissance planes had confirmed many more.'

frontline and also seriously undermine its supply chain, thus giving the Eighth Army the whip hand at El Alamein where the first battle had ended in stalemate.

Stirling was unhappy with the mission. His preference was to lurk behind the lines, nightly hurting Axis supplies by smashing up dumps and petrol bowsers. Classic small-scale, ghost in-and-out SAS hits over which he had direct control. Benghazi, however, was to be an operation with very few of the unit's usual hallmarks. Instead, Stirling's men were to combine with a Royal Navy detachment as well as SBS and Commando troops. Operation Bigamy, as it was called, was even assigned two tanks. All in all, the proposed raid did not look or feel like those that had caught the enemy off guard on so many different occasions over the previous nine months.

On the same Cairo visit as the planning conference, Stirling also attended a function at which he was introduced to its most important guest – Winston Churchill. The prime minister was sufficiently impressed to request a follow-up meeting the next evening. It was the ideal opportunity for Stirling to share his long-term vision for the SAS: his aspirations for the unit to grow into a regiment and for its future use beyond North Africa and into Europe.

That summer, another conversation involving Stirling was to have a direct influence not just on Reg Seekings, but also on his brother. A year earlier, after his traumatic Crete experiences, Bob had left hospital as Layforce was disbanding. He ceased to be attached to Middle East Depot Commando on 28 August and two days later was attached to Docks Camp at Port Tewfik.

There, on the southern end of the Suez Canal, Bob spent months doing general fatigues, including overseeing row after row of tents being erected. At the same time, he formed a strong bond with a Sudanese soldier who helped him keep the native workforce in line as daily duties were carried out. Bob also enjoyed going to have tea with elderly Egyptian men, shooting the breeze and picking up some of the Arabic language. It was a low-key period of the war for him but probably came at the right time after the fighting withdrawal from Crete and the ensuing hardships of the boat escape.

The extensive enemy thrust in mid-1942 changed the picture for Bob and his friend Eric Musk. Men of the calibre of the Commando-trained pair were needed to bolster the diminished Eighth Army's fighting columns; a factor that swayed Reg to take an irregular course of action. 'Stirling tipped me off that all those sorts of people were going to be drafted up into the frontline because Rommel was really pushing,' remembered Reg. 'So Stirling said to me, "What about this young brother I hear about? You better get him".' Reg also received the affirmative when he asked if Musk too could join the unit. Not long afterwards he made the 25-mile trip south to swoop on Tewfik. 'I went down, told them to pack their bloody bags, left a note for their OC and brought them back into the unit. That's how Bob got to be in the SAS.'

A rather fitting way for Bob and Eric to be brought into the fold. Not exactly by the book, but then not much about Reg Seekings – or, indeed Stirling's SAS – was.

Chapter 11

BATTLE AT BENGHAZI

Egypt's Kharga Oasis in late August 1942 was much to Reg's liking. Aside from the bathing available in the healing waters, the town was British administered, and possessed a railway station and tarmac roads. Then there was the tennis club – 'first class' in his opinion – where the members all spoke English. 'It wasn't hard to imagine you were back home.' Adding to the agreeable surrounds, there was the attraction of the local girls, whom he found 'very charming'.

But Kharga's comforts were a fleeting taste of the good life for the SAS. Three separate convoys were in the midst of a gruelling journey, travelling south of the Great Sand Sea and westwards across to Kufra in south-east Cyrenaica. From there, the trucks and jeeps carrying more than 200 men and extensive ammunition were to point north ahead of laying up within striking distance of the port of Benghazi. From base to Benghazi via the chosen route was an epic desert tour in the vicinity of 1,500 miles.

Stirling's force was scheduled to attack through the night of 13 September into the early hours of the next morning. However, it was a race for the unit just to get itself in position for the assault. Time was against them right from the moment preparations began at Kabrit. The workload was tremendous as vehicles were stacked and readied for weeks of desert travel. A herculean effort was required simply to mobilize the SAS for Operation Bigamy.

Around midnight one evening, Seekings' section had finished a lengthy shift when Sergeant Dave Kershaw asked for assistance with the men under his control. 'My lot have gone bolshie,' he explained. Seekings took a hardline response; he stuck the boot in – literally. 'That was when I got the name for being a rough, tough so-and-so,' he said.

The weeks in transit presented a different challenge as the trucks were often held up by soft sand. 'A number of the drivers had no experience in this sort of thing,' considered Seekings. All too regularly on the trek he was scurrying round with the steel sand channels and mats to help free vehicles that had come to a standstill. It was time-consuming and tested the patience of even the most mild-mannered. Not that Seekings could count himself among their number.

Diminishing essentials were another major concern. At one point, with the convoy enduring the Kharga–Kufra leg (a trip of around 600 miles), petrol supplies had run dangerously low and the ever-dependable SAS Original Jim Almonds went off in search of an Egyptian emergency landing strip that was understood to be in the locale. 'We spent two very anxious days waiting for him; at last he turned up with plenty to get us to Kufra,' wrote Seekings.

Kufra was full of hustle and bustle at the start of that September. Not only was the sizeable SAS unit assembled at the oasis, so were men from the SBS, LRDG and the Commandos. All were preparing to hit simultaneously various targets across the theatre. The Sudan Defence Force (SDF), who were also at the basin oasis, would launch their assault on Jalo a couple of days after the main wave.

For the SAS, a last-leg journey of more than 600 miles lay ahead, much of it alongside the west side of the Sand Sea. The men were bound for an RV in Wadi Gamra, around 40 miles south of Benghazi, and hundreds of miles behind the lines established at El Alamein. Advance, main and rear convoys left Kufra in the first week of September and the final hours prior to departure were spent with all hands engaged in feverish activity. 'It was really wicked, the way we worked the men,' wrote Seekings. 'It must have been nearly 2 o'clock in the morning when they had finished and I must have been the most unpopular man ever born, particularly as we were moving off at 4.30. I had to find a guard to wake us up.

'We drove all that day until late at night; then I had to find another guard as we were moving well before first light. The cursing was terrific in spite of the fact that everyone from the CO downwards was taking their turn, as they did with all fatigues. Once, at least, we drove all night. It got to be sheer murder to keep awake.'

That Stirling was prepared to do his bit during the long haul up country provided a timely reminder of the SAS's ethos. This was a far more egalitarian unit than usual in the British Army; one in which respect was earned by actions rather than deference to rank. And Stirling's force would need every ounce of its unique esprit de corps for what lay ahead in Benghazi.

The operation's first casualty was sustained long before a shot was fired in anger. One night a truck that was part of the rear convoy became unbalanced by a sizeable hummock, throwing off Eustace A.N. Sque. An armament quarter-master sergeant with the REME – and pal of Seekings from his time in the workshop near Heliopolis – he'd used up his leave to join the Benghazi mission. Sque wanted to be on an SAS patrol to find out more about conditions so that he could facilitate future modifications to equipment. However, the fall from the truck left him with his plans in tatters and a broken femur.

A couple of days later the calm of dawn was interrupted by a mighty bang. A jeep had been blown up by a Thermos bomb (an anti-personnel mine) and burst into flames. The driver managed to drag clear its other occupant, Royal Navy officer Richard A. B. Ardley, but both individuals were seriously injured. 'The naval man was very badly burnt,' recalled Seekings. 'He begged us to shoot him as he said he would only live about three days at the most and would be a hindrance to us.' In fact, Ardley died in the early hours of the following day.

● ● ●

All three parties, minus the two tanks, had arrived at the RV by late in the day on 11 September. The location in Wadi Gamra was a welcome change after days spent amid rolling banks of sand, white light and intense heat. Now the SAS were surrounded by the fertile uplands of the Jebel Akhdar – 'The Green Mountain'. They secreted their vehicles deep in an ancient waterway, out of view of any Axis reconnaissance planes that might choose to fly over.

It was here that Stirling received intelligence from Captain Bob Melot, an extraordinary individual who became attached to the SAS. A Belgium Air Force pilot during the First World War, Melot went on to settle in Alexandria where he became a cotton trader. But as a middle-aged man, the Desert War saw him return to action, this time for the British Army. He lived a nomadic existence, often deep inside enemy territory.

Melot had his own network of Arab contacts, one of whom returned to the RV from Benghazi on 12 September. The man, a private in the Libyan Arab Force (LAF), was the harbinger of concerning news: Stirling's party was apparently expected. His information included reference to the recent arrival of seventy truckloads of Italian infantrymen to supplement the German battalion camped to the north-east of the town. Most of the shipping had seemingly moved on, too. That was a big blow if true; causing chaos in the harbour was key to damaging Rommel's supply chain. Melot's contact also reported that the town had strengthened its defences, including the laying of a minefield – overlooked by machine-gun posts and pillboxes – on its outer circular road.

Stirling was concerned enough to signal GHQ with the details. But any unease he may have felt was not shared by those in Cairo. The reply he received, according to an official memo, 'showed that no great importance was attributed to this information'. The job remained on.

As for those from the ranks, it is unlikely they knew much about the enemy's defensive capabilities in the hours prior to the Benghazi offensive. However, Seekings later reflected that he was in no doubt that the Axis were ready for the SAS. Indeed, he was convinced that loose lips had undermined the whole operation. 'They were waiting for us,' he said. 'Any other circumstances, if it hadn't have been leaked, we could've walked in there like we had done before. We definitely weren't picked up by aircraft or reconnaissance going in; it was just a matter of they *knew* that we were going in.'

He believed those in Cairo were to blame for the situation. 'We had one or two people that were a bit loose-mouthed.' Whether his opinions regarding a leak were right or wrong, one thing was for sure in the early hours of 14 September: Stirling's force weren't about to walk into the town as they pleased. Instead, Benghazi would go down as 'the toughest job', according to Seekings.

The build-up to the raid included diligent preparation and boisterous singing. Guns were cleaned and haversacks packed. In went Lewes bombs and grenades, as well as more prosaic items such as a blanket and maybe a book. Precautionary escape kits were handed out, including Benzedrine (an amphetamine) tablets.

There was also a fair share of pensive contemplation around

the wadi. Mayne anticipated 'some hard scrapping' ahead and Almonds made a remark to the medical officer Malcolm Pleydell that it looked as if he was 'going to be kept busy'. Bill Cumper, the down-to-earth cockney captain, echoed the sentiment in his own inimitable style: 'Oy, Quack! Mind you've got yer knives nice and sharp before we're back!'

Fortification was required in the countdown to departure. Tinned sardines and a bite of chocolate. Tots of rum and maybe the odd Benzedrine tablet. After weeks of travel, it was finally time for action.

· ● ·

Four jeeps under the command of Captain Melot set off in the early afternoon. The aim was to knock out an Italian-manned fort that the main force would have to travel close to as it followed on slightly later. Melot's team was to silence the fort's wireless post, thus preventing Benghazi from knowing it was about to come under attack. A short but fierce scrap ended with the Italians surrendering but the objective was not achieved without cost; Melot and Captain Chris Bailey were badly wounded.

Melot's injuries meant he was now unable to guide in Stirling's party. Instead the task fell to the same LAF private who had carried out the reconnaissance trip – but on a pitch-black chilly night, his direction-finding skills proved utterly inadequate. 'He lost himself and it was a nightmare journey across the plain,' recorded Seekings.

Progress of the jeeps was slow as their engine sumps received a series of bashes from large boulders. The RAF bombing runs on Benghazi, planned for just before the SAS were meant to infiltrate, had long since finished by the time the force of more than 200 men reached the outskirts of the town. Indeed, it was approaching

04:30 hours, five hours behind schedule, when Stirling's jeep led the convoy down a track lined with trees.

'We were very late in the evening – or early in the morning, as the case might be – by the time we actually got there,' recalled Mike Sadler, who was up front alongside the SAS commander. 'So there wasn't a night left to make use of.'

Seekings was also in one of the forward vehicles and among those tasked to 'tear round the streets, blasting up the town to get the Ities and Jerries to get their heads down'. But the jeeps all came to a halt at a closed barrier, behind which lay a tarmac road and entry to the town.

In the ensuing moments, key conversations took place, including Stirling's request for Cumper – an explosives ace who had been secured from the Royal Engineers – to clear the way. Cumper found the humour in most situations. The Londoner once took off his cap in the mess and read the unit's famous motto under its badge before offering his own revised version: 'Oo cares, Oo wins'! Stood on the edge of Benghazi, again he opted for a touch of levity. 'Let battle commence!' proclaimed Cumper, hoisting the bar.

Barely had he uttered the words before the column came under attack. The narrow track on which the vehicles had come to a standstill was slightly raised and a torrent of fire swept up from either side. Up front, Almonds' jeep was soon in flames and hot lead continued to fly everywhere. Seekings had jumped from a vehicle to liaise with Corporal Anthony Drongin and Corporal Dougie Beard. As the men spoke a flurry of flashes erupted from under the trees. Seekings' luck held but both corporals were hit, with one burst of fire smashing into Drongin and knocking him clean off the jeep. 'It had gone through his hips, shot his penis off,' said Seekings. Barely had he lifted the Scots Guard onto another jeep before he was doing the same for Beard, who had suffered a serious arm injury.

'Clearly we had run into an ambush,' said Sadler, who reacted fast when the bullets began to rain on the SAS jeeps. 'I climbed into the back of David's jeep, got onto those twin Vickers Ks and fired away a great quantity of ammunition against the various flashes I could see. All we could do was keep their heads down by shooting at them on their flashes.'

Sadler could see the flames roaring on Almonds' jeep 100 yards ahead of him. It was a worrying reminder of the parlous position he found himself in. But alarm sat alongside another sensation; Sadler was 'vaguely exhilarated' as he let fly with the Vickers Ks.

The machine-gun fire ensured the enemy did not have it all its own way. And, as battle raged, Seekings was briefly unclear over the unit's immediate aim. Were they trying to fight their way through? He found Stirling towards the front, chewing on his pipe and 'directing things'. The CO was initially a little 'niggly' when questioned. Seekings probed again and was told, 'We'll get the convoy turned round and come back and have a go another day.'

The task was easier said than done. Seekings passed the order but getting the long line of jeeps out of a tight spot was far from a quick process. 'The column was jacked up behind us,' said Sadler. 'We weren't taking times or anything, but I could well imagine we were stuck there for certainly half an hour.'

Seekings hurried back to his own jeep where driver David Lee was also delivering gutsy machine-gun resistance. Lee, son of a Shanghai police superintendent, was known for his immaculate manners, neat moustache and an unflappable nature. 'Davy would not show any type of fear,' said Seekings. 'He must have experienced fear because he was an intelligent man and no intelligent man can be devoid of fear – but he wouldn't show it. No way would he back down to a German.'

Switching from the Vickers Ks to the wheel, Lee was asked to turn back. But much to Seekings' alarm, Lee began a high-risk manoeuvre. Instead of reversing, the driver coolly aimed the vehicle at the trackside blankets behind which lay the enemy. 'Davy, turn round!' roared Reg as he poured out fire in the direction of the masking blankets. 'For Christ's sake, I didn't say attack!'

'Don't get a flap on,' Lee responded with his usual composure. 'What do you think I'm doing? I'm turning round.' He advanced the jeep until it was bang in front of the enemy guns before reversing to head back down the track. Lee had pulled it off, much to his rear gunner's relief.

As the vehicle rolled away from the town, Seekings sensed a movement at the side of the track. He peered out to find a figure scuttling on all fours. Telling Lee to stop the jeep, he walked back and heard a familiar voice call out: 'Is that you, Seeky?' It was Bill Cumper, shaken up after he had been struck by a reversing jeep. Happily, though, a large element of his sense of humour remained intact. 'Christ, you are a mad lot of bastards,' said Cumper. 'This is no place for me!' Seekings loaded him onto the back of the vehicle, which promptly cleared the scene just as dawn was breaking.

Stirling had given the order to scatter and the run for cover was well and truly on. But escape to the escarpment, some dozen or so miles away across the plain, was a challenge – especially as visibility was improving with every passing minute. Travelling across ground that was largely open, save for the odd cluster of sheep, the vehicles were easy prey for enemy aircraft. And barely had the withdrawal from Benghazi begun when a pair of fighters and a reconnaissance plane were spotted in the skies.

Seekings' concerns were heightened by the fact that his jeep experienced engine problems. The sump plug had been knocked out during the night and a quick fix was required. He lodged in a piece of wood to hold the thing in place and then stuffed his ration of blue soap into the engine. 'This is what my vehicle was running on – melted soap!' said Reg. The subsequent clanking from underneath was unnerving, but luckily the jeep somehow kept on moving. In any case, the noise was nowhere near as unsettling as the sound of swooping aircraft.

'If a plane came our way we stopped while it roared overhead, praying hard all the time,' recalled Seekings. Once or twice he'd duck and dive in and around the small camps of local tribespeople, searching for camouflage. But that was no guarantee of safety. 'They didn't think twice about shooting them up. Chickens flying all over the place.'

Around noon, the small party finally reached the escarpment. Others had not been so fortunate in their attempts to elude the aerial threat. Seven fighters kept up heavy fire resulting in the loss of five 3-ton trucks and seven jeeps through the withdrawal. 'It was heartbreaking to see them dive with guns blazing, followed by a large plume of black smoke that meant another truck gone,' wrote Seekings. 'With it, most probably, some of your pals.'

Drongin's plight also caused Seekings significant distress. He had discovered the corporal, seemingly unconscious and his hips and buttock area 'riddled with bullet holes'. With flies buzzing around him, he was lying by a track at the top of the escarpment, not far from the fort that Melot's men stormed eighteen hours or so earlier.

Seekings moved his stricken comrade into some shade and made for the forward RV, where he hoped to find medical officer Malcolm Pleydell. It was to be another hazardous journey in the jeep. By this time, so many Luftwaffe and Italian Regia Aeronautica aircraft were in the air that Seekings was forced continually to stop and start, creeping forward while crossing fingers that he was not spotted by the scouts above. Eventually, his soap-fuelled jeep packed up and Seekings made the last mile or so on foot to try and get help.

On arrival at the RV, Reg discovered that the medics were busy elsewhere. His initial response was to try and organize transport to recover Drongin. But when night had fallen and there was still no sign of the injured man, Seekings – furious by this stage – decided to lead the mercy mission himself. He requisitioned two jeeps and it was not long before his rescue party were soon creeping past the fort, which was once again under enemy occupation. The vehicles trundled through the darkness until they located Drongin and loaded him on board. That was the easy part; placating a man in agony, unable to pass water, was to prove much harder.

'He wanted me to shoot him,' wrote Seekings. 'He told me he had married before he came out east and knowing the state he was in he couldn't have a family and would be no use to his wife. It was terrible to see him. I got him back to the forward RV and handed him over.'[6]

As the day of 15 September continued, Seekings worked with Stirling and Cooper from that hideout. They jeeped around the Jebel area picking up survivors from vehicles that had been shot up or bombed in the withdrawal from Benghazi. It was a risky business and the trio were relieved to end up unharmed after coming under fire themselves when stopping for a bite to eat.

Later that day Stirling sent Reg – with the dozen or so men that had been collected – off to the main rendevous. By night-time, Seekings' group had lost the track and had to camp out until dawn. 'In the early hours we saw some lights and heard trucks a few miles in front of us,' recorded Seekings. 'We couldn't quite figure this out as it came from the direction of the RV.'

Not long after first light, Seekings and his party reached a hill that overlooked Wadi Gamra. There they were presented with a

---

6   Corporal Anthony Drongin was reported to have been killed in action or died of his wounds, 16–19 September 1942. He was twenty-seven years old.

horrifying sight; a string of smouldering vehicles showed that the main RV had been discovered by the enemy. Seekings absorbed a scene of destruction. 'Burning and burnt-out trucks all over the place. Unexploded bombs sticking out of the ground like large darts. Dead and wounded.'

He walked down and learned some details from the injured men about what had happened. 'Apparently the previous afternoon a recce plane had spotted them, and for hours they were bombed and strafed continuously, sometimes as many as forty planes overhead. The lights I had seen (the previous night) was Paddy taking the rest out of it.

'I set my chaps to work on salvage; fortunately some of the petrol cans had not exploded and still had some in them, but it was a slow and nerve-wracking job with the scores of unexploded bombs lying around – and the planes were out again.'

It was during this time that he noticed one of the medical team busying himself on the hillside. The orderly was making a Red Cross sign (four seriously wounded men were not going to make the return journey to Kufra) with materials, including sheets. Seekings was concerned that the activities might again attract the enemy's attention. He gave the orderly 'a dressing down' and forced him to stop, which upset the wounded. 'They said they wanted help. I had to tell them I had thirteen fit men and it was my duty etcetera to get them to safety to fight another day. Also the enemy would more than likely bomb them again if they saw movement.'

Seekings started to walk away, feeling 'a lousy heel' and pondering the 'hardest little speech' he had ever made. He had not got far before the small party called him back. An officer among them offered an apology, followed by a similar sentiment from Sque, who had suffered a broken femur on the outward trip. They acknowledged that Seekings' approach was the right one in the circumstances.

Later that afternoon his group managed to get a 3-ton truck operational and soon they were off in pursuit of Mayne's convoy, which had set out in the direction of Jalo. The plan was to travel fast and light to clear away from the danger of the fighter planes that swarmed around the Jebel Akhdar. There was no time to waste during the night and the sun was already well on its ascent the next morning when Seekings identified a crop of bushes as an ideal place to avoid being spotted from the air. In the bushes lurked a pleasant surprise. 'As we came up to them I saw, to my joy, the main party well camouflaged.'

His elation was soon dampened by a firm word or two from Mayne. The Irishman 'soundly cursed' him as the truck had raised 'so much dust', a tell-tale giveaway to any recce plane that might have been lurking. Seekings also got short shrift when mentioning to Mayne that he wanted to return to the escarpment where Stirling and Cooper were still hanging on for stragglers. 'I was told I was "a bloody fool" and couldn't do any good if I went, which I suppose was right,' reflected Seekings.

The truck was a handy addition to the overloaded convoy, offering additional capacity. It also brought much-needed supplies. Even so, food and drink rations were at a premium on the trail back across the Great Sand Sea. 'It was a case of holding out your hand and receiving a very small portion of bully stew in your palm and about half a cup of tea. And, as we were travelling slowly, we got very hungry and thirsty.'

Food, significant amounts of which had been lost in the bombing of the RV, had pretty much run out by the time the vehicles closed towards Jalo – and a lack of petrol was at least of equal concern. If fresh supplies were not obtained at the fortress oasis, prospects would be bleak indeed.

But before stocks could be replenished, it was necessary to establish who was now in control of Jalo, which had been the target for the SDF. When initial reconnaissance patrols failed to return after a few hours, Mayne sent out a further party that evening led by Captain Scratchley and Lieutenant Maclean.

Seekings, who had last been in Jalo on the return from Bouerat in late January, was keen to go along as well. However, it proved to be a very uncomfortable sortie. Early the following morning the group moved 'past shell-holes and all the signs of battle' before almost reaching the fort, at which point a series of shells flew over, seemingly stemming from the far end of the oasis. A German bomber then dropped its load in the vicinity of the guns. The fight for Jalo was still ongoing and the SAS men appeared to be smack in the middle of it. 'We about turned very smartly and took cover,' noted Seekings. 'The fort was still occupied by the enemy and we had to stick there, practically under the walls of it.' The patrol was careful to keep a low profile, camouflaging the jeeps and then sitting things out until the opportunity to bolt arose.

To pass the time, Sandy Scratchley pulled out a Damon Runyon book and the men took turns to read aloud the American writer's short stories. It was another incongruous episode in the protracted desert war; a largely enjoyable interlude, although a tale featuring an eating competition proved difficult for the starving soldiers to take. As did one Runyon yarn that included details of a character's predilection for rye whisky. If only …

Late that afternoon a bomber attacked, having spotted the small party. Shortly afterwards 'the fort let us have it, so we made a run for it.' But it wasn't that much longer before Seekings was at last sating his hunger, if not – to his regret – washing the food down with a coveted whisky.

The two jeeps fled into the desert where they first bumped into the initial recce patrols ('What the hell they had been doing, I don't know'). Then, as darkness arrived, they made contact with the SDF and it was from them that the SAS men acquired much-needed supplies, including bully beef and biscuits. They also learned that, similar to the operations at Benghazi and Tobruk, the SDF had met with severe problems at Jalo.

The SDF duly received a signal from GHQ, ordering their evacuation. Mayne's party ended up joining them, using petrol that Seekings had helped plunder from an Italian dump. By the following evening the weary travellers were heading southwards once more.

Their spirits had been lifted by an additional detail contained in the signal to the SDF. Headquarters in Cairo deemed the multiple operations to have fulfilled their primary goal, despite the apparently underwhelming outcomes of the Allies' attacks at Benghazi, Tobruk and Jalo.[7] The raids had caused Axis personnel to be pulled away from the frontline at El Alamein to counter the threat hundreds of miles away. Similarly, enemy aircraft were ordered back to support the defence of its key rear positions.

Later, Seekings also took the perspective that the marathon across-the-sands haul to Benghazi, along with its series of accompanying challenges, had served its purpose. However, it had been a stressful and energy-sapping mission. He had been involved in a desperate firefight, run the gauntlet as enemy air patrols sought retribution, witnessed in close-up the pain of the wounded and also had to function on limited sleep and fuel. Hell, he'd even run 'short of smokes'.

But it was to stand him in good stead for all that he would have to deal with either side of the year's end.

---

7   The LRDG enjoyed a stunning success at Barce airfield where a patrol left over thirty enemy aircraft in flames or damaged.

Chapter heading
Chapter 12

ROAD WORKS

In the early 1950s, Reg wrote an in-depth account of his time in the desert. Exercise book after exercise book, they were full of information, intriguing detail and even an insight into his feelings. His thoughts on L Detachment's early days are chronicled, as are thorough reflections on the ill-fated Squatter operation and the subsequent success at Tamet. There are also lengthy reports on the operations at Bouerat and Benghazi. But by far the most words are reserved for his final months in North Africa. Reg gave his account to David Stirling. In turn, on 4 June 1954 Stirling sent this narrative, titled 'The Last Desert Operation', as a thirty-page document to Paddy Mayne.

Stirling's secretary attached a short covering letter, signing off with 'I'm sorry I have been so long in typing it, but it took longer than I expected.' Perhaps that is unsurprising, given how much material Seekings provided. Indeed, 'The Last Desert Operation' is a record of an extraordinary four-month period in his life. It

MS. from: A. R. SEEKINGS.

THE LAST DESERT OPERATION

We left Kabrit in November with the newly formed "B"
Squadron to do a series of attacks on the coast road from
Buerat-Misurata-Homs.

As the 8th Army were chasing the enemy hard, the road was
full of traffic and we proceeded in small parties to a R.V. in
a Wadi some miles of El Agheila.

The journey up the coast road was worse than any action.
The roads were full of shell holes, the verges heavily mined,
and the giant transporters would not move an inch over them. It
was a nightmare getting past them, with all the blown up trucks as
a grim reminder of what would happen if they moved over too far.
I can't say I blamed them. Colonel Stirling had his Blitz
Buggy, and I had a jeep with the thankless task of trying to keep
up with him; inspite of taking crazy chances on corners it was
hopeless.

We reached the first R.V. losing only one three tonner and
a jeep, to my knowledge; the three tonner on a mine, but no
casualties, and the jeep left the road and crashed down into a
wooded valley and I think one man was taken to hospital.

We now set off for Y Dump - I forget its location, but I
remember it was right out in the desert and was at the base of a
large mushroom-shaped rock. Davey Lee had been making these
dumps for the last few weeks.

I had the job on this journey of bringing up the rear and
keeping the convoy closed up. This was quite a task on account
of its size. In the afternoon of the day before we were due at
the dump one of the three ton trucks got stuck between two steep
sand ridges, breaking the half-shaft. The truck with the M.T.O.
and spares, instead of bringing up the rear as ordered, had gone
up to the front and by this time was several miles ahead. I
did not reach it until they stopped for the evening meal.

'The Last Desert Operation' – Seekings' account of his work behind the lines in late 1942 and early 1943.

covers late November 1942 to mid-March 1943 and was a time of extreme contrasts. He enjoyed his own physical prowess and yet also endured hardship so extreme that he could barely walk. He relied on the help of a young Sudanese chief, while on occasions was consulted by generals. He experienced both triumph and loss in close-up. It was a road trip that left an indelible impression.

● ● ●

Having returned from Benghazi, almost another two months passed before Seekings' next desert operation. By then everything had changed. Not just for him, but also for the SAS and – not least – the Desert War status. The Allied forces, under the command of General Bernard Montgomery (who had taken charge of the Eighth Army in mid-August 1942), launched a large-scale offensive at El Alamein on 23 October. Under the desert dust clouds, Montgomery masterminded a telling victory, and late in the afternoon of 4 November, his opposite number Rommel issued orders to retreat. Over the following days, the Afrika Korps continued to be driven back westwards and Churchill would later write: 'Before Alamein we never had a victory. After Alamein we never had a defeat.'

The SAS played its part before and during the fighting at Alamein. Mayne was in charge of a desert hideaway from where patrols were sent out to hit the enemy's extended supply chain time after time. In particular, the railway line heading east from Tobruk was blown up on a series of occasions. But as November unfolded, raids in the area no longer became necessary, such was the progress of the Eighth Army.

Also experiencing fast-paced development was the SAS, which had been upgraded to regimental status in late September. 'Special Forces' had been a discussion topic at General Headquarters through that summer and it was decided that L Detachment, 1 Special Service Regiment (which had grown out of the Middle East Commandos) and the Special Boat Section were to be combined. In less than a year, from a depleted detachment of twenty-something returnees from Operation Squatter, L Detachment had morphed into No.1 SAS Regiment with a strength of thirty-two officers and 574 other ranks. Accompanying its establishment was David Stirling's promotion to the rank of lieutenant-colonel. It had been an extremely rapid rise for the man and the unit.

The reorganized SAS was made up of four squadrons. Mayne was in charge of A squadron, full of experienced SAS personnel. B squadron mainly comprised fresh recruits, including Major Vivien Street (Devonshire Regiment) at command level. Stirling needed his new squadron to be ready for action fast as it was to be required for his latest bold plan. Over some weeks in December, coinciding with the Eighth Army's next major push, his intention was to deliver a series of blows to the enemy's supply lines and communications, targeting a 400-mile stretch of the main coastal road.

Dividing the men of A and B squadrons into sixteen patrols, Stirling allocated to each a sector of the coastal road and its surrounds. Mayne's patrols were assigned the area from Agheila to Bouerat. B Squadron was to focus on the section from Bouerat all the way across to the other side of Tripoli. During the first week, each patrol would strike twice at night and also, if possible, once by day. The objectives included mining the road and attacking transport. It was an operation to disrupt and further demoralize Axis forces that were reeling from the fighting at El Alamein and its aftermath. Meanwhile, coming for the enemy from the other direction was an enormous Anglo-American force following the Operation Torch landings in Morocco and Algeria on 8 November.

B Squadron left Kabrit at 23:00 hours on 20 November. Stirling, who had not long emerged from hospital treatment for 'severe desert sores', joined the newly formed unit along with two of his most trusted hands, Seekings and Johnny Cooper. Despite recent ill health, the CO was his nonchalant self at the wheel of the Blitz Buggy. 'I had a jeep with the thankless task of trying to keep up with him,' recorded Seekings. 'In spite of taking crazy chances on corners etcetera, it was hopeless.' It was a long and difficult journey, 'worse than any action'. Shell holes pocked the roads, the verges of which were heavily mined. Every so often the jeeps would

LEFT: Father and son: Albert Seekings (l) fought in World War I and always instilled a strong sense of duty into Reg. (*Courtesy of Mel Morley*)

ABOVE: Annie Seekings was an assertive and occasionally hot-tempered figure in the household during Reg and Bob's formative years. (*Courtesy of Mel Morley*)

ABOVE LEFT: Before the war Reg Seekings always wanted more from life than labouring on the Fen fields as an agricultural worker. (*Courtesy of Sheila Palmer*)

ABOVE RIGHT: Sporty and fit, Bob Seekings signed up for the Cambridgeshire Regiment when he was just 15. Like his elder brother, he also served in 7 Commando and the SAS. (*Courtesy of the family of Bob Seekings*)

ABOVE: Eric Musk: from talented football prospect to 7 Commando volunteer and SAS soldier. (*Courtesy of the Musk family*)

BELOW: David Stirling and Jock Lewes discussing plans for L Detachment. (*Courtesy of the SAS Regimental Association*)

ABOVE LEFT: Inspirational leader Paddy Mayne. (*Courtesy of the SAS Regimental Association*)

ABOVE RIGHT: Master navigator Mike Sadler. (*Courtesy of the SAS Regimental Association*)

BELOW: Seekings and Johnny Cooper became the firmest of friends. (*Courtesy of the Cooper family*)

ABOVE: Stirling at the wheel of the Blitz Buggy. Seekings and Johnny Rose (back seat) and Cooper (passenger seat). (*Courtesy of the SAS Regimental Association*)

BELOW: Bob Seekings and Eric Musk enjoying a leave period in Egypt. (*Courtesy of the Musk family*)

ABOVE: Reg Seekings DCM, MM, possessed a fierce ambition, unyielding inner strength and immense courage. (*Courtesy of the family of Bob Seekings*)

ABOVE: Members of the Special Raiding Squadron gathering around a pianola to celebrate their success at Augusta, Sicily. (*Courtesy of the family of Peter Davis MC*)

BELOW: A scene of destruction: the Termoli side street after the shell strike that killed 18 men from the section to which Seekings was attached. (*Courtesy of the family of Peter Davis MC*)

ABOVE LEFT: Back in a 'chute, preparing to jump into occupied France for Operation Houndsworth. (*Courtesy of the Cooper family*)

ABOVE RIGHT: Seekings took part in Operation Archway in Germany in early-spring 1945 (*Courtesy of the Cooper family*)

LEFT: Reg Seekings married Monica Smith in the bride's home village of Stanton, Suffolk in July 1945. (*Courtesy of the family of Bob Seekings*)

ABOVE L TO R: Bob Seekings, unknown, Eric Musk and Reg Seekings catch up in later life. (*Courtesy of the family of Bob Seekings*)

BELOW L TO R: Johnny Cooper, Reg Seekings, Jim Almonds and Jimmy Storie pay their respects to Paddy Mayne in Newtownards in 1997. (*Author's collection*)

pass a blown-up truck, serving as a stark reminder as to what may happen if they moved over too far when trying to get past snail-paced tank transporters.

A reminder of a different kind came as Seekings' jeep sneaked past a fort on the Bouerat desert track. A burst of 20mm shells that exploded alongside the vehicle was proof they were now in enemy territory. The subsequent pursuit from 'at least a half dozen armoured cars' made for another uncomfortable scenario. The situation worsened when Stirling's Blitz Buggy came to an untimely halt in a gully chosen as an escape route. Seekings gave covering fire as Cooper ran round the back and pushed; their commander remained sat at the wheel of the jeep 'cursing it and encouraging it rather after the manner of a jockey in a tight finish'.

Reg decided to help shove and started to dash across. Indeed, he might have found the whole scene rather amusing had he not then caught sight of a light armoured car looming up on a ridge behind Stirling and Cooper. Seekings tore back to his .50 calibre Browning machine gun, firing off just one round before the weapon broke. But that solitary shot brought the desired effect as it cracked on top of a rock in front of the car, which instantly withdrew to the other side of the ridge. Moments later Stirling's jeep roared back into life before fire from a handful of other men helped lead the enemy away from the main convoy. Once that was accomplished, an all-night drive into more rolling country with dense vegetation followed. By necessity, the pace slowed and two or three jeeps toppled over, resulting in some nasty bashes and bruises for their occupants.

It had been twenty-four hours or so of unwelcome surprises. And Seekings was in for another one when the convoy finally reached its RV in a branch of Wadi Bei el Chebir, south-west of the coastal city of Misurata, around 130 miles from Tripoli. It was there that Stirling revealed to Seekings his intentions of linking up with the

First Army as it proceeded into Tunisia. After that, the plan was to return to England. 'This was great news,' recalled Seekings. 'Then came the shock. I had got to go with Major Street and B Squadron … the last thing in the world I wanted to do.'

Seekings did not elaborate on the reasons for his unhappiness at the turn of events but they are not difficult to imagine. He had grown accustomed to accompanying Stirling in the desert and the pair, along with Cooper, had been involved in many assignments in one another's company through 1942. Now he was being asked to work alongside personnel he hardly knew and, in the odd case, disliked. Also, he was going to have to operate without Cooper. And perhaps it sat uncomfortably that Stirling was giving him to a squadron labelled B.

The bigger picture was that the recently formed unit was

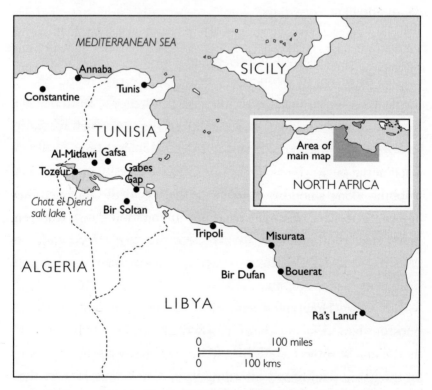

SAS operations in North Africa, December 1942 to March 1943.

full of men without desert raiding expertise. Stirling recognized that Seekings would provide the necessary know-how. Indeed, it is indicative of the faith the SAS commander had in his battle-hardened sergeant's abilities that he chose him to bolster B Squadron. It was a shrewd call, even if the idea went down like a lead balloon.

Despite his best attempts to get out of it – and by his own admission, he 'tried every way' – Seekings set off via jeep on 12 December with two B Squadron patrols to carry out assaults around Misurata. 'I was to take them up to their area and take charge of the first operations as officers and men were inexperienced,' wrote Seekings. 'After that [Street's patrol] would proceed on past Misurata, and I would, with my party, continue to operate in the area of the first op until I RV with the CO and Johnny a fortnight later at Bir Dufan airfield.'

Seekings was in a patrol that included Captain the Hon. Pat Hore-Ruthven. Seekings later recorded that the officer 'was under my orders', a situation that probably created a significant tension in itself at the outset. But aside from that, the chances of the two men rubbing along smoothly together looked decidedly remote. They appeared to have absolutely nothing in common. Hore-Ruthven, the elder by almost seven years, married a society beauty in Westminster Abbey just before the war and had two very young sons. Cambridge-educated, he was a son of the 1st Earl of Gowrie and wrote poetry. However, it was a clash in training at Kabrit that did most to shape Seekings' early view of Hore-Ruthven. They locked horns on the subject of driving speed; the officer 'seemed terrified at thirty miles an hour', according to Seekings. 'I had a very poor opinion of his courage.' Hore-Ruthven's negative feelings towards his sergeant were equally intense, if not more so. He detested him with a passion. And yet within days of going on operation alongside one another, the two men had completely revised their respective attitudes.

The thaw began slowly enough, prompted by Seekings' patient and commonsense approach after the jeeps encountered a wadi that was proving impassable due to thick mud. 'Major Street and Captain Hore-Ruthven asked me what we should do. I replied, "Wait until it dries up a bit." They were worried about being late, but after I pointed out it was one of those things that just couldn't be helped, they settled down. We got across at midday losing about six hours. It was then Captain Hore-Ruthven turned to me and said, "I am glad I have you with me sergeant, but I still hate your guts." I quickly let him know my feelings, but my opinion of him was gradually changing.'

Their first attack on the major coastal road was to take place on 15 December, just above the town of Tawergha, which lay around 25 miles south of Misurata. Seekings proposed 'a maximum effort with everything and everyone engaged' but this was initially resisted by Major Street. 'He had a plan entirely contrary to mine. He was going to insist on this until Captain Hore-Ruthven very bluntly informed him that I was in charge.'

The jeeps set off from the inner desert late in the afternoon. Passing Bir Dufan, enemy machine guns opened up on the patrols, forcing them to take cover under a small hill. With that alarm behind them, the party travelled due east and Seekings took the opportunity to grab some sleep. Awoken from his nap, he was told that trucks had been sighted. Closer inspection revealed that the 'trucks' were nothing other than bushes and an understandably irritated Seekings shut his eyes once more. He was still smouldering when the group finally did discover a transport convoy parked up for the night. 'I'll show you, damned novices,' thought Seekings to himself as he and Street crept up to investigate. The pair edged in among a large number of vehicles and got so close that they were able to identify the loads, which were machine-gun barrels and diesel oil. Seekings also spotted a card party taking place under a truck – but the SAS was to play the winning hand.

He swiftly organized the jeeps on his return. 'I ordered them to cross the road line astern at three or four yards interval. And – when the last one got over – to turn into line and advance to within ten or fifteen yards, turn broadside on to give the rear guns a chance and open fire with everything they had.'

The enemy was caught completely unawares, offering no resistance to B Squadron's firepower. Eventually Seekings fired a Very light – the cue for the guns to stop and for grenades to be thrown under trucks. The few vehicles that were not set alight straight away were targeted with bombs carrying ten-second fuses and he was soon enjoying the 'wonderful sight' of trucks and fuel drums exploding, his previous frustrations temporarily forgotten. Seekings checked the job over for his official report: 'Left fourteen in flames and six probables' was the assessment.

There was still scope for further mayhem. He and a handful of other men 'quickly destroyed four or five telephone poles and laid a few antipersonnel bullets around'. The sun had started to come up by this point and it was time for the jeeps to scurry for cover. Overall, it had been a textbook raid, exactly as Stirling had envisaged for the coastal stretch.

It was not long before Stukas were in the air, but Seekings' desert craft played a key part in ensuring the patrols went undiscovered. He decided to camouflage in more open country ('a trick I used all the time and I'm sure was the reason I wasn't caught') and watched as the enemy bombed and strafed areas with denser cover. Seekings claimed that 'out in the more-or-less open, we were laughing' – although that wasn't strictly true. He had ordered no fires and also for each crew to lie still by their jeeps. The men's discomfort grew as the hours passed and Seekings admitted that his decisions meant he 'was very unpopular'. Darkness fell allowing Street and his patrol to head off for their own sector, north of Misurata, but not before a final word from Seekings. During the previous night's attack, he noted that they had been keen to plunder the site. 'Although they had done a good job it had taken them far too long; their lives were more important than loot.'

The departure of Street's patrol left Seekings and Hore-Ruthven with three men plus a non-operative in Guardsman James MacDonald. 'Mac' as he was known, joined the original L Detachment in the summer of 1941 as Stirling's driver and batman. A Scots Guard, MacDonald was to prove an invaluable ally to Seekings – and not just in a driving capacity. 'Mac was first class. He'd had no training with us, but he was dependable and I could trust him,' he said.

The six-strong group and their two jeeps pulled back further into the desert for a couple of days' rest. By now Seekings and Hore-Ruthven were getting on famously around the camp fire. Seekings was particularly amused by the officer speaking out on the evils of youngsters consuming rum. As he did so, Hore-Ruthven was 'nursing a gallon jar between his legs and taking several good pulls from it'. This new-found respect and admiration for the captain was to grow again in the coming days.

On 18 December the patrol returned to the same area, north of Tawergha. Again using the cover of darkness, the jeeps closed in on the road before coming to a halt. Almost immediately the men became aware of Italian and German voices all around. 'We had driven slap bang into the middle of a big enemy camp,' recalled

Seekings, whose party was forced to stay put for hours. The situation was not helped by the non-stop singing of Italians in a nearby tent.

At long last, the camp went quiet and Seekings set off on a recce, noticing a large workshop and 'any number of trucks'. He re-joined the patrol and outlined a plan of destruction similar to three nights earlier, although first a punctured tyre required fixing. It was while the wheel was off that all of a sudden a red Very light illuminated the night sky. Immediately the camp was in uproar and engines sparked into life. The enemy had been spooked.

Seekings slammed his foot flat to the jeep's boards as the SAS attempted to extricate themselves from another tight corner. The vehicle flew over a ridge just outside the encampment when he realized 'quite a lot of lead' was whistling around his ears. Careering away from danger and through the blackness, the fleeing jeep struck a crevice, pitching Hore-Ruthven face-first into the guns. Given the force of the impact, Seekings was amazed by the captain's reaction. 'Not a murmur from him. After we stopped, I apologized for the speed and the injury to his face, which was nasty. My opinion of him changed entirely with his remark, 'Reg, we are in action now'. The two men were firmly on first-name terms.

Having motored to safety, it was just before dawn that the two jeeps were driven full tilt into some shrubs ('a good and easy way to camouflage'). A few hours later, the patrol awoke to the sound of goats and sheep. A tribal family, formerly from Sudan, were camped nearby and their pro-British young chief proved to be a handy acquaintance. Any time the enemy was in the vicinity he would drive his flocks to surround the camouflaged patrol. Not only did that help to disguise the raiders' presence but also served to remove any tyre tracks that may have been left by the jeeps.

As the men rested, recce planes patrolled in the skies. The Axis powers were onto them. This was also apparent on the coastal road where the enemy's traffic was stopping at armed points after dark before moving on at dawn. It meant a different approach was required for the next assault. Shoot-'em-ups from jeep parties were out; the next infiltration would have to be on foot with a small patrol dropped three or four miles back from the road. It was a return to the tip-and-run tactics that had proved so successful in the early days of L Detachment.

On the night of 20 December, Mac was left with instructions to flash his headlights at a certain hour to help guide the five men after the attack. A time limit had also been spelt out within which the raiders had to return. If they were not back by then, Mac was to head off back to camp and sit tight. 'If no one returned Mac was going to be in a mess; in all a rotten, nerve-wracking job,' assessed Seekings.

The action was to take place near the village of Gioda, a few miles north of where they had previously been operating. On arrival, they quickly recognized the potential for another rewarding night's work; a group of trucks were clustered and Hore-Ruthven went in for closer scrutiny. He was soon back, reporting that the vehicles appeared to be breakdown wagons and two or three looked to have tanks on them. It was decided to advance on the transport park-up after the road had been mined.

As the men made the final checks on their bombs, Seekings sneaked forward to assess the target zone. He spotted a lone sentry and, on the far side, what also appeared to be a guard tent. There was no way of getting in without being seen, so he made plans for Hore-Ruthven and the other three men accordingly. 'They would crawl up as close as possible and when the sentry challenged, all throw a grenade and follow it up quick; place their bombs, get out and not to worry about me.' Seekings was to go solo and take care of the guard tent with his Tommy gun. It was an attack that required split second timing and nerves of steel.

He had barely got in position when the sentry – 'in hysterics' –

challenged the SAS patrol. Moments later, the raid started to go wrong as the grenades exploded. 'In the flash I was horrified to see the captain hadn't waited for them to go off and had run right onto them. Even worse, if possible, the three men were running away like hell. If I could have got near them at that moment, I would have shot them down.'

With a fury matched only by concern for Hore-Ruthven, Seekings darted towards the trucks. He soon met up with the captain, who was badly wounded. To make matters worse, the pair were then discovered by a posse of Italians who had emerged from behind Hore-Ruthven. In desperation, Seekings pulled the pin on a grenade and hurled it into the group before grabbing hold of the injured officer. 'By now the air was thick with tracer bullets and shells from machine guns and 20-millimetre cannons. I carried him 150 to 200 yards to a sand hummock. Everything they had got was turned on us, it was a miracle we weren't blown to pieces. I then tried to get him to crawl. He begged me to get out and save myself as he was finished. I could see he was hit bad in the right shoulder and chest and side. He then passed out and I tried to drag him but couldn't manage. It was impossible to stand up and make a run for it as every gun had our range and was cleaning up our little sand hummock. Feeling very downhearted I was forced to leave him.'

The dramatic sequence of events was still not over. Seekings had just managed to crawl away when a lull in the firing enabled him to hear Hore-Ruthven shouting his name. This prompted the guns into fresh action and the tracer glow allowed Reg to glimpse a figure making a run for it. But Hore-Ruthven's escape bid was in vain; he soon fell to the ground and the shooting ceased.

Seekings' attempt to reach him was foiled by the Italians. His only option was to slip away into the night but not before he witnessed Hore-Ruthven being shot from point-blank range. 'The officer emptied his revolver into him as he lay on the ground.'[8]

With no clue as to the whereabouts of the other three men, Seekings hung around long enough to observe a large truck blow up. It was a small crumb of comfort after all that had played out. 'The captain must have used a time pencil and I was pleased he had got his target.'

With the Italians 'shouting and screaming their heads off', Seekings realized he had to make haste if he was to rendezvous with Mac. It was almost 03:30 hours and he was due back in less than twenty minutes with four miles to cover. 'I set off at a steady trot; I hadn't gone far when I saw the flash of Mac's headlights a long way off. I kept going, the lights getting nearer and nearer. By this time Mac should have been away. I was cursing him in my mind for disobeying orders but at the same time hoping he would not go before I got there. I thank God I had one good man left, a very good one, as it took bags and bags of guts to sit there all alone, flashing lights after seeing the fireworks going up.'

But as the first flushes of dawn flickered, Seekings heard the jeep start up. Long after the time that he was supposed to remain in place, Mac was – reluctantly, no doubt – pulling back. Seekings responded by hollering, followed by a burst from his Tommy but to no avail. So near and yet so far. It was then that he enjoyed a

---

8   The details of the raid in which Captain the Hon. Pat Hore-Ruthven was wounded have been taken from an account in Reg Seekings' private papers. Correspondence suggests the account was submitted to David Stirling's office in 1954. Seekings also gave a similar report to General Wilson's office on 18 March 1943. This is outlined in Hermione Ranfurly's book, *To War with Whitaker*. Seekings explained how Hore-Ruthven 'ran for about 30 yards' before he went down after renewed fire. The following moments he described as follows: 'The Italians fired many rounds from their pistols at something on the ground'. Ranfurly's book also includes a statement from an Italian doctor, who reported that Hore-Ruthven was taken to hospital in Misurata where 'he was cared for in the best possible manner, but bronchial pneumonia occasioned by the wound supervened, and this proved fatal'.

stroke of good fortune. The night chill had affected the jeep and it stalled. Before Mac could fire up the engine again, he heard Seekings' urgent shouts. 'Poor old Mac, he was nearly in tears at seeing me and what a relief to relax in the seat and have a smoke. I gave Mac all the news; he had seen the show from his position and was amazed that anyone had come out of it.'

A mile or so into the return journey to the hideout, the jeep picked up one of the three men before another was located (the final patrol member was to reach camp around noon). While they were briefly at a standstill, the patrol heard transport starting up followed by the sound of terrific explosions. 'They had hit our mines,' realized Seekings, as columns of smoke rose into the early-morning skies. It had been the toughest of nights, yielding some success but at a high cost. And to think, a week or so earlier Seekings had held a low view of Captain the Hon. Pat Hore-Ruthven's courage.

'How wrong I was!' he later wrote, adding an exclamation mark to emphasize the point.

Chapter 13

ROAD WARRIOR

The final days of 1942 and the first of 1943 were as demanding as any that Seekings experienced during his years in the Western Desert. Mac aside, he had little faith in the men with him and the shortage of supplies was starting to become a major problem. A slice of bacon or bully beef with a small portion of rice constituted the day's only meal and the patrol's water was running low, as was petrol. He also had two more bodies to look after. On returning to the desert hideout, the Sudanese chief and newly acquired friend of the patrol informed him that he had been harbouring two Indian regiment escapees from a Tripoli prisoner of war camp. Seekings was, as he described it, 'in a pretty pickle'. He spent a day or two mulling over matters before deciding to head back up towards Misurata. 'In spite of heavy patrol activity and aircraft, I was confident I could carry on and my presence in the area alone was doing the job I was sent here for.'

Before Christmas, Seekings led the patrol forward again. After a lengthy march, he and one other man (recorded only as 'Jock') went in to lay mines on the road. 'We came out near a large parking place which, although empty of transport, had a couple of sentries on duty. This gave me an idea; if I put a couple of mines on the road a mile or so further on and blew up a truck, the convoy would more than likely pull into this parking place, particularly as it was under guard. Estimating they would fill up the sides first, I laid three each side about ten yards from the edge and two about a third of the length from the road in the centre. It was pretty hair-raising crawling out the ten yards as it was moonlight. But when it came to go down the centre under the nose of the sentries with two armed mines on me, I nearly funked it. Inch by inch I eased along; at last the job was done.'

Despite the freezing cold night-time conditions, Seekings was streaked with perspiration as he made his way back to Jock, who covered him throughout with a Tommy gun. Two mines were placed further down the road to complete their work and, later that morning, the sound of distant explosions came as sweet music to the patrol's ears. 'Our mines had done their job again.'

Each foray was becoming more difficult. Not only was the Afrika Korps transport increasingly heavily guarded, but the daytime searches for the SAS men were also intensifying. One morning, just hours after Seekings had been active on the road, the sound of Volkswagens could be heard close to the patrol's camp. A German officer dismounted from a car to inspect a track before the Sudanese chief approached to point him in the direction of a small villa a few miles away. When the enemy had departed, the nomad advised Seekings he was leaving the area soon – and so should the SAS. A small chicken was given as a parting gift to the patrol, who began their journey to the main rendezvous intending to re-establish contact with Stirling.

After a day of testing travel, they reached the wadi that had been the starting point for their first operation alongside Street's patrol. 'That seemed a long time ago,' reflected Seekings. 'Then we had been well fed and fit; now we were feeling a bit weak from want of food. It was over a fortnight since we had a real meal.'

The tired group ate a little more substantially the next day, which was Christmas Day. The small chicken was cooked with a tin of tomatoes Seekings had saved and there was also a second course that was bittersweet given its source. 'Captain Hore-Ruthven had received a large fruit cake from his mother in Australia before we left Kabrit and he had brought it to eat on Christmas Day, he told us. Mac and I decided that no matter how hungry we got, that cake would wait until Christmas dinner. Silly perhaps, but we felt that was a way of paying our last respects.'

The quest for supplies received a boost on Boxing Day when two Germans were caught trying to fix a broken-down 3-ton truck. It was easy pickings for the SAS desperadoes, all wild hair, beards as long as Merlin and guns trained on the faces of the enemy. Seekings hopped out of the jeep brandishing his Colt pistol and had no trouble persuading the soldiers to hand over food, petrol and water. He then stuck a bomb on the truck and another on the accompanying ammunition load. Alerted by the sound of approaching transport, Seekings motioned to the Germans to jump onto the jeep bonnet. 'We hadn't gone far when the truck went up with a terrific explosion. I stopped and made the Jerries dismount. They were sure they were going to be shot; I gave them a water bottle and told them to beat it.'

By 30 December Seekings' patrol and the two Indians were back at the main desert RV. 'We could see no one had been here for quite some time.' There were a couple of stripped jeeps and some spare wheels but next to no essential supplies. Food prospects consisted of 'three or four large mouldy biscuits' that had been fried and discarded a month earlier. Also found was half a tin of lime powder, previously rejected because engine oil had been spilt in it. For Seekings, it was a case of needs must; 'That and the biscuits went down well, I enjoyed them as much as anything I've ever eaten.'

The lack of water was of grave concern and Seekings knew he must find a supply. During the journey to the RV, he recalled seeing an Arab and a camel with wet waterskins, which suggested the existence of a well within striking distance. His hunch proved to be correct, but he had to scramble inside the water source to fill the patrol's four-gallon cans as there was no sign of a rope. Bracing his shoulders and feet across the hole, he used his strength to descend deep into the well which opened out into what was a full-on river – 'a huge thing, travelling fast too'. Back and forth he went until three cans were full. 'I was buggered after that.'

The New Year's Day rendezvous with Stirling and his party failed to materialize. 'They never expected me back, apparently,' said Seekings. 'When they didn't turn up, I thought: "Well, they may have been knocked off …"' The CO had actually been back in Cairo to plot fresh moves, including his ambition to connect the Eighth Army with the First Army.

Seekings' patrol continued to sit tight as their already meagre rations diminished. 'Tea had been re-brewed and re-brewed', the last tin of sardines consumed on 3 January and a savage hunger existed within its leader. When an enemy truck roved into their RV on the following day and its occupants sat down to eat less than 100 yards away, the camouflaged Seekings wanted to attack. But the others failed to share his enthusiasm and the Germans left, taking the two stripped jeeps with them.

His 4 January entry for the official report noted: 'Decide things are too hot so we move out, expecting long walk back to our lines.' Later, in his own papers he would document another reason; the patrol had to push off 'before we got too weak from the lack of food'. That night they camped without eating a scrap.

They were still able to fuel a jeep and, heading east, the plan was to scavenge food from Afrika Korps camps. As the group of seven came south of Bouerat, the sights and sounds of battle were evident. Luftwaffe 109s patrolled the nearby desert track, while Seekings thought he could hear bombing and gunfire from the coast. It was an unsettling experience journeying through open country with the presence of the enemy all around. Their discomfort increased on the afternoon of 5 January as they crossed a large plateau. It seemed that they were being watched from armoured cars in the distance. Seekings decided not to hang around to find out if their observers were friend or foe. The patrol made a run for it but came to an abrupt halt on the edge of a high escarpment. Once again it was time for their driver to demonstrate his nerve and courage in a crisis.

'Mac with no hesitation drove the jeep over and down he went, almost standing on end,' wrote Seekings. 'Then we cut across two or three miles of flat to some rough ground, stopping to see what would happen. It was really funny to see the armoured cars as they reached the edge and the crews climb out and look around. We could imagine them [saying] "How the hell did they get down?" A little later we saw them coming across the flat and we moved on.'

At sunset the jeep broke from rough country to overlook a vast plain where the men were 'amazed to see hundreds of trucks all stopped for the night'. There was no way Seekings was going to settle for another day without grub. Gauging that the closest vehicles were about a mile away, he prepared to proceed alone on foot. Just before he set off, he issued some important instructions to Mac: if there was any firing, the driver was to carry on to the coast road, leaving him behind.

Seekings' physical capabilities had always been his strong suit, but as he trudged towards the trucks he knew he was running on empty. 'All I could manage when I started walking was ten paces at a time. I'd do it by counting. Deliberately counting up to ten and, stopping and resting. Doing another ten. By the time I got down there it was well dark and the fires had gone out. That mile or so was about the hardest I had ever done and it took me a long time to get there.'

The next challenge was to establish if he was among Allied troops. A page from a British periodical next to where a meal had been cooked was a positive clue but not sufficient to convince him. With a hand on his Colt .45, he moved in stealthily until he could hear voices. Still he was not quite close enough to detect the language being spoken, so he pulled the pin on his solitary grenade, preparing for the worst. The smell of cigarette smoke on the night air drew him in yet further until he was right next to the back of a truck from within which at last he heard an English voice – a north-country accent. 'Thank Christ,' said Seekings loud enough for those inside the truck to hear. He 'lifted the canvas flap up and could hardly speak', such was his relief.

The soldiers' reaction to his unannounced appearance was one of shock. A man with hair down his back, untidy beard, face the colour of stewed tea and clad in tattered clothing was stood inches away from them clutching a revolver in one hand and a grenade in the other. Seekings shared his credentials promptly, lest he be shot on the spot. 'Have a fag, mate,' was the response. Seekings had walked into a camp of the regiment known as the King's Dancing Girls – the King's Dragoon Guards (KDG). They were the parent regiment of Hore-Ruthven, which seemed rather fitting. 'A funny coincidence,' Seekings called it. It must have seemed that his old captain had held a light out when he needed it most.

Before pulling on a cigarette from the packet thrust into his hand, he asked for a piece of wire to make safe the grenade ('I had intended to drop it amongst them and run if they had been enemy'). Then he let the KDG men know about the rest of his patrol. 'They wanted to fetch them in as I was on my knees, but in view of their condition and nerves I thought it better I went.' Seekings reckoned his ragged and drained men – certainly Macdonald – were likely to 'shoot hell' out of anyone they didn't recognize. He staggered back down the wadi and called the patrol in from the darkness for a badly needed meal. Seekings warned his men to take it easy when they ate but understandably, given the deprivations they had been through, his message fell on deaf ears. 'They gorged themselves,' he said. 'They were screaming and groaning all bloody night, nearly died with pain. They'd had nothing for weeks – very, very little – and we'd all lost a tremendous amount of weight.'

But they had survived to fight another day, unlike many captured officers and men from other B Squadron patrols. Major Street and his companions, who had operated successfully with Hore-Ruthven and Seekings on 15 December, were caught just after Christmas.[9] They had all but run out of their supplies when they were forced to surrender, surrounded by enemy soldiers in the Bir Dufan wadi. Other patrols suffered similar fates along the coastal highway stretch.

Within a few hours Seekings found himself keeping high company. Initial discussions took place with Lieutenant-Colonel A. T. Smail of the 11th Hussars, and it emerged that the officer had been in one of the armoured vehicles tracking the SAS patrol across the

---

9   Street ended up in one of the most miraculous escape stories of the war. In January 1943 he was among a small group of prisoners being transported to Italy when the submarine in which they were travelling was targeted with depth charges by an aircraft. The captives ended up in a cold sea, and an American lieutenant, who happened to be a professional lifeguard, helped a spluttering Street swim to a Royal Navy destroyer that was in the area. Not long afterwards, Street returned to SAS service.

plateau the previous afternoon. Seekings was then taken towards the forward line to be interrogated by a brigadier. 'Colonel Smail introduced us as the men he had caught. I strongly denied this, pointing out we had reached our objective, otherwise I was afraid he would never have seen us again much less caught us. I told them we were very pleased with ourselves, making rings round the crack regiment of the Eighth Army. Colonel Smail didn't take this too well until the brig pointed out I had called them a "crack regiment".'

Next, Seekings was on his way to 7th Armoured Division to meet with General John Harding. As he waited in Division Headquarters, a major brought him some maps to pore over and gave him sweets and cigarettes. Having begun to get used to the upgrade in surroundings and treatment, he received a hearty slap on the back; General Harding had arrived. Seekings started by apologizing for his appearance ('I must have been a sorry sight'). He was still unwashed and had no laces in his boots. 'Never mind, sergeant,' said Harding, continuing in a matey vein. 'You will find some scruffy ones back at rear who never do a damn thing.'

Harding had acquired the reputation as 'a real fire-eater', a man whose drivers 'only lasted three weeks'. But Seekings felt instantly comfortable in his straight-talking presence and would come to refer to him as 'one of the finest chaps'. The general soon got down to business, wanting to know what his visitor thought of the division's maps. Perhaps feeling he was in the company of a kindred spirit, an emboldened Seekings offered a succinct 'Not much.' Harding then asked if the sergeant could 'put them right'. On receiving an affirmative answer, he told Seekings to be ready for collection at 20:00 hours. He was required for a conference not just with Harding but also the visiting General Freyberg, a Kiwi general (his family moved from England when he was a young child). Until then Seekings could relax over at the cook wagon. Harding told his major, 'Take the sergeant and see that him and his men have nothing but the best.' Seekings' stock had clearly risen as a result of his road work.

That night he sat down with Harding, Freyberg and Smail; the usual deference to rank was not required. Seekings particularly enjoyed the cut and thrust of conversation with Freyberg, who had fought in the Great War and earned a reputation for getting stuck into the action. The older man reminded Reg of his father. 'It was like talking to him too.'

The trio were especially keen for Seekings' take on the accuracy – or otherwise – of the existing maps relating to Tripolitania. 'Apparently I had the information Colonel Smail had been trying to get without success. Once I proved the accuracy of my navigation by immediately pointing to the spot Colonel Smail had first sighted me, and the course I had taken in meeting up with the KDGs, my information was never queried.

'It was very interesting and thrilling for a young sergeant to sit with two of the most successful generals in the British Army and to help plan the full-scale attacks on Tripoli and Misurata, accepting without question my answers on types of vehicles, width of front, speed, stores. At the end General Harding asked me, did I really think it possible? I replied, "The Germans are doing it, why shouldn't we?" To which he agreed adding, "and better".'

This was another world from the one Reg's former self had inhabited before the war. The isolation and drudgery of land labour, along with the relative lack of esteem afforded to it by other sectors of society, were long behind him. Seekings had become someone. The war, the SAS and, not least, his own iron will had earned him a level of respect and status he had spent hours dreaming of during his time in the fields.

● ● ●

Seekings was to have one last North African adventure after passing a few days at rear HQ, which was now located close to the Tripolitania–Cyrenaica border at a place the Allies nicknamed 'Marble Arch' – a huge monument built by the Italians along the coastal road. He was called in to General Intelligence for further map clarifications and report filing. There was also time for a welcome reunion. The SAS, too, had its rear HQ at Marble Arch and he was reacquainted with some familiar faces, not least his brother Bob. 'We found that we had been given up as lost, so that called for a celebration.'

Shortly afterwards, Reg learned that Stirling and Cooper were at a forward RV called Bir Soltan, 'getting ready to go through to the First Army'. There was a spare jeep in camp, so he asked SAS officer Bill Fraser about the possibilities of nabbing it. Fraser raised no objections, adding that if Seekings was suddenly to disappear he wouldn't know a thing. 'That was good enough for me.' With thousands of cigarettes, courtesy of a raid on the NAAFI carried out by a few of 'our' 3-ton truck drivers, Seekings was back on the road.

First he tagged along with some commandos who were off to clear the Bouerat track before going his own way to reach the forward RV. Frustratingly, he just missed Stirling, who had moved on the day before. Seekings duly received a signal from his commanding officer to meet up instead in Tozeur, a Tunisian oasis city on the far side of the vast Chott el Djerid salt lake. 'Late that afternoon a party of SBS came in with three jeeps on their way to the First Army, so I joined them and we set off next morning.'

Stirling never made that meeting. Not long after dawn in late January, his party – including navigator Mike Sadler and Johnny Cooper – passed through the narrow Gabes Gap where vast numbers of enemy troops were assembled. The jeeps drove over an airfield containing German aircraft and then, in the early-morning light, went by a car column parked up by the roadside. 'We were well seen at that stage,' said Sadler. A not too distant 'line of hills' was identified as a potential temporary shelter and the jeeps 'zinged off' in pursuit of some cover. 'What we didn't realize was we were doing that parallel to a road which was currently being used by the Germans.'

Sadler was in the front jeep when the party entered a wadi. 'I drove as far as you could until we couldn't get any further; everybody else came in behind me. We'd been several nights on the road and had a very arduous time.' As a result, once the vehicles were camouflaged and binoculars had scanned the surrounding area, it wasn't long before the men settled down for some badly needed rest.

Sadler and Cooper were in sleeping bags in close proximity to a jeep when their slumber ended in grim fashion. 'I found myself being kicked by a German,' said the navigator. But moments later the Schmeisser-carrying enemy and his accompanying colleague walked off down the wadi, offering a small window of opportunity to the men they had just awoken. 'I don't know what they had in mind, but I presume they just were doing the final touches of getting people captured,' said Sadler. 'We didn't stop to do anything. We just happened to be lucky enough to have our boots on, got out of our sleeping bags and shinned up the side of the wadi and vanished.'

Sadler, Cooper and a Sergeant Freddie Taxis (a Free French fighter) embarked on an extraordinary 100-plus-miles march, reaching Tozeur from where they were to link up with the American army. It was a miraculous escape, but they were the only ones from Stirling's patrol to emerge from the wadi as free men. 'Everybody else was rounded up, including David,' said Sadler.

Seekings would also soon make it to Tozeur, but his party avoided the Gabes Gap. The lake at Chott el Djerid was thought to be pretty much impenetrable, but a narrow camel track flanked by salt-encrusted mud provided safe passage. 'We were lucky,' he wrote. 'It was just wide enough for a jeep.' Travelling across the brilliant white surface, he was conscious that the jeeps would stick out like a sore thumb to enemy aircraft. But soft patches across the 30-mile stretch turned out to present the greater challenge. At one point, a jeep veered off the track and disappeared into the mud until it was almost invisible. The lengthy rescue operation was not completed until after dark.

On reaching the outskirts of Tozeur, Seekings and his travel companions were approached by a French Foreign Legion officer in flying white robes astride a white horse. Seekings thought the man was 'rather like something out of a story book'. With introductions complete, the Eighth Army men were offered a bath, food and a bed. The men deliberated but were swayed by the officer mentioning bread was available. 'I hadn't had a piece for months,' recalled Seekings.

With their guard down, the men walked into an ambush by Arab troops that was followed by an interrogation. The upshot was that Seekings and the others ended up being put on the road to Al-Mitlawi, some 40 miles to the north. The following morning they met up with a British attaché, who apologized for their overnight treatment, as well as providing an update on key matters that included a snippet of news about Stirling's party. 'He knew nothing definite but it didn't sound good.'

The men made their way, at the attaché's recommendation, towards the ancient Algerian metropolis of Constantine. The Desert War was now in its closing stages as the First and Eighth Army's squeeze on the enemy tightened by the day and en route they ran into an American roadblock at Gafsa. Seekings was unimpressed. The sentry barely registered the rag-tag desert warriors, 'in spite of our long beards and hair down to our shoulders'. When pressed on the latest news, the American was less than forthcoming. 'Don't know, don't know a goddamn thing,' came the indifferent response, delivered in a Deep-South drawl. The man spat on the floor. 'Better men than me don't know, why should I?' Seekings regarded him with equal measures of disgust and amazement. 'I never saw such a shambles of inefficiency in all my life.'

Seekings came across better-informed folk in the town and heard that Eighth Army people were further up country in Tebessa. Even more important were the details passed on by a private. The soldier told him of three individuals who 'had been beaten up by Arabs and that the names were Sadler and Cooper, with a French guy'. Seekings also heard that Stirling was either 'dead or captured'.

That Stirling was in the bag was confirmed when Seekings finally caught up with Cooper and Sadler. He had tracked them down to the First Army HQ in Constantine and noted the pair were 'looking the worse for wear'. Apart from the lack of food and water in their four-day march from the wadi, the trio had been stoned by a group of Arabs, who were planning at the very least to rob them of the clothes they were wearing. Cooper received a particularly nasty cut to the head and the blood oozed everywhere, including his eyes. 'Taxis and I rescued Johnny,' said Sadler. 'He called, "Help, I'm blinded", so we took his hands and ran him over a lot of stones, which got us away from these chaps who hadn't managed to get hold of our boots, although that was their intention. They wanted all our clothing.'

Reunited in Constantine, it was not long before the SAS old firm had mustered enough energy to attend a party held by their French counterparts. The evening began in orderly fashion with the hosts informing their English guests about the right glass to use. But once the wine started to flow it soon became acceptable practice to swig from the bottle. Seekings enjoyed himself to such an extent that he proclaimed it 'one of the finest dinners I've ever been to'.

With spirits revived, he and Cooper began to hunger for a bit of action. They met First Army commander General Kenneth Anderson and found him accommodating. 'He was very good and gave us a chitty stating that all help possible was to be given to the undermentioned sergeants,' said Seekings. They also paid a visit to Stirling's elder brother Bill, who had come out to North Africa with a Commando unit (Bill Stirling was soon to establish and command the 2nd SAS Regiment).

Next, Seekings and Cooper travelled to the Algerian coastal port city of Annaba to meet up with Major V. Barlow, SAS Original Dave Kershaw and nerveless Benghazi jeep-driver Davy Lee. 'Five old hands wanted to be dropped in Italy to get the CO out. Major Barlow tried to get it laid on but no one would play,' noted Seekings. In fact, 'The Phantom Major', as the enemy dubbed Stirling, was out of the war. He made a series of escape attempts and wound up in various prisoner of war camps, the last of which was Colditz Castle in Germany.

Stirling's seizure was confirmed in the SAS War Diary on 14 February 1943. The news soon filtered through to the men, bringing understandable uncertainty. They were concerned about the regiment's future without Stirling at the helm. The fear was that the SAS may be shut down by Middle East Headquarters, where Stirling and his unit were not popular with everyone. Cooper summed up the collective concern: 'I thought it was the end of us.'

Stirling's capture was arguably felt most keenly by Seekings and Cooper. After all, the three of them had been through so much together. From the shared disappointment of Operation Squatter to the three-man raiding success at Benina – and countless other adventures along the way – they had been a team. 'To John and myself, in losing David we'd lost not only a commanding officer, but a great friend,' said Reg. He regarded the blow as devastating on a personal level, as well as for the unit.

The other big question at the time was who would succeed Stirling should the SAS continue? But Seekings would not get any concrete answers until returning to base in mid-March. Before that he and Cooper briefly aligned with a Special Forces raiding unit commanded by Major Vladimir Peniakoff, known as 'Popski'. The short-lived association with 'Popski's Private Army' was not something he would look back on with any great affection. Indeed, Reg reflected that he and Johnny got so fed up with one another during that time they 'almost got to blows, which was very unusual for us'.

By this time Rommel had devised a plan to attack British positions south of the Mareth Line and the Battle of Medenine took place on 6 March. The great Afrika Korps commander was clear in his mind that if the offensive failed in its objectives, 'the end' for his army in the Desert War would be imminent. 'There was no point harbouring any illusions on that score,' he wrote. As the afternoon wore on and tank casualties piled up, Rommel saw the writing on the wall. By mid-evening he was 'forced to decide to break off the operation altogether' and on 9 March left for Rome, never to return to North Africa.

Six days later and Seekings was also on a plane. Along with Cooper and Barlow, he was bound for Cairo and then on to Kabrit where the SAS foundations had been laid in the summer of 1941. With bonhomie and testosterone in full supply, the sergeants' mess was the scene for a serious reunion bash. 'What a party we had,' wrote Seekings. Familiar faces from A Squadron were present including Paddy Mayne, who joined the throng 'immediately he heard we were back'. His squadron had been at the base for about a month after attending a skiing course (at a school that was then in Syria, now Lebanon). It was a point not lost on Seekings, who could not resist crowing amid all the revelry and rivalry. 'Johnny and I ruled the roost that night, proudly boasting first into action with the SAS and last out – it was battle service they wanted, not skiing in Syria.'

• ● •

The SAS's major impact on the North African campaign was even acknowledged by Rommel. For more than two years it had produced a long line of significant results: enemy airfields, installations and transport were constantly hit and the Axis commander conceded that Stirling's men 'had caused us more damage than any other British unit of equal strength'.

Recognition of Seekings' part was confirmed with the award of a Distinguished Conduct Medal, the second-highest gallantry honour for men in the ranks. Details of his feats were published in the *London Gazette* in November 1942 and referenced his role in ten raids. 'He has himself destroyed fifteen aircraft and by virtue of his accuracy with a Tommy gun at night and through a complete disregard of his personal safety he has killed at least ten of the enemy.' The citation highlighted how Seekings had 'particularly distinguished himself' in action at Benina in June 1942 when he operated alongside Stirling and Cooper as the SAS assisted in the attempt to relieve Malta.

The DCM was not to be Seekings' last high honour of the war. In the summer of 1943 he and the SAS were to excel again – this time in Europe.

Chapter 14

A BLOW TO THE SNOUT

On 13 May 1943 General Alexander reported to Churchill that the Desert War was finally at an end. Victory at Tunis led to the enemy's surrender and Alexander signed off his signal to the prime minister with the words, 'We are masters of the North African shores'.

At that point, plans had long been in development for the Allied Powers to strike at Hitler in Europe. The Soviets, who had been engaged on home soil against the Germans since June 1941, were very eager for the burden on them in the East to be eased by the Allies opening up a second European front. Their leader Joseph Stalin urged for a cross-Channel offensive, but Churchill lobbied for an alternative. His preference was to 'threaten the belly of Hitler's Europe' – and he got his wish. At the Casablanca Conference in January 1943, Churchill and the American president Franklin D. Roosevelt agreed upon a summer offensive on Sicily. The aim was to occupy the island and divert Germany's focus away from the

East. A successful assault on Sicily would also intensify the pressure on Germany's Axis partner Italy. The operation, entitled 'Husky', was to be the largest amphibious invasion of the Second World War – and both Reg and Bob Seekings would be in the thick of it.

• ● •

There must have been times when it was difficult to be the younger Seekings in the SAS. Reg's reputation for fearless fighting, along with his great strength of character, led to a growing reputation throughout 1942 and 1943. Bob was always aware of upholding the family's name throughout the war, not least when he joined the unit in the second half of 1942. At that stage there were few opportunities for him to undertake any specialized training as he had volunteered to be a truck driver at a time when the SAS needed them. 'My brother had never driven anything in his life, but told them he was a driver,' said Reg.

Bob often found himself under the orders of his big brother and, on occasion, that led to unpleasant chores. It got to the stage where Bob was sufficiently fed up to complain about his lot. Not unreasonably, Reg's response was that he could not be seen to give a family member an easy ride. There was no way the older Seekings was going to let anyone accuse him of favouritism.

Eventually Bob decided to request a transfer to another squadron (hence, he was with Captain Bill Fraser at Marble Arch in late 1942). But before his move, there was one occasion when he managed to put one over on Reg. The elder sibling's vehicle had broken down irreparably and he tried to take over from Bob, who was occupying the driver's seat of a truck. Bob was aggrieved and his subsequent appeal to the section's officer was upheld. Reg had to settle for travelling in the back. A gleeful Bob took great pleasure in making the journey as uncomfortable as possible by looking for potholes and jumping on the brakes, much to Reg's annoyance.

Change was coming and not just for Bob. The entry in the SAS War Diary for 19 March 1943 announced a major reorganization. The regiment was to be split, with Major George Jellicoe in charge of the Special Boat Squadron and Major Mayne taking control of the newly formed Special Raiding Squadron (SRS). Both units of the SAS were now under the central command of HQ Middle East Raiding Forces.

Bob's service records from the same date show that he was posted to the SRS, as was his elder brother. For Reg, there had never been any doubt who should succeed the captured Stirling. It could only be the Northern Irishman. 'Paddy Mayne was the man by now,' reckoned Reg. On the day the restructuring was announced, Mayne told the men that they were to embark on a rigorous training regime ahead of a vital operation.

At its inception, the squadron comprised three troops and a reserve. Bob, along with Eric Musk, was attached to C Section of 2 Troop and found himself under the command of Lieutenant Derrick Harrison, a pre-war trainee journalist and the son of a Fleet Street newspaperman. The section was split into two and within each were specialist sub-sections such as a light machine gun party and a rifle party.

It was from this point that Bob's war intensified again. The SRS temporarily moved to Palestine and a camp at Azzib, close to Nahariya. Salt on the air from the nearby Mediterranean Sea mingled with scent from the many orange groves in the area, which was located a handful of miles from the Syrian border. Early April saw Bob in parachute training at Ramat David airbase, about an hour's drive away. Mike Sadler also undertook the short course in Palestine and said, 'I can't say I enjoyed it too much; I did it as a necessity, not for pleasure.' That was a common feeling among the men, but it was worse for Bob – he had an intense aversion to heights. During his training he even asked to be excused from a balloon jump. But on 10 April he passed the parachutist's course. 'Five jumps and qualified,' his records show.

The rest of the month saw him in hard training with 2 Troop, whose overall command fell to Captain Harry Poat, a Guernsey native known for his immaculate dress, along with common sense and courage in combat. It was an all-encompassing, back-to-basics programme that even the most experienced SAS old hands such as Reg had to undertake. Every morning started at 06:15 hours with a gruelling fitness session, roared on by the relentless physical training instructor Company Sergeant-Major Glaze, who spared nobody. 'You can't say, "Carry on Sergeant" on this parade, you know' he would bark if an officer's efforts started to drop off. Just as in the desert, the unit had its own code of conduct.

The days were filled with everything from bayonet drill to memory tests, along with map reading, compass work, weapons training and other skills. There were also lectures and sports, including keenly contested football and rugby matches. And there was swimming. Bob was no natural in water (the family joke is that the Seekings 'swim like bricks'), but stamina was a strength and this was called on when 2 Troop undertook the Tiberias march. This gruelling endurance test carrying full equipment across 45 miles and more of rugged terrain – much of it hilly – had already proved extremely troublesome for the other two troops. Many from 3 Troop failed to finish, with the midday heat taking its toll. Meanwhile, 1 Troop chose a wrong turn and took almost forty-eight hours to complete the course.

The men of 2 Troop fared best of all. Late morning, in their sections, they began the march from the shores of Lake Tiberias, better known as the Sea of Galilee. Ahead lay a series of peaks, fast-flowing watercourses and rough country. Barely an hour had passed and the scorching sun proved too much for some of

Harrison's section, so the decision was taken to lay up until early evening. Conditions changed markedly after dark with a chill wind accompanying rainfall in the small hours. Sore feet were a common complaint, while there were various other aches and pains felt by the troop. But the hellish experience ended in huge satisfaction for C Section as Harrison's men managed to return to camp in the quickest time of all, thirty minutes before the stated twenty-four-hour limit. Bob, Musk and the others had earned the bragging rights.

The intensive and expansive training programme ensured that the SRS swiftly became a very competent and justifiably confident force. Mayne's leadership style was central to the unit's fast-track development. He had the total respect of every man under his command and not just because of his outstanding record in the Western Desert. His remarkable athleticism and stamina in training always stood out, while his sharp mind and studious eye missed nothing. The SRS were led by a man who demanded supreme standards and then exemplified them himself.

But there was still another level to reach to ensure that the troops were at their peak for the mission they were to be entrusted with – and bespoke training was required. The location for the next phase was on the coast a short distance from the camp. There they spent weeks practising invasion from the sea via landing crafts. Once on the beaches the men had to climb cliffs before mounting full-scale assaults on designated objectives. It was battle drill with live ammunition, carried out in a state of high focus – exactly the type of physical and mental preparation for the job that awaited them. Each troop's requirements became second nature as they worked relentlessly on their respective roles.

In mid-May the unit was visited by General Miles Dempsey, who was in charge of the Eighth Army's XIII Corps for Operation Husky. He watched on in admiration as the men carried out a thunderous and colourful night-firing exercise. It was all part of the build-up for the unit's attack on the gun battery at Capo Murro di Porco (which translates as Cape of the Pig's Snout – a description of the land's shape), just below Syracuse on the south-east coast of Sicily.

The coastal practice area was chosen to resemble a target that, at that stage, was still unknown to those under Mayne's command. 'It was practically identical to Capo Murro di Porco,' recalled Reg. 'We marked it out – boulders, everything – to full scale. What wasn't there, we marked according to aerial photographs. And we trained on that day after day. But we didn't really know what it was all about … we didn't know it was a replica of Capo Murro di Porco.'

That Mayne had accepted the challenge of his Special Raiding Squadron attacking 'Fortress Europe' was finally revealed when the troops were sealed off on the ships taking them from Port Said to Sicily. The SRS was to storm ashore in the early hours of 10 July 1943 and knock out clifftop gun nests to help pave the way for the Allies' huge fleet to moor safely later in the day. It was nothing like the raids that were often implemented by the SAS across North Africa. This was much more of a return to the Commando concept – Mayne's men were to be unleashed as frontal shock troops.

• ● •

Reg, part of 1 Troop under the overall leadership of Bill Fraser – who was by now a major – and Bob (with 2 Troop) travelled on a two-funnelled steamer called the *Ulster Monarch* that pre-war had conveyed passengers between north-west England and Northern Ireland. The *Dunera* provided transport for 3 Troop and the Mortar Detachment. Both vessels were part of a giant convoy of ships of all shapes and sizes that would join up for an industrial-scale offensive.

Reg had never seen anything like it: 'It was tremendous!'

The SRS left Port Said for open sea at 11:00 hours on 5 July. The previous days in harbour had been eventful. The War Diary recorded that a sergeant was placed on close arrest and was subsequently returned to his original unit (RTU'd) for unspecified 'disciplinary reasons' on 2 July. Twenty-four hours later, the unit went ashore as part of a major route march and the following afternoon SRS padre Captain Ronnie Lunt held a church service on board the *Ulster Monarch.*

Once the steamer was in transit, the War Diary instalments for the dates 6–8 July stated: 'Nothing to note'. In truth, there was a flurry of activity as the men of the SRS geared up for the real thing after all of their months of meticulous practice. A large model of the target area went around each troop, maps were scrutinized and aerial photography was absorbed. 'We also had some very good photographs taken by some of our own people,' said Reg. 'Taken from submarines of the actual coast. We were able to pick good landing spots. Their photographs stood out in relief; they were a bit better than some of the aerial shots.'

Also, equipment had to be primed and organized. It was a matter that required care and thought, not least because of the possibility of it coming into contact with seawater. But the SRS had the answers to most problems – Lieutenant Peter Davis noted that 'certain rubber articles designed for a very different purpose were placed over the muzzles of our weapons and our watches'!

The first glimpse of Sicily came late in the afternoon of 9 July. The *Ulster Monarch*'s loudspeakers announced that Mount Etna could be seen from one of the ship's bows, leading to a mass clamber up to the decks. If the men's systems needed an adrenaline shot at that stage, the sight of the island's loftiest summit is likely to have led to a fresh surge. For Reg this was a familiar feeling – a buzz that he savoured, almost craved. It was different for Bob

SAS operations in Sicily, July to October 1943.

and Musk: just over two years had passed since their exposure to sustained fighting on Crete. Yes, they had stood up to everything the SRS training programme had thrown at them, but this was not a dress rehearsal. And for Bob the countdown was an excruciating period as he was suffering from wave after wave of seasickness. The previous few days of calm waters and glorious sunshine had been replaced by towering swells and stormy skies. The steamer lurched and rolled on the whitecaps as the winds whipped up yet further through the evening. Gale force conditions were far from ideal for an amphibious landing, nor for the 140-plus gliders in the accompanying airborne invasion.

It must have felt eerily familiar for the few on board the *Ulster Monarch* who had jumped into the darkness from Bombay troop transporters on the doomed Operation Squatter in November 1941. 'The seas were very, very bad,' said Reg. 'We thought it would be called off.' But in passing the wardroom he overheard a conversation between Mayne and the skipper of the ship, a fellow Irishman (nicknamed Haile Selassie, apparently due to his impressive, curly black beard). 'We've got to land,' declared Mayne. 'We've got to go in.'

As the clock ticked past midnight and onwards, Bob's nausea refused to lie down. It even got to the point where he questioned his own fitness to fight. He was far from alone as others fought their own giddiness to rush to the steamer's sides (the offer of bacon and eggs for the men was probably not as tempting as at other times). And all the while a naval officer's low-key voice over the broadcasting system issued the latest status instructions. Final preparations were made through the early hours until the command came: 'SRS, embark!'

Six Landing Craft Assault (LCAs) – and a further three from the *Dunera* – were to be lowered into the raging waters from the davits of the *Ulster Monarch*. In the embarkation process, one man ended up in the drink before he was fished out without his rifle. It was not the ideal start. Once the motorized crafts were underway, the spray from the rough seas repeatedly swept across the 280-strong raiding force. Bob remained thoroughly groggy on the three-mile trip to the landing area, which could not be reached too soon for him.

Reg was in the prow of a boat that carried the badge of the Isle of Ely. The bosun on board was also from the Fens and the pair had painted the insignia onto the vessel as a nod to their roots. Seekings was up front with his trusty Vickers K, prepared for opposition when suddenly his attention was drawn to a sizeable object rising and falling on the sea. 'I thought it was a sub that had come up ..."Oh Christ!"'

It was actually a glider that had ended up in the turbulent waters. The occupants had bailed out and were desperately clinging to the aircraft. Seekings could hear British voices calling out to be rescued but the landing craft motored on past them. 'We had a job to do,' he said. 'We couldn't stop to pick them up. We were called a few names as we left them – they were crying out for help.'

Eventually, they were saved by the bosun. Once the section from 1 Troop were on dry land, he returned to collect the stricken men and ferried them to the *Ulster Monarch* (the naval man was to earn 'quite a high decoration for his rescue work' according to Seekings).

The glider was one of many that failed to make it, with the adverse weather a major factor in blighting the airborne offensive. Seekings saw further proof of their problems when the LCA conveying A Section of 1 Troop was manoeuvring in ahead of the disembarkation process. As the craft edged closer to land, an isolated figure became visible at the bottom of the cliffs. Seekings challenged him, demanding to know his identity. 'He garbled out bits of the operation and I thought, "Only a British chap would know this". So I hauled him in ... it was the adjutant of this airborne outfit. He'd made it to the cliff.'

●　●　●

The landings were successfully negotiated between 03:15 and 03:30 hours. At that point there was barely a sign of the enemy, who had been on high alert because of the ongoing aerial pounding from Allied bombers. Perhaps the violent winds through the second half of 9 July and into the early hours of the next day had persuaded them that the Allies would have to be mad to invade in such conditions ...

With the cliffs climbed, Seekings' customary single-minded

approach was heightened by the pressurized circumstances. 'Get the hell out of my way!' he roared at a party from another SRS troop and pressed on with his own section across an unnerving stretch of ground. Mines were said to be protecting the guns, prompting him and Sergeant Jack Terry to step forward. The two men had similar credentials. Both had been commandos and were the recipients of DCMs. Terry's high-ranking gallantry honour was awarded after his actions in a luckless 1941 mission to try and stop Rommel[10].

'We did the usual minefield procedure,' said Seekings. 'You had to be very careful and clear a path. It was perhaps the wrong thing, two senior men doing it. But we've always found, Jack and I, that if you were prepared to do those sort of things yourself, you never had any problem later on in any action with telling a person to do it. They'd just do it.'

A few hundred yards to the west, Lieutenant Alec Muirhead (initially commissioned to the Worcestershire Regiment in 1940) had organized the mortar platoon on a ridge. Soon, as the official report documented, his men were 'lighting fires in the defended area'. The invaders' presence was no longer in doubt and 1 Troop came under increasingly heavy machine gun attack after cutting the barbed wire defences directly in front of the battery position. But as the time approached 04:30 hours, Lieutenant Johnny Wiseman, the officer commanding A section which included Seekings, led his men forward in decisive and gallant action to capture the gun nest. 'Immediately the mortar fire finished he went straight in achieving complete surprise, killing, capturing and wounding 40 of the enemy,' confirmed the citation for Wiseman's Military Cross. The swift surge was a complete success, as the operation report

---

10   Jack Terry was one of only two commandos to avoid being killed or captured in Operation Flipper, an unsuccessful attempt to seize or kill Rommel at a house thought to have been his Libyan headquarters. The German general was not even present at the property on the night of the raid in mid-November 1941.

recorded. Four heavy guns, three light anti-aircraft guns plus other weaponry were claimed, fifty to sixty prisoners of war bagged and a further fifty enemy killed or wounded. Confirmation of the SRS's superbly efficient attack was provided by the figure 'NONE' typed in capital letters next to the heading 'Own Casualties'.

Wiseman's section then went off to round up personnel from a nearby deep bunker. Booming shouts demanding that those inside 'Come out!' bounced down the long tunnel. 'Our blood was up then, we was ready to kill anybody I think,' said Seekings. But he was jolted from his mindset when, along with Italian soldiers, a bewildered and dishevelled bunch of civilians from the local population began to emerge into the first flickers of pre-dawn light. Among the last to step out was a young girl whose poise and dignity caught Seekings' eye.

"She came out with head held up, so proud,' he said. 'Then a grenade or something went off close – most of the firing had died down by then – and that broke her down. She started sobbing. That sobered me up ... I thought, 'Christ, like my sister'.

For a few moments he considered the war in a different light as images from home of his youngest sibling Evelyn, now in her mid-teens, flashed through his mind. But it was not the time nor place to let thoughts drift for long.

Harrison's party, including Bob and Eric Musk, had also experienced an eventful early-morning infiltration, starting when they collected five men from the wing of one of the many gliders that had plunged into the sea. Daylight showed thirteen of them still afloat on a now-becalmed surface. On reaching shore, Harrison made for the cliffs, but others from his section found a different route in the darkness. 'Here we are, let's go this way,' said Musk. He had seen a path that led from the beach to the top, ensuring that he, Bob and fellow ex-Commando Bob McDougall had no need to engage in any risky clamber up the rocks.

With the section reassembled, Harrison led a 'left flanking movement' that brought his men in behind the coastal battery for a southwards assault, the opposite direction to 1 Troop's approach. With only the odd low stone wall for cover, they kept as near to the ground as possible but were unable to disguise completely their presence. Green tracer flashed through them before the section's Bren gun duo retorted to silence the enemy position. Next it was red tracer that was skimming uncomfortably close to the group. The section had been mistaken for Italians by one of their own parties, leading to an urgent shout of the agreed challenger call of 'Desert Rats'. The response of 'Kill the Italians' duly came, but still the red tracer poured across. It took a while for Harrison's spread-out party to clock on that they had been shouting to each other and were possibly being targeted by other Allied soldiers. Once the penny dropped, they let rip with a collective roar that reached the ears of the other section, and at last the 'friendly fire' ceased. It had come from Lieutenant Tony Marsh's A Section of 2 Troop. Soon the two parties combined to arrive at the coastal defences and the sappers, brought in by Harrison's section, blew the guns at approximately 05:00 hours.

Shortly afterwards, the SRS signalled their success to those waiting at sea just beyond the range of heavy guns. Green flares confirmed to the massed invasion fleet that it was now safe to proceed: the coast was clear. Or was it? The men had not been resting for long when the unmistakable sound of a big gun boomed from further inland, around a mile and a half to the north-west. Further explosions followed and a rising swell of water from where a shell had thumped into the sea indicated that the convoy was under attack from another defence battery position. Mayne's operational orders had been to destroy a specific emplacement with 'subsequent objectives at own discretion'. With the ships clearly still facing the threat of a hammering, the Irishman wasted no time in organizing another attack by his squadron.

Harrison's section moved north-westwards across the peninsula. Frequently they faced sniper fire from defence positions at various farmsteads dotted across the arid terrain. After a hail of bullets from one farmhouse a handkerchief was raised, but on this occasion it was not Italians who subsequently appeared. The building contained a party from the glider force, many of whom had failed to make their intended drop zone. ('They came down in the sea and all over the damn place,' remarked Reg. 'They lost quite a lot of men.')

Harrison's men proceeded in two groups. One was to snuff out another farmhouse and the other made directly for the gun positions. Bob later related to his family how he became involved in a lethal scrap with an Italian machine-gun position protecting the battery. He and Musk worked in tandem, inching forward using a fire-and-manoeuvre tactic that they had practised together many times. Confidence provided by all of their training was key, but this time the enemy threat brought a whole new level of intensity and an even more important factor was required: sheer courage. Adrenaline coursed through the pair as they edged forward, covering one another's moves until the gun crew was fewer than 25 yards away. Almost instinctively, the Fenland friends dovetailed until they finally neutralized the Italian post after a decisive close-contact exchange.

In the immediate vicinity of the gun battery defences, Reg was occupied in another pocket of fierce fighting. He was heading up a sub-section held at bay by the sweeping crossfire from a pill box, its occupants supported by an enemy mortar team in another building. But Seekings was not prepared to accept a protracted skirmish. Discussions before the operation about methods of attack had focused on the squadron aiming to force the issue. 'We reckoned there was only one way; that was direct, straight in,' said Reg. 'None of this business of waiting round, doing feinting movements – just in. If you broke through and your mates were having a bit of trouble then hit from the rear, bring them forward. What we wanted was sharp, fast penetration. We mustn't allow ourselves to get pinned down or in a prolonged shootout.'

Having weighed up matters, Seekings led his sub-section in a dramatic surge. As the opposition machine guns chugged away, his men advanced via a flank before, as the subsequent citation noted, 'Sgt Seekings himself rushed the pill box'. An extraordinary act of guts, quick-thinking and quick feet ended with him forcing grenades through the building's slits. In the same clear and single-minded vein, his next move was to sweep round to the front, under covering fire from his sub-section, to 'finish off' the enemy with his Tommy gun.

On the face of it, Seekings' tactics might have appeared off the cuff – or, more likely, downright reckless. But nothing could have been further from the truth. It was a calculated assault, borne out of considerable thought and reckoning. During his early war days with the Cambridgeshire Regiment and 7 Commando, he had spent a lot of time around pill boxes under construction across north Norfolk and then near Felixstowe. The interest he took in the buildings was sufficient for him to retain a strong impression of them in his mind and he put his knowledge to good use on Sicily.

'I had worked out how to attack these pill boxes on board ship – we had a lot of time to do it – gambling that all pill boxes were the same, which they are, given a maximum field of fire. So I worked out heights and distances and realized these chaps would be pulling the guns round and firing at acute angles to get crossfire. That would mean on the high ones the fire would cross at a certain point and on the low ones the same thing. I worked out that at a certain distance I could run in, jump the low ones and duck the high ones, get up alongside and push my grenades through into the pill box. That's what I was doing whilst the lads were covering me.'

In later years, with a chuckle Seekings would reflect that it was 'quite simple, really'. Perhaps it was in his mind. But it was not the type of conventional attack that every soldier was capable of, a point reflected in the fact that he received a Military Medal for his gallantry under fire. His citation also outlined how he 'collected his sub-section and advanced on and wiped out the mortar post, thus allowing his Troop to continue their advance'.

At times the fighting had been ferocious, as was recorded in the War Diary's report. But the guile and craft of 1 and 2 Troop, matched by their determination and ballsy approach resulted in another triumph for the SRS. The 'decisive assault' was led by 2 Troop's Captain Poat, who along with his men 'swept through the gun positions'.[11] Another key defence emplacement had been taken out by the squadron, as well as a substantial haul of weaponry commandeered.

Their morning's work was still not complete. A short while later the War Diary recorded that 'No 1 Troop went forward' and a section cleaned up a further gun nest. The battery commander joined an ever-growing multitude of prisoners of war. Under Seekings' supervision, the officer was allowed to say a brief goodbye to his wife. Memory of the moment gave Reg a good laugh. 'I think his wife was glad to see the back of him,' said Seekings. 'He looked a supercilious type.' Funnily enough, the paths of the two men would cross later in the war. 'They came over on the side of the British. Some wag put him on point duty … quite funny.'

For hours, Seekings had been involved in much of the key action,

---

11   Poat's 'inspiring example to his men' was referenced in the citation for the Military Cross he was awarded for his part in silencing the Capo Murro di Porco guns on 10 July 1943.

enjoying spectacular success. He also had a narrow escape when a shell burst between his legs. Flying shrapnel 'blew my pants a bit' and 'a sliver went through my nose', but otherwise he emerged unscathed. It was not the last time that Seekings enjoyed a slice of good fortune during the SAS's activities in Europe. In fact it was to become a recurring theme.

A memorable highlight of the action was the part he played in a bayonet charge that saw 1 Troop crush a command post. Long hours of training at Mayne's rigorous insistence came to fruition as the men from 1 Troop terrorized the Italians, 'working the bolt and firing on the step'. Seekings found himself admiring the section's work; the 'sparkle of fire on the bayonets' was 'an awe-inspiring sight'. The picture stayed with him and, doubtless, also with the enemy. 'It was very impressive,' he said. 'No wonder they didn't want to know anything about it!'

He also witnessed in close-up an act of gross treachery in which a member of his section was mortally wounded. As 1 Troop headed north over the peninsula, a group of enemy soldiers offered a white flag, but before they had been taken prisoner an Italian opened up with a machine gun. Corporal Geoff Caton (South Lancashire Regiment) was hit and died hours later, while Guardsman Alfred Allen (Coldstream Guards) received such severe injuries that the following January he was discharged, deemed unfit for further service. More than forty years later, Seekings would speak only briefly about the despicable trick. 'That's where I lost two of my best men,' he said. The sentence was delivered slowly as if he still keenly felt the cold fury that surely flowed through him at the time. His only other words on the deadly deceit: 'I dealt with that.'

Caton was the solitary loss experienced by the squadron as they delivered on their 10 July objective. As well as leaving a trail of destruction across a series of coastal defence batteries, Mayne's superb leadership had resulted in significant seizures of weapons all over the peninsula. More than 200 enemy personnel were thought to be killed or wounded, while at least 500 prisoners were rounded up. Most important of all, their activities significantly contributed to the main invasion force being able to sail into harbour. A clear indication of the point was provided on 11 July when Mayne's men came to a main road and saw a huge numbers of tanks rumbling inland to bolster the advancing Allied forces.

The 1st SAS Regiment had recorded a stunning success in its first operation on European soil. And that was just the beginning …

Chapter 15

BLUE-SHIRTED DEVILS

A pianola hauled to a street corner from a café in Augusta, Sicily proved to be a star attraction in the early-afternoon sunshine. Sat in front of it was a man sporting a rather incongruous top hat and to one side stood Eric Musk, part of a growing throng ready for a sing-song. A cymbal and a tambourine were also soon procured to help the party swing (see page 6 of photographic section).

The smell of recently cooked food filled the air as pop-up fires lined the pavements. Alcohol supplies in the area were rapidly diminishing and the mood was one of jollity. Bob Seekings enjoyed the moment, happily clutching a smart silk pendant. It had been recently liberated from the Sicilian town's 'Fascisti' headquarters as something of a souvenir to show the family back home one distant day in the future. A reminder of fun in the sun Sicily-style. And also an item to stir recollections of the night before …

• ● •

The Special Raiding Squadron had barely returned from the offensive on the guns of Capo Murro di Porco when rumours of a fresh operation started to circulate beneath the decks of the *Ulster Monarch*. The speculation was confirmed on the afternoon of 12 July when Paddy Mayne informed his troop commanders that the specialist invasion skills of the unit were required for another spearhead amphibious attack on Sicily, this time at Augusta, just a few miles up the east coast from Syracuse. The squadron was to take the town, home to a major naval port, ahead of the 17th Infantry Brigade's imminent arrival.

It was hoped that the enemy had already cleared out of Augusta, located on a jutting strip of land flanked east and west by the sea. Reconnaissance indicated that a white flag had been spotted above the historic citadel. Certainly the waters were becalmed as the LCAs were readied to relay in the men from 19:30 hours.

'We had split up into two groups,' recalled Musk. He and Bob were in the latter party but it was not until 'nearly up to dinner' before they reached Augusta. The early evening tranquillity had been interrupted – and how – just as the first wave of LCAs prepared for departure. The deafening sound of heavy guns from a clifftop battery across the bay made it crystal clear the coastline was defended, after all. A succession of shells smacked into the sea all around the *Ulster Monarch* and dark thoughts crossed Bob's mind: this might be it. The relentless pounding continued as the men of 2 Troop and the mortar section anxiously waited for the return of the LCAs from the first drop-off.

But as the War Diary report spelt out, the enemy guns were soon hit by a fierce response from the sea. Coastal positions to the west and north (from where a hail of machine gun bursts targeted the raiders) were 'superbly counteracted by LCAs MG [machine gun] fire and gunfire of *Ulster Monarch* and supporting ships'.

Bob was especially impressed by the dramatic actions of one

particular destroyer from Greece's Royal Hellenic Navy. The *Kanaris* swept past the *Ulster Monarch* and proceeded deep into the harbour to unleash in lethal fashion on the enemy. It was a sight to behold and one that remained imprinted in Bob's mind. He maintained that the *Kanaris'* fearless, bravura performance played a major part in saving the landings. His section commander Derrick Harrison also watched on in awe. 'The God of brave men sailed with all the men in that destroyer,' the 2 Troop officer later reflected.

Harrison's section was eventually brought to shore as dusk approached. The troopers crouched down as low as possible in the crafts as the threat from enemy machine guns lingered. Hardly had the men set foot on land when they saw two of their own medics stricken on the ground, felled by small-arms fire.

For the imminent penetration into the town, Harrison called on his section to divide – a group on either side of the street. The final trio in each small party faced backwards as they moved in order to guard against an attack from the rear. As the men advanced, what swiftly struck them was just how creepy the streets were. Aside from isolated rifle shots and the odd distant chatter from a Tommy gun, the place was like a graveyard. The desolate atmosphere served only to heighten the tension and yet the SRS sensed they were not alone as they advanced with extreme care. It was almost as if enemy eyes, imaginary or otherwise, were burning into their backs as they walked through an ever-darkening Augusta.

The narrow streets had to be cleared of any possible hidden menace. Even though the first wave had rigorously dealt with the secreted snipers, Harrison's men were watchful and wary. Any hint at movement in the shadows or suspicions about a building had to be followed up. One such vigilant investigation led to Bob and Musk adhering to the usual protocol for such situations when cautiously they assessed a tiny courtyard. In short time, a grenade was thrown to clear out any potential enemy that may be lurking, but on this occasion it struck a window frame and bounced back towards the two friends. The three-second timer meant there was no time to run – all they could do was get flat to the ground, and fast. Happily, their luck held and the blast missed them both.

Minutes later they were with Harrison's men in a public green space and joining other sections already using the flower beds and bushes as handy cover.

• ● •

After the initial hammering from the coastal battery and the northern peninsula's accompanying machine-gun fire, the operation had achieved its primary objective, albeit with two men from the Royal Army Medical Corps losing their lives during the landing. Mayne's report for the War Diary stated that the town was successfully captured, having only encountered 'light sniper opposition'. However, the position changed significantly as the evening unfolded. The invading 3 Troop had advanced to the railway on the west side of town and also north towards a tactically important crossroads position when the enemy retaliated. Mortars whirred into the station area and German patrols let fly with incessant machine-gun fire from a stronghold near a bridge. Also, three tanks had been spotted. The situation had changed markedly – and there was still no sign of 17th Brigade.

There were other problems such as that the vast majority of the squadron's wireless sets were out of commission due to water damage incurred during the landings. A shortage of ammunition was a further cause for concern. Mayne duly read the situation superbly, realizing that further offensive movements that night brought unnecessary risk. Therefore he ordered the squadron to take up defensive positions behind the only two bridges that offered access to the vital port area.

It was a nervous time, with sub-sections spread out just in case the Germans emerged from their strongholds to try and drive out the raiders. The cold night air added to the discomfort. Conditions were far from conducive to comfortable dozing, despite the darkness. Reg Seekings, not in the mood to sleep in any case, was doing a stint as sentry when he heard footsteps nearby. Keen to establish if he was about to confront friend or foe, he barked out the challenger code … 'Hobbs!' This was a reference to the famous England cricket batsman of the 1920s. The agreed retort was 'Sutcliffe' – the name of Hobbs' opening partner when he played for his country – but the codeword was not immediately forthcoming. In fact, there was a prolonged period of deathly quiet.

'I shouted out again: "Hobbs!",' said Seekings. Still nothing came back. 'The fingers are getting tighter and tighter on the trigger.' He was right at the point of preparing to fire towards the direction of the footfall when at last an urgent yell of 'Sutcliffe' could just about be deciphered. The reason for the delayed reaction soon became apparent: a young officer had struggled with a stammer at the worst possible moment and found it almost impossible to get beyond the 'S' of Sutcliffe. The sergeant accompanying him had found himself so mesmerized by the agonizing tension of the situation that he hadn't been able to say anything either.

In the early hours of 13 July, events took a turn that perhaps even Mayne could not have predicted. From across the town the sound of tracked and wheeled transport on the move could just about be heard by some within the SRS sections. It crossed a few minds that the Germans were gearing up for the secondary stage of their counterattack at Augusta. In fact, the opposite was the case. The enemy were pulling out of the strongholds from where they had troubled 3 Troop hours earlier. Just before dawn an advance patrol from 17th Brigade made contact with Mayne's men to share the good news.

Reg made his way back to the main square, diving into a café for much-needed refreshments. While inside, the sound of shells bursting indicated that the enemy had not completely disappeared from the locale. But there was no concerted onslaught in the vein of the previous evening's fightback. Following on from their success at Capo Murro di Porco, the SRS had stormed inland during daylight to take a 'big naval port' with very few casualties. The men could hardly have done any more in their spearhead role, clad in striking new blue shirts. 'Very smart but they stand out,' said Seekings of their Indian-made uniform. Indeed, he recalled how it was the Augusta operation that led to the squadron acquiring a nickname: 'The Blue-Shirted Devils'.

The three troops had been outnumbered and outgunned. But they had out-fought and – thanks to Mayne – outwitted the Italians and Germans. 'They ran from us, I'm telling you,' was Seekings' enduring opinion on the battle for Augusta.

For a few hours in its aftermath, the men in blue shirts could be seen letting their hair down around the town's sunlit streets. Pent-up emotions were released after the stresses and pressure of the previous few days. All sorts of high jinks unfolded through the late morning and afternoon – much of it accompanied by copious consumption of the local vino.

Trophy-hunting proved another popular way of passing the time in a town that, aside from the Special Raiding Squadron and the incoming 17th Brigade, was by now apparently deserted. Bob Seekings decided to go for a tour of his surroundings. Piles of propaganda leaflets confirmed one building as the base for the local fascists. Bob picked up a navy pendant on which the words 'Giovani Fascisti, Augusta' (Young Fascists, Augusta) were written. On the reverse side, in mustard and plum, was inscribed the Italian fascist motto *'Credere Obbedire Combattere'* – believe, obey, fight.

By late afternoon, the men had boarded destroyers and were

whizzing off to reunite with the *Ulster Monarch* in Syracuse harbour. The ships carried some unusual booty, not least a load of ladies' hats that the raiders wasted little time in selling to the Greek sailors on board. Seekings recalled how a 'beautiful radiogram' had also been procured for the *Ulster Monarch's* skipper (other reports suggest it was a pianola). On welcoming back the squadron, the naval man issued a warning about not having 'drunken men' or 'loot' on his vessel. But while he spoke, a hook was hoisting up the requisitioned musical item, accompanied by good-natured shouts of 'a present, you black-bearded bastard – keep quiet!'

Early in the second half of August, the Allies forced the Axis to relinquish its grip on Sicily. Fighting on the island had lasted thirty-eight days from the early-hours invasion by 1st SAS's raiding squadron. Mayne's force had been put on notice for a couple of further assignments in July and August, notably Operation Walrus on 6 August. A road and a stretch of railway at Capo Ali, between Catania and Messina, were to be destroyed after an amphibious assault from an LCI (Landing Craft Infantry). Final preparations had been carried out but the job was cancelled at the eleventh hour.

As Montgomery's Eighth Army and the US Seventh Army – under the command of General George S. Patton – advanced against an increasingly German-only resistance, the Special Raiding Squadron's time was largely spent in camps. General training remained relatively exacting, as recorded by the War Diary. For example, 1 August saw 'cliff work, PT etc' undertaken. Standards and behaviour codes were kept at the highest level and those that slipped below expectations were weeded out. On 8 August three men were returned to their original units for 'disciplinary reasons'.

A further diary instalment recorded that another seven suffered the same fate eight days later.

At the same time, pride in the squadron was fostered with official recognition of its members' achievements at Capo Murro di Porco and Augusta. The War Diary for 20 August referenced: 'Immediate awards of Bar to D.S.O [Distinguished Service Order], M.C [Military Cross] and 6 M.Ms [Military Medals].' The Bar was Mayne's latest gallantry decoration. On 21 September Reg Seekings was individually named in the War Diary for his Military Medal. In the same entry, Poat's Military Cross was also recorded.

Bob Seekings had a moment to savour in late August when it was 2 Troop's turn to tackle the 11,000-foot Mount Etna. Never a boastful soul, Bob was very proud that he was first to the summit of the volcano. In a group of exceptionally fit and hardy men, his running ability and supreme stamina came to the fore. There were no medals on offer, but he always carried a glow for his prowess on the famous Sicilian mountainside that day.

It was on 27 August that 2 Troop returned from Etna. Four days later and the SRS prepared to move on: the Allied invasion of mainland Italy was about to commence. The start of September saw the squadron leave camp at Cannizzaro to embark in two LCIs (each with a capacity of around 200) from Catania and move up the coast to Riposto. From there they were to sail from the north-east of Sicily and make the short voyage across the Strait of Messina. A strength of 243 men from all ranks was to secure Bagnara in the south-west heel of Italy as well as several targets nearby the large village.

Bagnara was built into the lower reaches of overhanging hills that looked across the Tyrrhenian Sea. In one way it was similar to the Augusta offensive in mid-July: the force was to arrive by boat and capture their objective, then hold before handing it over to the advancing Eighth Army. However, on this occasion the assault –

part of Operation Baytown – was designed to take place several miles behind the lines. It was thought that attacking the Germans' rear would force them to draw back troops and thus ease the route for the Eighth Army's progression north. The SRS were due to land during the first hours of 4 September.

Problems with the two LCIs saw the men jumping from one to the other. In the end only one embarked, joined by five LCAs, which were much smaller in size. 'There was so much nonsense, it wasn't true,' said Reg Seekings.

Aside from the delay to their departure, there was another matter playing on his mind … 'the Amazons of Bagnara'. In their briefing the men had been cautioned about the village's female population, who had taken on mythical status, at least in Seekings' head. An Eighth Army intelligence summary warned how history told of the women of Bagnara conveying poison from their mouths when kissing invading soldiers. The message was to be very wary of them. 'Only the day before one of them had shot a German officer,' said Seekings. 'The women there are peculiar to this area. You get women over seven foot tall there – huge. And some of them most beautiful too. Built in proportion, you know. They said they were very moral, they'd defend their honour and we'd got to be careful of them.'

Known as 'Bagnarote', the women of the village were renowned for their striking good looks and strength. Many of them were involved in selling freshly caught fish and could often be seen transporting on their heads sizable wicker baskets laden with fish. The apparent effect must have been that they were seven-foot tall – certainly it was an image that captured Seekings' imagination as he geared up for the invasion.

But such thoughts vanished as the SRS endured a less than straightforward infiltration. The navy took the crafts beyond their intended landing site, just south of Bagnara, and by 04:45 hours the operation was running late. Seekings sensed that certain navy personnel were 'getting jumpy and wanted to turn back'. He was far from amused, offering a blunt response: 'Land us.'

By 05:15 the whole squadron was on a beach on the northern edges of Bagnara. There were signs of gun emplacements 'pushed up in the sand', but the landings were trouble-free even if the day's first glimpses of sunlight increased the chances of the raiders being detected.

Major Fraser with 1 Troop HQ and Wiseman's A Section passed through Bagnara as quick as possible. 'We had got to climb up the cliffs, get up into the mountains and hold the bridge,' said Seekings. 'That was what the army wanted.' However, not everything went to plan. Before the invasion force moored up, the sound of an explosion inland was heard from the landing crafts. Enemy sappers had got to work in the pre-dawn, blowing the main bridge.

● ● ●

Reg was among members of 1 Troop who had scrambled up into a hillside vineyard. The men had not been in position long when he chose to take a recce. As he progressed stealthily, Reg caught sight of a German mortar team descending the incline and instinctively began to move back. 'They must have spotted me,' he thought. Even so, such was the sheer angle he was not overly concerned about being fired upon. But it was one of the rare occasions Seekings got it bang wrong. Within seconds he was under fire and puffs of dust accompanied the thud of shells that exploded around the arid land at the base of the vines.

'Sergeant Seekings has had it,' muttered Fraser, who was watching on from nearby. 'Christ, we'd better get our heads down if he's had it,' replied Wiseman. Barely were the words out of their mouths and Seekings emerged, covered in muck thrown up by the mortars that had fallen all around him. 'What's the trouble?' he said, apparently unfazed. But the truth was he had enjoyed another lucky escape: the enemy mortar men proved far more adept than initially he gave them credit for. 'They got right ranged on me – they really hammered it,' he conceded. The onslaught was just the start of furious fighting across the steep inclines. Wiseman took his section higher into the hills, the men's Palestine training coming to the fore as they scaled a near vertical cliff to reach a place from where there was less chance of them being visible.

Bob and Eric had to be mindful of sniper's pot-shots as C section from 2 Troop kept their distance from one another while making their way out of the town. Watchfully, they proceeded on the road that weaved its way up through the hills. As they passed the bridge that had been damaged by enemy sappers in the early hours, Harrison became aware of a party of marching men turning a corner behind the last of his own troops. With an urgent shout, he pointed in the direction of the threat. Immediately, the Bren gun sub-section spun round and bullets whined through the air, causing panic among the unsuspecting Germans. Shortly afterwards there was further contact with the opposition, who once again were caught in the line of fire as they rounded one of the area's sharp roadside bends.

Other sections were not so lucky. Dead and wounded started to add up as the Germans made use of hidden defensive positions in the hills. There was hardly an Italian among the enemy, which mainly comprised well-motivated infantry troops from a Jäger (light infantry) battalion and a Grenadier regiment. Some were already battle-hardened from time in Russia or in North Africa and they made for stern opposition.

There were other problems besides the danger posed by German hostilities. The failure of wireless communications became an increasing issue for the squadron's signallers, who were not helped by battery shortcomings or the hilly, tree-covered country which severely hindered transmissions.

However, more and more of Mayne's men began to populate the elevated vantage points, including – in a hillside vineyard – Reg Seekings. He was part of a group well placed to oppose possible danger arising out of high ground to the north. Indeed, it was from that direction, and from a little village nestled into the heights about half a mile away, that a counterattack came. At first the Germans were checked, only for a Tiger tank to join the fray. The feared armoured vehicle 'started to give us a bit of trouble', forcing into retreat a Royal Navy destroyer that had been called up. But the tank was then stopped in its tracks in the most fortuitous fashion. 'We got the mortars on it, eventually, and we had no more firing from it,' Seekings explained. 'One of the mortar bombs had dropped through the open turret. A bloody lucky hit!'

From the heights Seekings had already fired a shot at the bridge below to check the range – 600 yards. Later, when he saw it being approached by what he assessed was a German demolitions team, he eyed up two men and turned to a sniper, Corporal Tom Rennie, with a plan. 'You take the right-hand one, I'll take the left-hand one.' Seekings grabbed an ordinary rifle, got the target in his sights and from long-range 'made the finest shot of my life'. The bullet smashed into the German's upper legs, cutting him down instantly. 'Rennie got his smack in the stomach but the one I hit in the thigh died first. That's the only two we got; the others … that broke them up and they crawled away in the ditches I suppose.'

Seekings had his own close shave on an increasingly hot day in which the section's water supplies would run out. At one point he sought alternative refreshment, his head popping up among the vines. Barely had he begun to reach for 'a lovely bunch of grapes' and it was practically shot from his outstretched hand. 'Grape juice squirted all over me.' Given his position, he was dead lucky.

Midway through the afternoon of 4 September the forward elements of the York and Lancaster Regiment made contact with Mayne's force. This was a moment after their series of amphibious landings that always brought elation and relief to the men of the SRS. It meant that the main army were closing in to reinforce and consolidate the raiders' gains. And in the instance of Bagnara, it was the sign for the enemy to run to the hills. The morning of 5 September opened with a mortar blast, along with a few outbreaks of machine-gun fire, but they were the Germans' parting shots. At 09:00 hours orders were issued from squadron headquarters, located in the centre of Bagnara, for the sections to leave their overnight positions in preparation for the return voyage across the Strait of Messina.

Harrison and his section were the last to get back, very late in the afternoon. The officer, along with a sub-section, had enjoyed an eventful day in which contact was made with the Green Howards from the 15th Infantry Brigade. Harrison's group also discovered a deserted gun post from where the Germans had offered a deadly threat a day earlier. It had been mission accomplished for the SRS, but not without loss. Five of their own were killed and a further seventeen wounded in the fighting at Bagnara.

By the following day the squadron were back in Sicily. The men could reflect on another important contribution to the Allied efforts. The door to mainland Europe was now unlocked, albeit still only ajar. There was further encouragement just two days later on 8 September when Italy's unconditional surrender to the Allies was confirmed with the announcement of the Armistice of Cassibile.

● ● ●

Seekings was pragmatic when it came to the deadly implications of war. Indeed, the hillside shooting of the soldier from the German demolitions team suggests he was detached and even cold-hearted. But a scene from his brief time in Bagnara showed that he was far from untouchable. He was leading a party back towards the village from the vineyards and the descent had been tense. There was 'a lot of firing and stuff' still unfolding in the heights, forcing the men to dive for cover on occasion. Finally the SRS personnel made it onto the twisting hillside road, where they passed a bombed-out house. A donkey-cart had also been struck, resulting in its owner's belongings being strewn everywhere. Amid the devastation a 'horrifying' spectacle stirred Seekings' emotions.

'All that was left were bits and pieces scattered around,' he recalled. 'And there laying in the gutter of the road was an old woman's arm with a wedding ring on. I think it affected the whole party more than anything we'd ever seen. That was all that was left – old hands with a wedding ring on.'

The memory of that elderly brown hand never left Seekings. Many years later he would reflect on it as the 'the thing that affected me, upset me more than anything during the war'. That was a strong statement, given what he confronted at Termoli just a month later.

Chapter 16

TWENTY-FOUR HOURS IN TERMOLI

Reg and Bob Seekings never forgot Tuesday 5 October, 1943. It began calmly enough, albeit the brothers found themselves in contrasting situations. Reg slept in a Termoli monastery the previous night, while Bob shivered outside under a single blanket about a mile and a half away. He was among three sections of the SRS called on to strengthen the defensive line to the north of the town, which is located approximately halfway up the east coast of Italy.

Two days earlier, the squadron – its overall strength now reduced to 207 – had been involved in a behind-the-lines attack launched from the Adriatic Sea. Along with 3 Commando and 40 (Royal Marine) Commando, they went in under cover of darkness for a Special Service Brigade operation entitled 'Devon'. The amphibious offensive was similar in design to Bagnara; the raiders had stolen ashore to secure and hold Termoli before being relieved late in the afternoon by the Lancashire Fusiliers, an infantry regiment that was part of Montgomery's Eighth Army.

But not everything had gone to plan early that morning. While 40 Commando drove out the German garrison from the town, the SRS forged further southwards, fighting as they went. The squadron's objective was to hold two bridges – to assist the advancing regular army – only to discover they had already been blown by the enemy. The bridges' destruction was to slow down significantly the infantry and tank units' progress. However, that was not the only problem that the Allies faced. Strategically, Termoli was worth fighting for and Field Marshal Albert Kesselring (commander of the German forces in Italy) immediately demanded that the town must be recaptured, whatever it took. He wasted little time in ordering the formidable power of the 16th Panzer Division with its tanks, artillery and crack troops to travel from one side of the country to the other to spearhead a retaliation.

The counterattack threat led to three sections from the SRS joining the forward elements of the main army through the bitterly cold evening of 4 October and into the early hours of the next day. Harrison's C Section had anxiously kept watch from one side of a ridge near to a farmhouse. Not long after dawn the officer sent his men, two at a time, across to the building to have their rations cooked by the farmer's wife and one of his daughters. Unquestioningly, the large family accepted the soldiers into their home, serving up smiles and warmth, along with nourishment. The Italians appeared oblivious to the danger that was almost guaranteed to descend on the area that day. 'They refused to go,' recalled Musk, who, along with others, suggested the family should leave without delay to seek out a safer location.

The tension increased mid-morning when a German fighter plane flew in, almost directly above C Section. Around the same time, the sounds of an air attack could be heard coming from the harbour. Then came the whine of the first shell targeting Harrison's men. It landed well behind them, but soon more began to burst ever closer. Shrapnel fragments began to fly as enemy artillery fire confirmed the renewed scrap for control of Termoli.

The full force of the panzer division, including tanks, let rip on the town's thin defensive perimeter, with Bob and Eric in the eye of the storm. At one stage C Section laid low in a wooded area on a side of the valley, but the trees offered minimal cover. 'It wasn't long before we were pasted with mortars firing non-stop at our position,' reflected Musk in a handwritten private record of events. 'It was absolutely hell let loose.'

The SRS toughed out the onslaught, but it proved too much for some regular infantry soldiers. Outgunned and outnumbered, it was the first time many had experienced such a formidable enemy formation. In panic, men turned on their heels to escape from the lines. Meanwhile, long columns of British support were largely static to the south of the town on the other side of the Biferno River. Engineers attempted to install bridging to allow armour and personnel to cross waters swollen by recent heavy rainfall. But the German presence on the nearby high ground endangered the sappers as they tried to work through the daylight hours of 5 October.

Reg had not been called on in the early part of the day. He was back in Termoli where the first shells had fallen just after dawn and continued to shower the town throughout the morning. With A Section of 1 Troop in reserve, he and a couple of mates bided their time in a café. A cluster of non-SRS officers sat close by and Reg's antennae went up when a captain arrived with a briefing on the German counterattack. 'We better get the SRS on this,' responded the senior officer, prompting Seekings to hurry off to inform Mayne that something was brewing. The ferocity of the enemy push and the ever-mounting strain on the Allies' line meant that more hands were required to staunch the tide. Those sections of the squadron that were not already defending Termoli were placed on half an hour's notice to move. But it was not until after lunch that the order was given for all remaining SRS personnel to board the trucks lined up on a street nearby. As the men assembled, a local family came out from their home to watch. The family had recently done a bit of washing for the SRS and turned out to wave them on their way.

Initially there was a kerfuffle surrounding which section should travel in a certain vehicle. The truck was to be driven by the injured Sergeant McNinch from 2 Troop, who was quickly joined on board by fellow members of its B Section. However, Wiseman soon scurried up to claim it for A Section of 1 Troop. The officer got his way, resulting in men piling on and off trucks in the narrow road next to some gardens. Seekings grew more bothered with each passing minute of the hold-up. He was concerned the spectacle might not go unmissed by the enemy. 'We had known for days that there had been an OP (observation post) in the town,' said Reg, who believed its sentry had been feeding back information to the Germans on where shells had been landing so the artillery guns could be adjusted accordingly. 'It was obvious to experienced men that there was an OP somewhere and he was ranging all the different spots in the town.' The thought played on Seekings' mind as the respective sections loaded, unloaded and reloaded that afternoon. His worries were not in any way eased by the knowledge that every man was carrying in his pack a large grenade with enough explosives to blow the tracks off a tank.

'We got on the truck, we get off the truck, on the truck – oh god, we were browned off. All of us were saying, "Next bloody minute we'll get blown to hell", because we knew that the Jerries had the range.' And Reg's worst fears were realized shortly before 3 o'clock. Wiseman jumped from the truck to speak with Mayne's messenger;

it seemed there was a further delay. 'They'd just had the order, "Get off the truck", and I was kicking the fastening loose on the back of the tailboard,' recalled Seekings. As he did so, an awful but familiar roar drowned out all other sound on the little street. It was the first of six heavy shells that fell in quick succession in the area. Lieutenant Peter Davis, in charge of 2 Troop's B Section, climbed from the back of a truck to be confronted by, in his words, 'a gruesome disaster' – a scene of 'death, destruction and confusion'. The little street had, in a matter of seconds, been completely transformed by the missiles. Houses were unrecognizable, huge chunks of masonry lay strewn across the road and clouds of dust hung over the area.

Amid the devastation sat the remains of a truck – the one McNinch had been preparing to drive. Its back half had been blown away. 'A couple of shells landed in different places and this one came and landed right smack in the bloody truck,' said Reg. 'It landed right behind me; I suppose nearer to me than anybody.' The explosion blew him clean off the lorry, but the only damage he incurred was to a fingernail, which beggared belief given the carnage all around him. Reg picked himself up and, 'smothered in bits of flesh', stumbled back to try and offer assistance to the casualties. The majority of A Section were already dead. As well as the shell damage, some of the grenades carried by the men had also exploded, adding to the chaos. An incredulous Seekings looked around and saw 'chaps sort of hanging on the telephone wires, on the roofs'. He spotted twenty-three-year-old parachutist Alex Skinner, his dead body in flames. It was the first time Reg had ever encountered a burning man and he was horrified. 'I didn't realize how fast a body can burn.' Seekings stepped over other victims to reach a jug of water inside a nearby house before returning with it to pour over Skinner.

Nearby, Seekings came across two men clinging to life with their chests blown open. The first of them was Sergeant John 'Jocky'

Henderson, asking for a Tommy gun to be taken from his chest – 'it's hurting me,' he explained. Reg was struck by the composed manner of the man, who proceeded to pull off an arm. 'It's a bad one this time,' he told Seekings, who tried to offer reassurance that the sergeant would be all right in hospital. 'I knew bloody well he wouldn't.'

Reg walked off to fetch Henderson a glass of water but was stopped in his tracks by a voice from the ground. 'Sergeant, can you get me a drink please, I'm thirsty.' Seekings peered below and struggled to identify the disfigured man below. 'His face was pulped,' said Reg. Eventually he recognized the man from his voice; it was Lance Corporal Charles Grant from A Section. 'You could see his lungs and his heart beating away.'

At one point Seekings passed what was left of the truck and saw McNinch still sitting in the cab with a broad smile spread across his face. Reg wondered if the man's nerve had been shattered by the shell strike. 'Christ man, what the hell's wrong with you?' he roared at the volunteer driver. 'Come on, get out and give us a hand. Don't sit there grinning like a bloody Cheshire cat.' But McNinch remained in his seat, still beaming. Angrily, Reg yanked open the cab door and was ready to belt the man in an attempt to bring him to his senses when he discovered the true situation. The popular sergeant had been caught by shrapnel and 'was as dead as a bloody doornail. A bit had gone through the cab and straight through the heart. There wasn't a mark on him, just sitting there with a big smile on his face.'

Eighteen of Mayne's men were killed as a result of the shell. But they were not the only ones dead or seriously injured. Members of the family that had helped with the squadron's laundry lay in a heap. Among them, Reg noticed the women had been 'split open' and a man was 'disembowelled'. His initial assessment was that the entire family was dead. But all of a sudden, a young lad clambered from the top of the tangled pile and started to run around screaming. His guts were clearly visible, 'blown out like a huge balloon'. Seekings felt the only option was to shoot the boy, such was his pitiful condition. 'There was absolutely no hope for him,' said Reg. 'You couldn't let anybody suffer and run around like that.'

• ● •

The same afternoon was every bit as testing for men in 2 Troop. C section, alongside Captain Tony Marsh's A Section, were under unremitting attack from German mortars, and Harrison chose to take his men forward to cover the front of a Commando unit which had also been drafted in to reinforce the line. The move down the valley was a bold call and one that was likely to surprise the enemy, given the state of the battle. Harrison pushed on alone to find a suitable position offering decent protection for the rest of his men. At one point, a bomb hit the ground just spitting distance away from him. It was a close shave, but his section would not be so fortunate.

Bob Seekings was making his way across a patch of open ground when a mortar round smashed into the ground just behind him. The bomb's violent impact sent him flying forwards, but his luck held, just as his brother's did at a similar time that afternoon back in the town. Stunned and grateful to be alive, he scrambled to his feet without a mark on him before his thoughts quickly turned to the man who had been directly behind, Private Benjamin McLaughlan. Bob glanced back and instantly saw McLaughlan had also been hurled to the floor by the bomb – but unlike himself the Scot had not escaped its blast. The mortar landed 'right under him' according to fellow C Section member Eric Musk, who hurried to assist. 'Bob and I ran to an outbuilding, took the door off and used it as a stretcher,' said Eric, who noted that McLaughlan was 'in a terrible state'. The twenty-three-year-old had been a painter and decorator back home in South Lanarkshire before the war. He joined the SAS not long after Bob and the pair's friendship blossomed during their time under Harrison's command. To see his good mate's grievous injuries was deeply distressing for Bob, who was still imperilled. As was Musk as he set off in a small party tasked with taking the mortar round's five victims to a field hospital near the town's railway station. He, Bob McDougall, James McDiarmid and Ginger Hines made slow progress on a journey that was fraught with danger. 'We were under fire as we made our way,' remembered Musk. One man, Lance Corporal John 'Ginger' Hodgkinson, would not make it to hospital – his injuries proved fatal well before reaching town. Later, Bob also learned that McLaughlan had died (on 12 October).

The ferocious German counterattack continued, forcing those that remained in A Section and C Section to fall back. Harrison's depleted unit slowly made their way before taking cover in a culvert under the railway that was situated close to the coastline. As darkness came, the group left the culvert and filed down the beach to find the right flank. But the withdrawal had not gone smoothly for others from the squadron. The enemy pinned down a small unit in a farmhouse, forcing Corporal W. F. B. 'Kit' Kennedy to jump on a horse and ride back to friendly lines.

Mayne received Kennedy's news that men had been cut off and were in urgent need of assistance. 'How about it?' he asked calmly, turning to Reg Seekings, who had reported to the CO after the tragedy of the truck strike. Reg had little sympathy at first. 'To hell with it … they got into the trouble, let them get out.' It was then that medical officer Captain Philip Gunn chipped in. 'By the way,' said Gunn, 'where is little Seekings?' The penny dropped immediately for Reg. 'You better go and find out and see what you can do,' Mayne told him.

Big-brother responsibility principally fuelled the solo mission, which began with Seekings quickly tracking down the Germans. Their fire zipped across a ploughed field, homing in on a farm building sited a couple of hundred yards or so away. The predicament of the farm's occupants was clear, as was his own. How was he going to change the tide single-handedly? Unconventionally, Reg decided his best option was to enter the fray from within the enemy ranks. 'I more or less joined in the German attack on the place,' he said. His thinking was, 'The only way I can get there is if I just walk across and don't do any firing and just hope that they think it's somebody gone mad.' It was the long-odds gamble of a man willing to do whatever it took to save a family member – desperate and illogical. But it proved a masterstroke. 'I walked through the Germans laying there firing, and the firing stopped.' In fact the only bullets near Seekings fizzed out of the farmhouse from the gun of his old boxing buddy Pat Riley. Thankfully, Bob prevented a friendly-fire disaster. 'My brother stopped him,' said Reg. 'He recognized me.'

Seekings' mind ticked in overdrive as he covered the last yards of the ground. It was one thing reaching the building, but quite another to magic away everyone inside. His eyes landed on a section of 'dead ground' on the beach. Hidden from the view of enemy guns, it presented a potential escape route. Having reached the buildings, he proceeded to send groups of four or five towards the beach with the instruction for them to rendezvous at the culvert under the bridge. Steadily, the pinned-down party slipped away to safety. Reg was among those last out.

The SAS War Diary report detailed how, by early evening, the squadron gathered in strength in the 'right sector' to the north of Termoli. Mayne positioned all the troops available to him in the area between the beach and the railway station to face the sharp end of the enemy's thrust. The commanding officer, whose battle brilliance was matched by a sensitivity for his men, knew that many of them had been on the defensive line for over twenty-four hours. They needed to be fed and watered ahead of the next major confrontation, which was likely to prove decisive in the battle for the town. Mayne called on Seekings and the equally experienced Bob Bennett to ferry supplies to the sections dotted around the railway area. For the job, the two SAS Originals were to carry a tin bath, piled full of essentials. There was little chance of the enemy missing such an incongruous sight.

Reg knew of the danger that lay ahead. Earlier, he had darted over the railway a couple of times and come under attack from an enemy mortar detachment. The Germans let fly at him with 'Moaning Minnies', a sequence of rounds fired in quick succession that made a peculiar screeching sound in flight. Seekings warned Bennett of the likely threat as they approached the track. 'Look, we've got to run like hell when we go across this railway line because they'll blow us to hell. We can't stop once we get going. We've got to go – and pray!'

It did not take long for a salvo of mortars to whistle in their general direction. 'I'm not kidding, one bomb went between Bennett and I under the bath and dived into the deck just a yard or two in front of us,' recalled Reg. 'Fortunately for us it was a dud.' Seekings had survived the day.

• ● •

Hostilities raged again from 05:00 on 6 October, but by mid-afternoon the Germans were defeated following a concerted combined Allied effort. Reinforcements at last flooded into Termoli in the hours before dawn. The Irish Brigade was among the influx at the town's harbour and the Canadian Trois-Rivières Tank Regiment arrived over the Biferno after the engineers defied the attentions of the enemy to put in place a pontoon bridge. Mayne's force was badly depleted by the time of the final battle, but it was heavily armed and stared down the enemy in magnificent style. Spread across a ridge, the men repelled a series of attempted German advances along the railway line. To its left was a cemetery, the scene for further bitter exchanges with mortar units deployed alongside tank power. But at 15:00 hours, under covering fire from the SRS, the Irish Brigade moved through positions that had been defended expertly and for so long, to send the Germans fleeing back up the beach in their hundreds. The Allies' infantry attack also finally brought to an end the stubborn resistance from the cemetery. On 3 October Termoli had been taken; on 6 October it was held after this intense and unforgiving battle. 'One of our sections was actually fighting Tiger tanks with bare hands. My young brother in the churchyard even got singed by the muzzle blasts of tanks,' recalled Reg, a whiff of admiration in his voice.

At last, the squadron withdrew to its billets. Early that evening, Seekings went back to the narrow street by the gardens where the Italian family had cheerily gathered to wave them off less than thirty hours before. The unit was planning to bury those who had been killed by the shell, and Reg was searching for 'bits and pieces' to assist with identification. Particularly on his mind was Sergeant Jock Findlay, an 'absolute first-class chap' by Reg's reckoning. Findlay was engaged to be married and had been studying to become an auctioneer. 'I wonder where Jock is?' mused his fellow sergeant. Seekings and others were cutting back some mock orange bushes on the inside wall of the gardens in preparation for the burials when Findlay was finally discovered. 'As I hacked that away, there was Jock – just a bust of him, a grin on his face. It had been so sudden, all of this.'

As dusk drew in, just yards from the worst losses the SAS had experienced in its two years or so of existence, the unit's padre Captain Ronnie Lunt quietly conducted a short service as the dead were laid to rest. Musk's written notes recorded the event: 'After Sergeant Seekings had collected all the arms, legs, heads etc and made sure they were all belonging to the right person, we then buried them. We also buried an Italian lady and her baby, who were both killed whilst watching the lads getting into the trucks.' Musk's words appear matter of fact, almost blunt. Perhaps it was the only way he could process what had happened.

For Seekings, the hard-earned victory at Termoli was always inextricably linked with the truck tragedy. Months earlier in Palestine, he had been instrumental in moulding the section during its training. In Sicily and Italy, the men – to Reg, *his* men – had fought brilliantly on a series of occasions. Indeed, within hours of landing at Termoli, they successfully pulled off a roadside ambush on German paratroopers and then overcame another party of the elite fighters in a vicious farmhouse scrap. After surrendering, the major in command of the enemy spoke with Seekings. 'I said to my men, "This is strange, I have never known men to fight this hard",' the officer told Reg.

Such shared encounters deepened the bonds between those within 1 Troop's A Section. The twenty or so soldiers in it were not just colleagues to Reg – they meant far more. It was devastating for him to lose so many mates in the moments of chaos created by the shell strike. Decades passed, but the experience never left him. 'Termoli was bad, very bad,' he reflected.

Chapter 17

INTO FRANCE

At around 02:00 hours on 11 June 1944, a stick of parachutists undertook last-minute checks before squeezing through the hole in the floor of a Stirling bomber. The aircraft was one of two flying from a Gloucestershire airfield where the passengers had spent recent weeks under conditions of the highest security. RAF Fairford had been like 'a concentration camp' according to Seekings. 'Three security checks to go and have a shower and that was under armed guard.'

Fairford's barbed wire, watchtowers and machine guns were well behind him now as he waited expectantly for the Stirling's inboard motors to ease off and for it almost to glide in for disembarkation. But the pilot seemed to be following a different script. Somewhat unnervingly for those on standby in the fuselage, the plane proceeded as if it was heading in for a bombing run. 'Christ, what's he doing?' thought Reg. He steeled himself, briefly pausing to reflect on the wisdom of his habit of hurling himself out of a plane without a helmet ('a stupid thing of mine'). Next moment, the green light appeared and his worst fears were realized: 'It was like jumping into hell.'

Seekings plunged into the night, a heavy kitbag – topped up with supplies of soap for use as a potential bartering commodity – attached to his leg. Immediately, the Stirling's slipstream lashed his ears so violently it 'nearly took my damned ears off'. Pitch-black skies and pounding rain made him feel as if he was being 'tossed around like feathers in a whirlpool'. Split seconds later, he was instantly grateful when his chute cracked open, offering some welcome relief, but the rest of the descent still had to be negotiated.

The stick headed towards the unknown, having been dropped miles from the intended drop zone. Darkness turned the final stages of the drop into even more of a guessing game, and Seekings barely caught sight of the trees beneath before he had hurtled unceremoniously into them. He was still strung up in the boughs gathering his thoughts when he became aware of a healthy fragrance wafting on the night air. The scent seemed strangely familiar and then it dawned on him. Soap! Just before impact, he had released the leg-bag – dangling on a rope 12 feet below – and much of its contents had erupted on landing. 'With it raining, you could smell Lifebuoy for miles!' In his own inimitable way, Seekings introduced himself in France without even setting foot on its soil.

• ● •

Reg landed five days after D-Day and was part of a mission that was much closer to David Stirling's original strategic vision for the SAS than the frontal assaults assigned to Mayne's men in Sicily and mainland Italy. However, by the time Reg crashed into that woodland in the middle of France, the SAS had become unrecognizable from Stirling's original small detachment. It was reconstituted at the start of 1944 and became the Special Air Service Brigade that soon boasted a combined strength of 2,500 men. Under the brigade umbrella, Mayne remained firmly in command of the 1st SAS Regiment – the unit reunited with its original title after fighting as the Special Raiding Squadron through much of the previous year (Mayne's force eventually sailed for home shores in late December 1943). The 2nd SAS Regiment was part of the new formation, alongside two French parachute battalions, a Belgian parachute squadron and a reconnaissance and signals squadron known as 'Phantom'. Brigadier Roderick McLeod, who had primarily served as a Royal Artillery officer, had been installed as overall commander after a stint with the 1st Parachute Brigade in 1943.

Seekings also took on new responsibilities early in January 1944. With 1 SAS setting up base in Scotland, in the small Ayrshire town of Darvel, some 25 miles from Glasgow, Mayne – now a lieutenant colonel – summoned him to a hotel to discuss the regiment's immediate future. The Irishman explained that he required additional officers, promptly showing Reg a list of possible candidates. At the top was Reg's own name. He instantly crossed it off, muttering 'No way.' Mayne tried another tack. 'Will you take warrant rank, then?' The chance to step up to the highest level for non-commissioned soldiers again drew a swift response. But unlike Seekings' previous reply, this time he accepted his commanding officer's offer. 'That's all I want – I'm happy.' His personal documents show that on 7 January he was promoted to squadron sergeant-major status, no mean feat, considering he was just twenty-three years old. His experiences from the previous two and a half years stood him in good stead for the lynchpin role and ensured he had the respect not just of the men beneath his new rank, but also those above it.

The opening weeks of the year were spent on leave for many in the SAS. After that it was time for everyone to knuckle down to some tough training. As plans for the invasion of north-west Europe were being shaped, the men were put through their paces across the Ayrshire countryside and beyond. Day and night, different exercises were designed to recreate the work that was likely to lie ahead. Docks, railways and even a power station were chosen for study and schemes as sabotage activities became the SAS's priority, just as they once were in North Africa. The Home Guard and even the local police were sometimes called on to act as opposition. Then there was parachute practice, including three jumps at night, which took place at an airfield close to the west coast of Scotland. Those that had learnt their skills in the desert had to adjust to jumping from an aperture in the fuselage floor, rather than out of an aircraft door as they had done in the past.

Everything was geared towards supporting the Allies' eagerly anticipated invasion of Western Europe, but Bob Seekings played no part in any of it. He returned to Britain after his SRS operations in time for a personal landmark on 13 February 1944, which did not go unnoticed by his commanding officer. Reg was present as Mayne called Bob before him and noted that it was the young private's birthday. Bob confirmed that he had reached the age of twenty-one, to which his CO offered congratulations. 'He said, "Well done … you've done well",' recalled Reg, who watched on as Mayne thoughtfully gave Bob an extra couple of weeks' leave. 'That was typical of Paddy,' said the elder Seekings.

Perhaps the highly perceptive Irishman had already noted that the strain of war had started to take its toll on Bob. Soon, more obvious physical signs of wear and tear became clear. 'His insteps went down,' said Reg. 'He buggered them up jumping.' But issues with his feet were not Bob's only problem. He was fatigued, spent, mentally exhausted – and haunted by events from the previous four years. It proved impossible to shake off the experience of Termoli, especially that afternoon on the side of a valley where his close friend Ben 'Ginger' McLaughlan suffered a fatal wound in the mortar blitz. Indeed, Bob had not been in Scotland for long when he travelled to Hamilton to meet William and Agnes McLaughlan and talk to them about what had happened to their son.

Bob also fell in love during the spring of 1944. As SAS men mingled with the locals in various social contexts, he became acquainted with Agnes Elliott. Agnes was a girl from Catrine, ten miles to the south of Darvel, and worked in a weaving factory. She had not long recovered from a sixteen-hour operation after an abscess developed on her brain following an accident at work. Agnes was left with scar tissue and subsequently suffered bouts of epilepsy that plagued her for the rest of her life. But the petite Scottish girl became a breath of fresh air for Bob, lifting his spirits after the trauma of Termoli. Aside from the usual courting at dances, there was a more serious aspect to their fast-developing relationship. Agnes was a Presbyterian Scot, always ready to debate politics and ethics with Bob, who had his own deep-thinking side.

The other major change in his life resulted from the collapse of his feet arches. On 20 May he was transferred from 1 SAS to the brigade's Headquarters Squadron at Sorn Castle. It meant swapping intensive training for a much slower-paced life and mundane duties. But that summer he was often accompanied in his work by a Golden Labrador, given to him by Lady Sorn (Madeline Scott Moncrieff), who recognized Bob's passion for animals.

Inside Sorn Castle, SAS involvement in Operation Overlord – the name given to the Battle of Normandy – was a hot topic of conversation. It took time to iron out the details of the unit's role, but during May it was decided that Mayne's men were principally required for action well away from the beaches. Looking at the likely eventualities after the Allied invasion, the planners were keen to slow down the progress of German reinforcements – in particular, the elite and vast 2nd SS Panzer Division ('Das Reich'), which had been resting and refitting in Toulouse. This was where the SAS fitted in. Two of 1 SAS's squadrons were ordered to drop deep inside central France and disrupt Das Reich's movement north to Normandy. The men were to operate against the enemy's lines of communication and key targets were the railway networks, which were to be attacked relentlessly. The code names given to the operations were Bulbasket and Houndsworth. For Bulbasket, parachutists jumped into the Limoges area. Further to the east in the Morvan region, A Squadron – including Seekings – arrived under the cloak of night for Houndsworth.

Wild and almost impenetrable in places, the hilly and heavily forested Morvan was in many ways ideal terrain for the SAS to establish a stronghold. It was also home to resistance cells of the Maquis. The guerrilla fighters, known as Maquisards, had become increasingly organized and grown in number to an estimated 100,000 by the time of D-Day. They were a mix in terms of age, included young girls and women, and joined from all walks of life; some came with military backgrounds. Similarly, there were differing political views among the clandestine groups. But the Maquis had one common denominator: a hatred of German occupation and its Vichy-régime collaborators. As such, their importance in the fight against the occupation forces was recognized by the Allies. Indeed, the two SAS squadrons that dropped behind the lines were to link up and help supply the resistance groups living in camouflaged woodland camps. As Reg understood it, 'Our job was to support and push the Maquis into operations.'

Contacting the local resistance following touchdown in France was a high priority for the main recce party from A Squadron, 1 SAS,

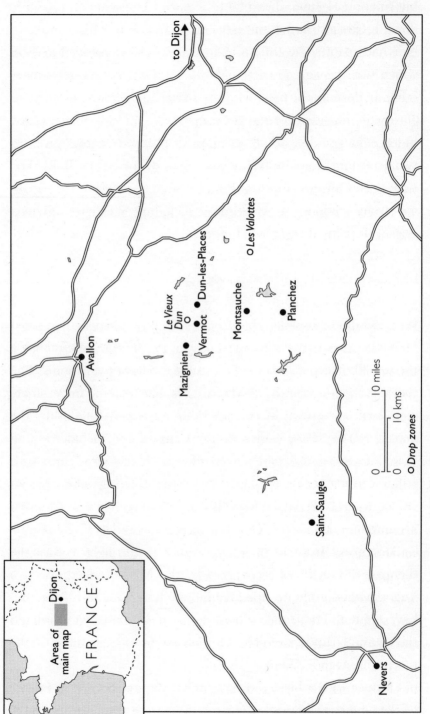

SAS 'Operation Houndsworth', June to September 1944.

but first, on 11 June, they had to reassemble. Seekings scrambled down a tree just as Johnny Cooper stumbled upon him after the pair had spent some time attempting their best owl impressions, which was the agreed method of identifying themselves to each other. In the end, the two friends resorted to old-fashioned hollering across the hillside. Clearly, the enemy or its agents were not out in force, maybe dissuaded by the heavy rain. Cooper now sported two lieutenant's 'pips' on a shoulder epaulette, having completed his time at an Officer Cadet Training Unit. By dawn all bar one of his ten-strong section were back together, kitbags located and chutes buried. It seemed the pre-arranged hooting enjoyed some success after all. 'You've never heard such a collection of owls as there was in France that night,' reflected Seekings. The sole member of the stick not rapidly accounted for, Trooper Docherty, was picked up later that day.

As the wet weather continued, Seekings and Cooper climbed to the top of a steep hill to pinpoint their whereabouts. The bearing told the pair they were 'exactly 21 miles' from the intended drop zone, which was close to the rural outpost of Le Vieux Dun. Reg persuaded his mate that they should venture into the nearest village in an attempt to make contact with the local resistance group. The risk of coming across an informant – or worse, the Vichy regime's Milice (a pro-Nazi paramilitary organization) – was one they would just have to take.

A sergeant from their stick called Ange Zellic accompanied them on the sortie. Zellic's background – he was an Italian-born Yugoslav who grew up in France – made him an ideal person to have around. The three men approached a couple of farmhouses then hummed and hawed about which door to tap on. After an eeny, meeny, miny, moe moment, they struck lucky with their choice. An old farmer with a big handlebar moustache opened the door and worked out straightaway who the strangers were. He whipped the trio inside and with good reason. It turned out the other farmhouse was owned by 'a big favourite of the Germans', according to Reg.

Their fortuitously discovered protector told the SAS men they would have to stay put for the time being because he could not permit the possibility of the other farmer spotting them. It required bravery to harbour the unexpected visitors as discovery was likely to result in death for them all. Hitler had issued the *Kommandobefehl* (Commando Order) in October 1942, responding to means of warfare by 'British saboteurs' that he deemed were against the terms of the Geneva Convention. The order stated: 'Henceforth, all enemy troops encountered by German troops during so-called Commando operations, in Europe or in Africa, though they appear to be soldiers or demolition groups, are to be exterminated to the last man, either in combat or in pursuit.' The command continued: 'If such men appear to be about to surrender, no quarter should be given to them – on general principle'. Allied behind-the-lines fighters were to be shown no mercy under the terms of the order. And any Frenchman suspected of assisting such operatives was highly likely to be considered in the same light.

Seekings soon struck up an easy rapport with the farmer, who had served with a French cavalry unit. It seemed the man and Reg's father, once of the Bedfordshire Regiment, were linked by common ground from the Great War. 'The two units were stationed together for quite a time during the war. I'd often heard Dad talk about this French unit. Him and my old man most probably had been on the booze together.'

The farmer's trust in the soldiers extended to informing them that his daughter was a messenger for the local Maquis. 'We couldn't have hit better,' said Seekings. But before the girl arrived, a French youth burst into the house with news of smoke rising from the woods. The remainder of the SAS stick apparently had lit a fire in an attempt to dry out their saturated clothing and kit. Villagers saw the telltale plumes rising in the woods and were anxious that it could lead to reprisals from the Milice, who Seekings quickly understood were a 'bad crowd'. The teenage lad remained suspicious of the strangers, since informants and collaborators were a constant concern for the resistance networks. But eventually he was satisfied by a courteous gesture from the SAS men: Seekings and Cooper immediately rose from their seats when the farmer's daughter arrived. 'Ah, now I know you're English – the Germans never stand up like that,' he told Reg. It was an important lesson for the SAS men to remember. Next moment, the youngster allowed a copper-headed mallet to shake loose from his sleeve, satisfied that he had no immediate use for the makeshift weapon. 'I would have attacked you,' he told the soldiers. An amused Seekings responded, 'Where do you think this gun is pointing?' His Tommy gun had never moved from the French boy's guts from the moment he entered the room. 'He hadn't spotted that.'

The farmer's daughter facilitated contact with the local Maquis fighters, who arranged transport to take the stick to the intended infiltration area. However, it took several more days before Major Fraser established squadron headquarters in the dense Morvan forest, not far from the entrenched camp of another Maquis force. Fraser's stick, who had been in the other Stirling bomber on the same night that Seekings flew across, had taken some time to reunite after a series of scattered landings across the French countryside. But by late on the evening of 17 June every member of the original nineteen-strong main recce party was camped in the Bois de la Pérouse. Now all they had to do was endure the soaking wet hours, to which there seemed no end, and await the imminent arrival of the bulk of A Squadron.

Mist and rain made for further gloom as the reception committee peered up at inky skies during the night of 17–18 June. Eventually, the rumble of a Stirling could be heard in the distance.

The sound of its engines increased to a roar as the plane honed in on the designated Les Valottes drop zone where bonfires blazed as a guide to those high above. But the drop failed to materialize – the weather was just 'so heavy' according to Seekings. 'They just couldn't see our ground lights.' In the days that followed came crushing news. One of the returning planes, containing a bunch of the squadron's NCOs (an SAS Headquarters document specified a total of one officer and fourteen other ranks), appeared to have vanished without trace. 'It just disappeared,' recalled Seekings. 'And there was some good men in that.'

Incessant downpours lowered morale yet further and the shortage of food became a major concern. Barely a scrap remained in the camp. But in the small hours of 22 June, relief came, even if the weather remained resolutely grim. Stirlings flew across the two drop zones, delivering eighty containers of badly-needed supplies. As they began to thud onto the ground, the sound of voices could be heard in the air. More than sixty men had jumped to bring up the numbers of Fraser's squadron, enabling them to focus on achieving the planners' objectives for Operation Houndsworth. A dramatic few days lay ahead, not least for Seekings.

The first contact with the enemy took place on 24 June when a night-time ambush, in conjunction with the Maquis, was staged just outside Montsauche. Captain Alec Muirhead led the SAS party, which included Seekings and Cooper, who were armed with Bren guns. Muirhead's official report documented that four trucks were destroyed and a motorcycle was captured, while thirty Germans and an officer were killed. The Maquis suffered one death in a battle primarily fought from roadside ditches.

A badly injured lieutenant was bagged by the SAS after the fighting. He was a Russian, who spoke about his situation under interrogation from Cooper and others. Previously captured by Germans during the protracted battle at Stalingrad, the man was informed at the time that he would be spared from starvation in a snowy prisoner of war cage if he were to 'volunteer' to support their efforts in France. The Russian explained how he had been placed in a desperate position, but now it had become far worse. To Cooper's eye, the man was not going to survive his wounds. And on top of these, the 'Grey' Russian – as those aligned with the enemy in France were termed by the SAS – feared being turned over to the hands of the ruthless Maquis. Anxious not to face the French, the stricken officer pleaded to be shot. Cooper detailed how his wishes were heeded by a single bullet to the head from Seekings.

Just forty-eight hours later Reg suffered a very similar experience.

Chapter 18

FAITH AND HEALING

Religion seemed to hold little appeal for Reg Seekings during the war, but he always credited Reverend J. Fraser McLuskey with saving his life. The twenty-nine-year-old, Edinburgh-born McLuskey accepted a posting to the SAS Brigade after successfully completing his parachute training in early 1944. It followed his enlistment as an army chaplain the previous year, having filled that role at the University of Glasgow. Physically, the broad-shouldered and six-foot-plus Scot certainly looked the part within 1 SAS Regiment personnel at its Darvel base. Indeed, the padre's genuine, warm and likeable manner soon served to dissolve just about all the curiosity that might have surrounded his connection to the unit. However, Seekings clung to a dismissive opinion, viewing the individual with the clerical collar as 'very prim and proper' and refusing to moderate his own language around him. 'Parsons didn't particularly interest me.'

Reg's apparent reluctance to embrace religion, or those that represented it, did not prevent him from joining the SAS's worship on 26 June in the Morvan woodlands, halfway between Paris and

Lyon. McLuskey addressed his unusual congregation just days after a particularly nasty parachute landing. The padre had clattered into trees, within which he found himself suspended upside down. McLuskey succeeded in cutting himself free, only to plummet head-first from about 40 feet before thudding into a grass bank and promptly falling unconscious. On stirring, he heaved with the first of several bouts of violent sickness. It was the most unpleasant of starts to the chaplain's French stint, but he recovered sufficiently fast to be able to stage his first open air service at Major Fraser's camp.

An altar cloth, carrying the regimental emblem of the winged dagger, was laid over the communion table on which a cross was added. Hymn books were handed out as the men of A Squadron assembled in a half-circle. McLuskey recognized that few men attended church on a regular basis, but singing seemed to lift them all. A lesson was read, followed by the address and then everyone stood for the Lord's Prayer. Some partook in communion as the smell from the logs on the fire blended with the pinewood. A towering canopy of trees, up above the throng, gave its own cathedral-like feel to proceedings. It was a service that provided measures of reassurance and calm during a time of uncertainty and anxiety. But within hours the spell was broken. 'All of a sudden, bullets started to whistle through the tree-tops,' said Seekings. Fraser's headquarters camp near Le Vieux Dun had been caught unawares as the German retaliation for the convoy ambush of 24 June spread through the locale.

The enemy response started in nearby Montsauche and Planchez with civilians bearing the brunt. By the time Fraser's party became aware of the danger, reprisals had extended to an early-evening attack on the Maquis hospital at the Château de Vermot – a temporary home for a handful of SAS personnel recuperating from injuries sustained from their parachute jumps. The aggressors, said to be 250-strong, composed of heavily armed Germans and Grey

Russians, were intent on snuffing out the Maquis group secreted in the woodlands. Mortar and machine-gun fire, supported by sniping, soon began in earnest. However, a messenger sent from the guerilla fighters' camp alerted Fraser to how the enemy had left itself vulnerable to an attack from the rear. The Scot duly planned for his squadron to swing behind the Germans and take up positions to strike back in the Battle of Vermot.

Fighting showed no signs of easing as the SAS were guided towards the scene by a partisan. As they drew closer to the enemy guns, Seekings became increasingly unhappy with the situation. Looking on from the undergrowth, it seemed to him that men from the Maquis 'were going down like ninepins'. Turning to Fraser, he said, 'This is bloody hopeless.' Hastily, Seekings assessed the options. 'Look, I'll gain that higher ground,' pointing to a ridge on one side of the valley. Fraser gave the okay to the suggestion from his sergeant-major, who, along with Captain Wiseman, took a small group of men and set off to scale the steep slope. Having made the vantage point without a hitch, Reg glanced over the vale and, perched on the hillside around 800 yards or so away, was a gunner protecting enemy transport. Seekings was eager for the sub-section to deal with the trucks, so he informed Sergeant Jack Terry that he planned to proceed in more open territory, using an area of dead ground from which the party would emerge and mount an attack. The experienced Terry immediately understood the dead ground was out of sight for the hillside gunner, but Reg was unsure if all the others would see the situation so clearly. The majority were 'green troops' who had 'never been in action before', and he had no wish to alarm them or complicate affairs. 'I won't upset them, I won't scare them, I won't tell them about it until I get them over,' he thought as he pressed on across the valley. Whether the matter remained a nagging distraction for him or if he was able to forget about it and retain his usual single-minded focus is unclear. Either way, a few minutes later Seekings made a rare error of judgement that almost left him dead.

The party made its way the required distance to the other side of the valley, where Seekings emerged from cover – and found himself staring down the barrel of a machine gun. He and the enemy gunner were 'face to face', barely more than a handful of yards away from one another. His foe 'reacted fast' and, 'half-crouched, he dropped behind the gun,' said Reg, whose own instincts told him to dive to the deck. But this time there was to be no escape. Moments after shouting a warning to the rest of the section, Seekings was nailed by a single bullet. The shot slammed into his head and 'blasted through' before 'it lodged between my spine and my skull'. He sank to the ground, blood instantly oozing from the gap just under his hairline.

Seekings suffered no immediate feelings of pain. Instead, he found himself in an otherworldly state in which he was being swept along 'going like the clappers of hell' in what seemed like an underground river. 'My whole past from the time I was a kid, my mother, girlfriends – the lot – all went through,' he later reflected. 'It was like watching a film. Fantastic. Then, I was going deeper and deeper and deeper away.' Eventually, another part of Seekings' mind began to exercise some control. It stemmed the tide of the raging river sensation and returned him to the reality of the French hillside. 'I seemed to subconsciously, somehow, pull myself out of it.' Reg was unsure how long the ethereal episode had gone on for: he could not determine how long he had been unconscious. But throughout the eerie experience his trademark good luck held – and beyond.

In contrast, the enemy gunner endured little fortune from the moment he fired first in the skirmish. Immediately, his weapon seized and he resorted to slinging two grenades. They landed with 'a tremendous bang and flash' a foot either side of Seekings, who 'never got a scratch' from either. The SAS soon countered. Notably, Lance Corporal David Gibb's Bren gun began to chatter. Gibb, originally from the Royal Armoured Corps, 'distinguished himself' with 'prompt and accurate fire', wrote Wiseman in his subsequent report.

Seekings, his grasp on the situation apparently returning, tried to join in the shooting. He reached for his carbine rifle and found his right arm was useless. In those moments he was unaware of his physical state, but it seemed the bullet's position had affected the efficacy of his nervous system. Despite his urgent efforts, the limb remained 'flopped' and stubbornly unresponsive. 'With the creases in my battledress, it looked just as though my arm was blown off. It was all a mass of blood and what-not there,' he said.

Terry reached the injured man first, having crawled up to him from behind. He cottoned on far quicker than Seekings regarding the bullet's location and began to manoeuvre his head. 'Jack, get a tourniquet on my arm!' roared Reg. 'It's my arm, not my head.' It took days before he finally began to accept that his arm was unscathed and actually the shot had hit home at the base of his skull.

Wiseman's section withdrew behind a nearby hill without any further casualties. Seekings, despite the serious nature of his injury, found the will to run 50 yards or so towards a giant fallen tree. Barely had he ducked behind it for cover when he realized that his tobacco pipe had fallen from a pocket during his adrenalin-fuelled dash. 'Like a bloody idiot, I went and picked the bloody pipe up,' he said. 'That was the last I got up on my own after that for a day or two.'

Seekings began to wilt as he lay behind the tree. With darkness closing in, Trooper Elliott was selected to help him head back to camp. The pair had only just started their trek when Reg became aware of the first flash of lightning fizzing across the skies. He trudged forward, supported by the lanky Elliott, as the storm became more and more violent. At one point, he could even smell the sulphur from the lightning, such was its intensity and proximity. But the booming thunderclaps and accompanying electricity seemed to benefit Seekings, rather than add to his problems. 'It was terrific – cleared my head a lot,' he said.

Reg possessed a good idea of his bearings, having previously studied and memorized maps of the area. Even so, he hesitated when the duo reached a fork in the path. 'I can't afford to go wrong. Not the state I'm in,' he stressed to his companion. 'Go up there,' added Seekings, pointing to one track, 'and you should, within 100 yards, see a little white hut.' With a few more words, he sent him on his way and crawled under a bush to wait. After a few minutes, the young man stumbled back, unaware of Reg's presence. 'All right, Elliott,' came a gruff call from the dense vegetation. 'Where are you going?' The startled young trooper almost leapt from his skin, which tickled Seekings, despite his own troubles.

Eventually, the two men made it to camp where Reg's blood-soaked uniform had to be cut off to allow for an initial examination under tarpaulin. The medic peered at him, while Padre McLuskey assisted by shining a torch on the patient's head. Seekings' discomfort was obvious as a series of attempts failed to extricate the bullet from where it was trapped next to his skull. At last, the medic admitted defeat and left the bullet inside Reg, whose condition deteriorated further by the following morning. Relentless rainfall did nothing to lift A Squadron's spirits on a day of heinous enemy activity in the surrounding area. An extract from Fraser's operation report spelt out in stark form the atrocities that took place on 27 June. 'The village of Vermot was burnt down. Dun-les-Places was given over to rape and murder, 21 men being shot.' Innocent civilians suffered the worst indignities, having been dragged into the fight for France. The Dun curé's fate was as shocking as anything that occurred: he was publicly hung from the church belfry.

Fraser completed his daily review by stating details of a camp relocation, brought about by the ongoing reprisals. His squadron, including a wounded and understandably out-of-sorts Seekings, sat tight before moving under moonlight to a safer area at Mazignien, which was situated some miles to the north-west of the unrest. A gruelling march, including a slog through a bog, ended just before dawn. 'I'd had enough,' said Seekings. 'I was feeling bloody terrible.' He dozed off for a bit, awakening to find the sun beating down at long last. Wiseman wandered over to him: 'Come on sergeant-major, where's that old grit of yours?' The warm rays and Wiseman's attempted levity succeeded in briefly putting a smile back on Seekings' face.

Shortly afterwards Fraser identified a nearby clearing on a slope within the woodlands as a suitable setting for his new headquarters. The commanding officer consulted Reg, just to check that he was also happy with the location. Seekings, hardly in the best of shapes to extend the search for a base elsewhere, readily agreed. He knew little about the following week, except that, 'It rained and rained and rained and we had no bloody food.' But the time laid up in camp allowed his exhausted body to stabilize and strengthen after the trauma of the shooting and subsequent exertions. Through those sodden days, Padre McLuskey kept more than an eye out for him, which Seekings never forgot. 'He nursed me, really looked after me.' But McLuskey's care went beyond just making sure the casualty was fed and watered; he offered support with a lightness of touch that was valued by the men – even Reg.

One morning, with Seekings beginning to show signs of improvement, the padre volunteered to give him a shave. He added words to the effect that he was something of an expert with the razor and would sir like a light or heavy shave? Reg went along with it, then, when McLuskey had completed the job, the Scot owned up to a 'little fib'. It transpired that he had never shaved another man in his life until that point! From that day, Seekings' previous dismissive attitude towards the padre started to change. 'We got talking and he said, God willing, if he ever got back to Scotland, he could preach real religion, not what he had been preaching. He had seen real religion lived those last few days; men without a thought for themselves, sacrificing this and that, really helping one another.' Seekings understood the sentiment before adding his own observation. 'Yes, padre and, if they didn't listen, you could also swear at them!' Reg's language had been more colourful than normal in the aftermath of his gunshot wound and McLuskey concurred, 'I could do that, too.'

In mid-July, again Fraser chose to move camp, this time to a picturesque valley near Chalaux, a handful of miles to the north-west of Mazignien. Seekings, with a sizeable bandage wrapped round his head, continued his recuperation by nipping out for a cognac in village cafés or bars. Over time, he became a familiar figure in various hostelries around the Morvan, as did others from the squadron. McLuskey, as a man of the cloth, proved invaluable when it came to smoothing the way with the local population and helping to build useful networks around the area. 'He'd get along with anybody,' said Seekings. 'He was very handy for liaison work and with the public, in particular. Having him with us made it so much easier. We could get better information from the French public, because they put trust in the padre.' That summer Seekings learnt to do likewise, although it cannot be said that he discovered religion in the manner that some soldiers did. Instead, he forged a meaningful and enduring friendship. McLuskey later wrote how A Squadron's sergeant-major 'could be as smart as he was tough and good-hearted'. For his part, Reg grew to appreciate that 1 SAS's padre offered something 'really wonderful' to the men during their time in France.

● ● ●

Fraser's squadron stepped up its activities through July and August, helped by supply drops that not only restocked theirs and the Maquis' firepower, but also included the parachuting in of jeeps. One vehicle landed precariously on a woodland bank. It took hours of hard graft and the cutting down of forty trees to release it, all before breakfast! Not all such jeep drops were successful – there was more than the odd 'prang'. But the mobility provided by those vehicles that did withstand their theatrical mode of arrival helped significantly, as did other requisitioned transport. Houndsworth really began to impede and hamper the enemy in accordance with the operation's original objectives. Railway lines were blown up with increasing frequency and, on a number of occasions, forced train derailments, including on 9 August between Nevers and La Charite. Five days later, a turntable and points were destroyed at Tamnay. Sandwiched in between, an Alec Muirhead-led party unleashed mortar bombs and incendiary fire on a synthetic oil plant at Autun. Alongside much activity of a similar nature, a telling series of important signals were relayed to England, passing on information to help set up air strikes on targets such as bomb dumps and petrol tanks. Meanwhile, the vast Allied forces pressed on from establishing beachheads in Normandy to capture the region's city of Caen in July. Just over a month later, on 25 August, Paris was liberated.

Seekings recovered sufficiently, albeit with the bullet still lodged just above his spine, to play a part in the latter stages of A Squadron's ongoing sabotage work. McLuskey regularly acted as his driver, the pair enjoying one another's company as well as finding themselves in the heat of the action on occasion. The padre's proximity to the fighting led to him one day bringing up the subject of carrying weapons. 'I didn't think it was a good thing, neither did the boys,' said Reg. 'We thought he set an example. He kept things on a sort of civilized level and people admired him for that and there was enough of us to protect him.'

McLuskey remained without arms, but that did not stop him from heading into a few tight spots to help his fellow SAS men. He often encouraged others at times of strain – indeed, in life and death moments. 'When there was an action and we were attacked, or anything like that, he knew the men that were a bit nervous,' observed Seekings. 'Although he was unarmed, he would crawl up alongside and have a little chat, a little laugh with them until he saw they were nicely comfy,' said Reg. 'Then he'd crawl off, peer up and talk to another chap. Chaps really appreciated that, it really calmed them down.'

Seekings watched on, his regard for the man of the cloth having grown beyond all recognition from his initial disdain. In return, he broadened McLuskey's reading list after the older man noticed the New Testament and the Soldier's Handbook were hardly well-thumbed by the squadron. McLuskey gave the matter some thought and quizzed Reg about books that the men might like instead. 'Lemmy Caution,' responded Seekings, giving the name of the American-based private detective created by British writer Peter Cheyney. The padre acted on Reg's suggestion and in due course Cheyney's books arrived as part of a parachute drop. With the books in high demand, McLuskey decided to pick up a copy and see what the fuss was all about. Next thing, he started to use a smattering of Caution's streetwise lingo. 'Carry on, I'm just gumshoeing around,' the padre was heard to say.

As August drew to a close, the Germans were in mass retreat through France after the Allies launched a campaign across the south of the country. Around the turn of the month, the SAS focused much of their efforts on ambushing enemy forces as they withdrew eastwards. This involved hours of reconnaissance work gauging column movements on the *routes nationales* (trunk roads). Fraser, Seekings, McLuskey and a handful of others spent time based in Saint-Saulge, which was around an hour's drive to the south-west from the main camp. This enabled the party to observe the main road heading north from the nearby town of Nevers. One day, Reg, the padre and a couple of others were driving back to Saint-Saulge when they became the target of an ambush of a very different kind. Children and girls from a rural village spilled onto the road to stop the vehicle and shower the men with flowers. 'We were being greeted as the liberators!' said Reg. Bouquets tended to be strewn all across the jeeps after return trips from those intelligence-gathering days.

In similar fashion, Seekings and McLuskey received the gratitude of a couple living in an isolated farmhouse. 'They saw us go past and must have recognized us,' said Seekings, who by this stage was wearing a tunic with his ribbons on display. 'Later on, they heard the vehicles come back, saw it was us, stopped us and took us into their house and insisted that we have tea. She got an old tea bag out of a vase on the mantelpiece – there was, I suppose, only two or three spoonfuls of tea. This was the last of their tea from the time that France capitulated and they'd saved this with the idea that the first English soldier that they saw when France was being freed again would have a cup of tea. So we sat down and had this old tea. Quite an experience …'

It was 6 September when, for the final time, the majority of Fraser's force departed the base camp at Chalaux; not for action, but to return home. Their fleet of civilian cars, half a dozen jeeps and a couple of purloined German lorries moved northwards, snaking through the back roads at first. Swifter progress was provided when the strange-looking column ventured onto a *route nationale* travelling in the direction of Auxerre. Wherever there were houses, tricolour flags could be seen flying, but the SAS men remained

Fraser McLuskey: the Scottish padre became a great friend to many
SAS soldiers, not least Reg Seekings.

vigilant. They were in no man's land, so the prospect of running
into German transportation was still a very real threat. The time
to relax came finally after an alarm-free 70-mile journey that
concluded at Joigny. It was there that the convoy was met by a
gum-chewing, baton-toting American military policeman. Not
much of a welcome party, but the men of A Squadron cared not a
jot. They had re-crossed the line and were back on Allied territory.

The ensuing revelry went on long and late into the night in the city built around the banks of the River Yonne.

Tired eyes, along with sore heads, moved west the following day. Liberator bombers were bringing in huge quantities of flour from across the English Channel to an American-occupied aerodrome near Orléans. But there the US Air Force initially seemed reluctant to let the men from the SAS hitch a ride home on the aircraft. 'The Yanks had strict instructions that under no circumstances were they to fly anybody out of France,' said Seekings. As squadron sergeant-major, he made sure he took part in the talks, aiming to satisfy the men's strong homing instincts. During a lengthy discussion, Seekings noticed that a US colonel seemed to take a shine to A Squadron's Bren guns. The US officer confirmed they would be just the job around his ranch back in Texas. Reg sensed a deal in the offing and his bartering instincts kicked in: Bren gun for a lift home. 'Eventually we talked him into it. We gave him three or four Bren guns and, the first dozen Liberators, we piled onto those and flew out of France.' Once in the plane, Reg was one of those who almost gave the crew a heart attack by sitting next to an open hatch, 'watching the ground below', as if strapped into the luxury of a regular flight's window seat. 'They were frightened we were going to fall out.'

Eventually, the Liberators landed at Middle Wallop airfield in Hampshire, bringing down the curtain on another rollercoaster period in Seekings' war. Operation Houndsworth had enjoyed significant successes, but it had also brought extreme hardship for many in A Squadron. On his return, McLuskey prepared an insightful report in which he flagged up the huge stress experienced by men asked to work behind the lines for months at a time. 'Although they are not always conscious of the fact, the men can never relax and the resultant state of tension leaves its mark ...' he wrote. 'The effects of strain could be clearly observed in some of the best soldiers we have … carelessness, impatience, edginess and depression'.

In France, Seekings put up with extreme hunger, as well as days of apparently never-ending rain – and had to survive a gunshot to the head. It was his closest call yet in a charmed existence. At last, that autumn, he underwent surgery at Chelmsford General Hospital to remove the bullet from his skull area. Reg spoke to the surgeon about the circumstances surrounding the shooting, including the surreal sensations immediately after being hit, those moments in which he was swept along at breakneck speed through the underground river. The doctor responded by citing Seekings' fitness and strength as reasons why he had pulled through. He also pointed to one other factor – Seekings' hardwired survival instincts, called on so often in the ring pre-war. 'I think only a good boxer could have done what you did; you dragged yourself out of it,' the surgeon told him. 'If you'd let yourself go, you would have died.'

The specialist passed the time by describing another case he had dealt with. A man had been shot in the head with the bullet flying all the way through his brain and yet somehow there had been no lasting damage. All the man required was treatment for a flesh wound. Evidently, Seekings was not the only soldier to enjoy remarkable good fortune.

Chapter 19

IN HITLER'S BACKYARD

Reg Seekings departed for the Allied spearhead into Germany in the second half of March 1945. This time, there was an added incentive for harbouring hopes of a safe return: he had fallen in love with Monica Smith.

A blue-eyed Suffolk country girl with lustrous, golden-brown hair, Monica served as a private in the Auxiliary Territorial Service (ATS). She enlisted on 22 April 1943, the day after her twenty-first birthday. In the autumn of 1944, she transferred from her posting in Nottingham to 731 Company of the Royal Army Service Corps, under the auspices of what was to be re-designated as the No.1 Essex Group ATS. At a similar time, Seekings also arrived in the same East Anglian county. He was with 1 SAS Regiment at its latest base – Hylands House, on the outskirts of Chelmsford. How the couple met remains a mystery, but a whirlwind romance developed over the winter of 1944–45. Perhaps Seekings asked Monica to dance at a forces social function – she was a keen dancer, according to her younger brother Ronald. Mike Sadler, the desert navigator who became an SAS intelligence officer, also remembered a vibrant scene around the Chelmsford hostelries. It is possible Reg and Monica shared a first drink together in one such establishment. But one aspect is certain: by the time that Seekings went off to invade the Rhineland he was engaged to be married. And not only did he leave with love in his heart, but also on it. Anyone looking closely at Reg's battledress could see a medal ATS badge pinned to his left breast, a symbol of his keenly felt affection.

Brigadier Mike Calvert took charge of the SAS on 14 March 1945 as his predecessor Roderick McLeod departed for the position of Director of Military Operations in India. Calvert had previously excelled in the Far East and was decorated with a Distinguished Service Order after leading a behind-the-lines operation in Burma when attached to the long-range penetration specialists, the Chindits. A week after assuming command, the man known as 'Mad Mike' provided a stirring rallying cry to his soldiers. Calvert wrote: 'You are special troops and I expect you to do special things in the last heave against the Hun. There will be plenty of worthwhile jobs to do.'

Seekings was sent on one such assignment as part of an SAS jeep force that sailed into Ostend on 20 March, just forty-eight hours or so before the Allies began their major offensive east of the Rhine. Lieutenant-Colonel Brian Franks (whose parent regiment was the Middlesex Yeomanry) headed the unit labelled Frankforce, consisting of 284 men from both 1 SAS and 2 SAS. The composite regiment's operation was entitled Archway and its initial objective was reconnaissance work to be conducted in the area to the north of a bridgehead established by airborne invaders. Once the Allies' advance began in earnest, the SAS were then to push forward through the enemy and harass its lines of communications, as well as continuing in a short-range recce capacity. 'Wherever anybody was held up, our job was to hit hard, drive through the German lines, shoot them up the rear and make a gap for the ordinary army to come through,' summed up Seekings.

But the fighting was no longer taking place in a distant desert scene in North Africa or even much closer to home in French forests. It was about to unfold in the enemy's very own backyard. Hitler's heartland included some of his most obsessive supporters, not least sections of the Nazi Party's paramilitary Waffen SS organization. There was no question that such opposition would offer the stiffest resistance – and uphold the notorious Commando Order. To try to protect themselves, the SAS swapped their red airborne berets for black ones. Similarly, newly issued pay books classified the men of Frankforce as tank corps personnel. Carrying his false credentials, Seekings boarded a Buffalo (a tracked amphibious transport craft, suitable for land and water) to traverse the River Rhine on 25 March. The crossing passed off successfully with the SAS disembarking at Bislich, a few miles to the west of the city of Wesel.

Signs and sounds of fighting were apparent almost immediately. Hastily vacated trenches and jettisoned belongings could be seen – as well as the odd corpse – around the woodland area where Frankforce gathered before their activities got underway. Outbreaks of sniping fire kept everyone alert and the 'bullets flying around' compelled Seekings to take cover under his jeep. Trooper McKenzie, sheltering under the same vehicle, produced a bottle of rum from somewhere. ('Mac was a great scrounger,' said Reg.) The Scottish tough nut could be relied upon for lively company and sharp humour – although he was not everyone's cup of tea. Seekings referred to him as one of 'the roughest bloody rogues in creation', and the previous year had raised a few eyebrows when selecting the Glaswegian for his jeep crew prior to Operation Houndsworth. 'He'd done two stretches in prison for arson,' said Reg. 'Five pound a time for setting fire to a factory before the war.' McKenzie also had something of a chequered history during his years in the army. Seekings recalled how the 'rough little Scots lad' was a 'first-class medical orderly', but ended up getting the boot from the Royal Army Medical Corps 'for taking up arms against the Germans at Sidi Rezegh [in Libya]'. Mac and Reg also clashed early on in their acquaintance during the SRS's Italian operations in the summer of 1943. McKenzie took a shine to the teenage daughter of a local woman who had been helping out with some of the men's washing, but Seekings put a stop to it. Mac swore night-time revenge applied by the tip of his bayonet. 'Don't worry about him,' Reg told those who were alarmed by the Scotsman's murderous threats. 'He needs me to lead him into action, so he'll keep me alive. He'll never kill me.'

By the time the two men swigged rum together under Seekings' jeep in the Rhineland, an understanding, maybe even a friendship,

A jeep patrol during Operation Archway. (L to r) Reg is pictured with Sergeant Jack Terry, 'Mac' (assumed to be Trooper McKenzie) and Trooper 'Swag' Jemson.

had developed. Mac, by now a recently married man, mentioned he had heard that Reg was also due to walk up the aisle. 'Yes, if I get through this,' came the reply. The trooper absorbed the remark and then rather cheekily asked if he could attend the wedding. 'Mac, you would have been invited anyway,' said Seekings, providing a good indication as to how far their relationship had progressed. But next, McKenzie took the conversation in a far darker direction. He spoke of how he was going 'to cop it'. Seekings immediately tried to dismiss such talk – he had heard similar premonitions before and they had turned out to be uncannily correct. 'Don't be so bloody silly, Mac,' he said. But the feisty little Scotsman refused to be silenced and asked for a promise. 'I want you to write to the wife and tell her I went down shooting your guns.' It was an unnerving conversation and the words returned to Seekings' mind before the week was out.

• ● •

Seekings' first scrap on German soil was a deadly affair, typical of those that were to unfold in the eastwards advance. Late in the morning on 27 March, twelve heavily weaponized jeeps led by Major Fraser teamed up with Canadian paratroopers, whose initial attempts to clear a copse had been frustrated by the enemy's fire from bazookas and Spandau light machine guns. With the Canadians ready to renew their attack, Fraser opted for a left-sided outflanking manoeuvre that took the SAS transport across dead ground. His jeep managed to close to within 30 yards of the Germans, but then came into the sights of a well-camouflaged gun position. Moments later, the officer commanding A Squadron had been shot in the left hand and his vehicle was lying stuck in a ditch. In response, the other eleven jeeps fanned out before the SAS served up a withering onslaught of their own from the familiar

Vickers Ks, supported by .5 Brownings (Browning M2 .50 caliber machine guns). 'We blasted hell out of the German paratroopers – knocked them for six,' said Seekings. During a fierce fifteen-minute assault, the enemy guns were suppressed one by one.

Next, Reg dismounted and selected a group to sweep the area and snuff out any lingering threat from solitary snipers. Firing had ceased in the copse when he suddenly found himself facing a young German paratrooper poised with a couple of stick hand grenades (nicknamed spud-mashers by the British). Reg was in a tricky spot, made even more uncomfortable by the feeling that he was being observed from behind the trees. His instincts told him not to shoot, at least not straightaway. Instead he called out in German, demanding that the kid put down the grenades. But his words appeared to have fallen on deaf ears. If anything, the teenager's body language suggested he was about to hurl the spud-mashers. Then, with Seekings on the brink of adopting Plan B, the youngster must also have had a change of mind as he dropped the grenades to the ground. The subsequent pressure release was almost audible, as every moment of the little scene was played out in front of an unseen and unfriendly audience, including a colonel from a parachute regiment. The officer, who that day was among those to surrender to the SAS, told Seekings: 'If you'd shot him, we would have fought to the death.'

It had been a fierce passage of fighting that morning. The official report stated ten enemy were killed and a further thirty-two were captured. By comparison, the SAS troop escaped relatively lightly from the skirmishing. Fraser ended up as its sole casualty and took no further part in the action on German soil.

The following morning saw Seekings attached to a large jeep party commanded by Captain Ian Wellsted. Their task was to support 6th Airborne Division – a British airborne infantry division, formed two years earlier – by forging ahead to secure positions by the railway line on the far side of the town of Rhade. But the seven-mile journey east from Erle proved far from straightforward, as a short and nasty clash unfolded with enemy soldiers who were hell-bent on the sort of ambush tactics adopted so often in the past by the SAS itself. One vicious fight began after a German emerged from scrublands armed with a Panzerfaust (a portable, single-use anti-tank weapon) and torched the scout car travelling with a British tank just in front of Wellsted's unit. Seconds later, figures lurking in nearby woodlands opened up on the line of jeeps sat behind the lead vehicle, which was now ablaze. In return, the SAS guns roared out with Seekings using the partial cover provided by a culvert to blast away. But amid all the angry sounds of battle, there came a warning shout. 'Behind you sah-major!' Somebody had caught sight of a German Home Guard patrol moving down a ditch, ever closer to Reg's vehicle. By the time that he had turned away from his mounted gun and raised a Bren, the Home Guard were within a few yards' range. 'I think there was eleven of them, all in single file,' said Seekings, who shot first and asked questions later. 'Whether they thought I was German or whether they thought they could capture us, I just don't know.'

The SAS also suffered casualties in the bloody engagement – including Mac. 'I'm hit,' exclaimed the gunner, who initially got short shrift after a quick glance from Seekings. 'Get back behind the bloody guns,' roared the SSM. Around the same time Trooper Perkins, the other crew member, shouted out that he had also been struck. The gunner-wireless operator was sat on the rear seat and had been stitched all the way down an arm by a long burst from a Spandau. Meanwhile, Mac continued to cry out in discomfort, believing that he was bleeding to death. Seekings pulled him from the jeep for a closer look and still failed to be convinced of any major concern. It was only when he went to lift the Scotsman back behind the .5 Browning that he noticed a big pool of blood on the seat.

Within seconds, Reg ripped off the sleeve of McKenzie's battledress and finally discovered the full extent of the stricken man's injuries. 'A bullet had gone through and exploded and blew all his bloody armpit.' The gaping wound was so huge that Seekings 'stuffed in' two big shell dressings to try and plug it. But the injured pair, especially McKenzie, required prompt specialist medical care. 'I shouted out to the lads to carry on, that I was going to get my two wounded men back,' said Reg, who knew there was an airborne dressing station not far behind them across the valley. But before the jeep set off, he heard a defiant bellow of 'You bastards!' Mac had garnered a burst of second wind and was attempting to retaliate one-handed from behind the Browning. 'Mind you, he would only have hit aircraft, but there was the effect – we were firing,' said Reg. McKenzie's bravado rubbed off on Perkins, who also set aside his suffering to let fly from the Vickers K in the back of the vehicle.

Seekings drove like the clappers to get to the medical tent. As he sped along, Reg cast his thoughts back to a few nights earlier when Mac had predicted his own death. The memory unsettled him and he shot on, determined to reach help with his man still breathing. The only time he briefly slowed was when an airborne officer attempted to stop him. 'I just bashed past and nearly knocked him down,' said Seekings, who eventually reached his intended destination and made sure McKenzie received immediate treatment. According to Reg, his roughneck gunner lost an arm. 'A few more seconds, he'd have been gone,' a doctor informed Seekings. 'I couldn't have helped him.'

With Seekings confident that his two men were in receipt of good care, he jumped back in his jeep to re-join Wellsted's troop. An official report documented how they had prevailed before the infantry moved in to clear up the woods 'assisted by fire from the jeeps'. The enemy suffered an estimated eighty deaths and almost the same number of prisoners were captured. Wellsted's party pressed on in the vanguard before delivering on their orders issued earlier that day to 'Get the infantry into Rhade.'

As for McKenzie, he survived (as did Perkins), although Reg never saw him again. 'Mac got very bitter,' he said. 'I was away when he came back to camp and picked his gear up. The only man he wanted to speak to was me.' McKenzie's loyalties lay with Seekings, and not just because Reg had saved his life on the edge of a German wood: the pair had experienced so much in one another's company. Reg always wondered what became of the 'rough little so and so' from a very different walk of life with whom he shared cross words, laughs and slugs of rum – not to mention manning the guns side by side. 'He was good,' said Seekings.

Sunday 1 April provided a window of peace for some of the men from 1 SAS as Fraser McLuskey organized an Easter service. The padre laid his by now familiar maroon cloth carrying the regiment's crest across a table in a farmhouse and Wellsted's troop sang resurrection hymns while the farmer's family watched on. A week later the same unit suffered its worst losses on German soil. Working alongside the Inns of Court Regiment, the troop was travelling just behind two Dingo scout cars and an armoured car as part of a recce when they fell prey to a trap to the north-west of Hanover. Enemy fighters were initially glimpsed on one side of the Neustadt-Nienburg road, prompting the SAS to respond with a belligerent burst from their Vickers into the trees. Next, Wellsted took a group from the jeeps to probe, but it was not long before the woodlands echoed to the sounds of booming Panzerfausts and furious fire from Spandaus. Hidden in the ditches and concealed among the undergrowth, the Germans let loose with a murderous ambush.

Battle raged for ten minutes – Trooper John 'Taffy' Glyde was

SAS 'Operation Archway', March to May 1945.

killed – before the armoured car led the SAS in a fast, fighting withdrawal to an intersection; not that the troop's problems were at an end. The enemy started to surround the jeeps, leaving them cut off from their own lines. The main threat emerged from the south in the shape of two armoured vehicles firing down the sandy track that the SAS had used earlier on their way across from Schneeren. Also, away to the east, Seekings caught sight of unknown uniformed men, while there was still a danger from the enemy in the woods where the ambush had begun. But the squadron sergeant-major appeared relatively unflustered as he and troopers Neil McMillan and Geordie Younger prepared to make a stand from their jeep. McMillan heard Reg mutter something along the lines of, 'There's a lot of the buggers, aren't there?' His demeanour had a positive effect on the others and McMillan took cheer from knowing that Seekings was fighting alongside him. 'He was never one for looking concerned.'

But this was one occasion when Seekings' feathers became ruffled. With the enemy closing in on three sides, the SAS position looked ever more unsafe, especially the jeeps that contained Lieutenant Denis Wainman and Sergeant Jeff Du Vivier and their respective crews. Defiantly they faced two 20-mm cannons, as well as persistent small-arms fire from within the scrub to the side of the track. Wellsted called on their own armoured vehicle, which rallied to fine effect, scoring direct hits on the two armoured enemy cars, the leading one of which had advanced to within a mere 50 yards of the squadron. But Germans still appeared to be marauding everywhere, with support from an armoured personnel carrier piling out to join the battle. The SAS began to incur further casualties. Also, a clutch of jeeps was knocked out and ammunition was diminishing rapidly. Seekings, armed only with his Colt .45, dived down next to an old tree, tears of frustration swelling his eyes. As he took cover in a ditch, Reg experienced an uncomfortable sensation: for the first time in his life he understood what fear felt like. A thought fizzed through his mind: 'We've got to get out of this or we'll just be cut to ribbons.'

Options were rapidly running out for the SAS fighters. Assessing the situation, the cool head of Major Poat realized that those under his command were both outnumbered and hemmed in. There was only one thing for it: he gave orders for a break-out. Seekings planned to 'bash through' with the help of a 2-inch mortar that he had thrown on the back of his jeep, but first there was also the important task of collecting the casualties. He numbered off half of the men, urging them 'to load up the wounded and prepare to fight themselves out with me'. Next, Reg grabbed the mortar and pounded enemy positions on one side of the road before making a dash for it with his little party and their blazing guns. With the first objective achieved successfully, Seekings turned round and this time pointed the mortar in the direction of the opposite side of the road to assist the remainder in their getaway bid. In due course, the remnants also shot their way out from the enemy's clutches before the SAS jeeps still remaining in service sped off on an easterly course.

In sombre mood, the troop eventually returned to the safety of the Allied lines. Trooper Jim Blakeney, from Wainman's jeep, had been shot dead in the trackside crossfire; at the same location Trooper Roy Davies suffered a fatal body wound. Trooper Douglas Ferguson (Poat's batman) tried in vain to reach Davies, but was hit in the shoulder. Heavy fire prevented anyone from attempting to rescue Ferguson, who was never seen again by his fellow SAS soldiers. There were several other casualties from the brutal encounter, with Wellsted (who would reflect on it as 'my worst defeat') hospitalized after being struck in both legs. Seekings later reported that his own jeep was riddled and his raincoat pocked with holes. As for his bedroll, it simply fell to bits. 'I was in tatters,' he said, 'but I hadn't got a mark on me.'

The 8 April encounter turned out to be the last hard fighting in which Seekings participated in the war. Over a four-year period, he had seen intense action in North Africa, Sicily, mainland Italy, France and now east of the River Rhine. Involvement in a litany of hostilities had shown him the starkest realities of conflict and he had become as battle-hardened as perhaps any man in the British Army. But nothing could have prepared Seekings for what lay around the corner in Germany.

Chapter 20

BELSEN AND BEYOND

Seekings sat on the roadside, watching German tanks harmlessly roll by in front of him. Every now and again he chatted amiably enough with passing enemy soldiers. Similarly, others from the SAS talked or sometimes hollered to men with whom they had been in opposition for so long. Seekings found it all 'most peculiar'.

The novel experience stemmed from a local truce. This had been agreed on 12 April 1945 after the Germans called for no fighting within a zone that included a large concentration camp, which lay in the path of the Allied advance north-eastwards. The enemy concern was that fighting in the vicinity might lead to escapees and widespread transmission of serious diseases such as typhus that were known to be rife within the camp. It was decided that an SAS patrol would attend the site to help pave the way for medical teams from the British Army and the Red Cross. The party was ordered to assess 'medical requirements', according to Johnny Cooper. In advance, the travellers received appropriate inoculation updates and were given a yellow armband to indicate non-combatant status. Their destination was Bergen-Belsen Concentration Camp.

Seekings smelt the place long before arriving there. Driving through the forest in Lower Saxony, he noticed a 'horrible stink'. The stench remained in the air, unpleasant and pungent for the next day or so, until on 15 April the patrol came across wire fences, overlooked by towering fir trees, guarded by Hungarians wearing unusual orange-brown uniforms. This was Belsen, its main gate framed by well-kept flower beds alongside smartly painted kerbstones. SS officer Josef Kramer received the SAS men. It seemed as if just another military base lay behind him, further down the drive.

Over the previous four years Reg had been confronted with a long line of extreme challenges, physical and mental. He had hurled himself from a plane into the black oblivion of night during one of the worst desert storms in living memory; he had avoided capture, surviving dire starvation and thirst when behind the lines; he had been at the tailgate of a truck almost in touching distance of his section members when most of them were killed by a bomb blast; he had been shot in the base of his head at near point-blank range. And yet none of his previous encounters or emotional responses to his catalogue of experiences could have prepared him or his comrades for what they witnessed at Belsen. 'We looked in and it was a hell of a mess,' he said. Death and deprivation in large scale were apparent all over the sprawling site.

The camp and its wooden barrack huts, surrounded by barbed wire, held an estimated 60,000 prisoners, many of whom were starving and sick. Some lay dead in their bunks amid the filthiest of human conditions. But going deeper into the camp, the reality of Belsen presented its very worst to the SAS detachment: deep trenches containing partially clothed or naked bodies, rotting, emaciated and piled on top of one another (approximately 13,000 corpses were discovered in the camp). The sights all around them shocked the SAS patrol. 'I've seen people die of starvation and there was not much difference in them,' said Seekings. 'But these, it was systematic. They were just a skeleton. Terrible. It's hard to credit that people would go to those extremes to do things.'

Lieutenant John Randall later gave an account of how Reg meted out a small slice of his own justice in response to an incident of casual violence in Belsen. Randall, the first Allied officer to enter the camp around half an hour or so before he was joined by his SAS colleagues, recalled how a guard was beating a prisoner with the butt of his rifle. He and Seekings were among those to glimpse the scene, which took place by a hut. According to Randall, Reg ('a very tough man' in Randall's opinion) asked Major John Tonkin for permission to intervene. The officer immediately gave his consent, resulting in Seekings approaching the guard and punching him to the floor. Once the man had struggled back onto his feet, he was 'knocked out by another punch to the head'. Given how Cooper also wrote of the 'utter rage' that consumed his old friend in Belsen, it is easy to imagine those moments as they unfolded. Not only had Seekings unleashed his blows with the conviction of an army boxing champion, but also with an utter contempt and revulsion for all that was surrounding him. The power shift within Belsen was confirmed when Tonkin gave orders for Kramer to be taken to the guardroom where he was held with Irma Grese, who had been in charge of the camp's women prisoners. Tonkin told the pair that the Allies now had control and that any subsequent mistreatment of prisoners would lead to punishment. The camp had been liberated with the SAS at the vanguard – or, as Seekings later phrased it: 'We were the first in Belsen too.' A major medical relief operation got underway at the camp from that day and the SAS patrol moved on. 'We got out quick,' Reg said, relieved not to have to spend another moment surrounded by the horror of Belsen.

●　●　●

For three days from 19 April, a troop from 1 SAS joined forces with a Field Security unit to flush out prominent SS and Gestapo personnel who were seeking to avoid capture during the inexorable Allied advance. 'We were after the war criminals,' said Seekings. In particular, they wanted to find a general considered to be responsible for 'a lot of dirty work in France'.

Seekings took on the role with his usual blend of brawn and guile, but only after the convoy survived a scare in the proximity of Lüneburg. Jack Terry and Reg got together for a chat after their sixth senses kicked in during a transport break in a dell. Seekings decided to investigate a ridge, which had been the main focus of his suspicions. Sure enough, his and Terry's hunch proved spot on. They came across trenches packed with young cadets, unsure, scared and without leadership. Seekings reckoned that most of them were around eleven years old. One of them said that they had been trying to weigh up what to do. 'They could have knocked hell out of us,' Reg said.

The combined SAS and Field Security party arrived in Lüneburg and quickly got to work. 'We were running around, picking up all these people and holding them until the leading elements of the army got through,' said Reg. 'Then, we took over the gaol and put them in.'

One of the more polite encounters saw him and Cooper knock on the door of Willy Messerschmitt, the renowned aircraft designer. An interesting situation followed in which the bold Messerschmitt seemed intent on quizzing his visitors about the Perspex used to stabilize the screens in British aircraft. 'He said, "If you can give me the secret, I can guarantee you'd be the richest man in the world",' said Seekings. Eventually, it was Messerschmitt who divulged information, rather than the other way round, and the SAS men moved on.

On another occasion a woman, strongly suspected of being

the mistress of an enemy adjutant, underwent a grilling about his whereabouts, but refused to talk. 'She was tough,' said Reg. 'We stood her up against a wall and put bullets alongside her ear – she wouldn't flinch.' Finally, the woman, who maintained she did not know the man in question, was left alone on the understanding that she was to be kept under scrutiny. But soon afterwards, Seekings devised a smart method of eliciting the required information with help from an unlikely source: a local photographer-chemist. The man was developing films taken to him by some of the SAS soldiers who had briefly been inside Belsen. With the kernel of a plan in his mind, Seekings asked him if he had any pictures of pretty women. Initially, the chemist misunderstood, imagining that the British soldier sought something risqué for his own enjoyment. Seekings soon set him straight: his idea was to superimpose a photo of an attractive female onto one in his possession showing the German adjutant. 'Can you fake up such a picture as though she's being very intimate or sitting on his lap?' Once the chemist grasped what was required, he set about arming Seekings with this very different sort of weapon. Reg returned to question the tight-lipped woman and theatrically produced the mocked-up photo. 'You mean to tell me you don't know this man?' Confronted by what appeared to be damning evidence of her lover's apparent infidelity, the woman 'blew her top' and promptly blurted out his whereabouts.

Seekings employed much harsher tactics when he and Cooper finally tracked down the officer, who was lying low in a village. A woman responded to their presence at her front door but maintained that the hunted man was not there. She claimed her husband was the only male frequenting the property. Seekings persisted, which led to the appearance of a man who denied any military involvement. 'Silly bugger, he'd left his jackboots on,' said Reg, who straightaway caught sight of the footwear typically associated with the Wehrmacht and the Waffen SS. A fierce and lengthy interrogation ensued, but the German gave nothing away. 'Eventually Johnny found stuffed in his mattress an SS truncheon, this steel-core thing. So we used it on him; across his shoulder blades, shins, shoulder blades, shins, shoulder blades. He still wouldn't talk. How the hell he stood it, I don't know.' Seekings ended up losing his temper, 'which is a bad thing when you're doing that sort of work'. The process escalated to the point where he thought he had killed the man. 'I had to work like hell to save him,' admitted Seekings. The German came round but realized he had been taken to the very edge. 'He broke down and said, yes, he was number so-and-so, Hauptman [usually translated as captain] so-and-so, and wished to be treated as a prisoner of war.'

Seekings also got involved in the detention of Lüneburg's gauleiter (regional Nazi Party leader). Monocle and all, the Nazi official had been captured, but was arguing the toss with a regular British Army major about where he had been told to sit in the vehicle that was to transport him to prison. 'Why don't you kick his arse?' Reg asked the major, who replied that such an action would likely end up with him being hauled over the coals. 'Don't be bloody ridiculous,' said Seekings, promptly sticking his boot in. 'You get in there … don't bloody argue with me!' he barked at the gauleiter.

The following morning saw Seekings take a similar hard line with the high-ranking German as a draft of prisoners were prepared for handover to a special police unit. After the cell doors clanged open, the gauleiter failed to appear. It transpired that the man was still conducting his ablutions, testing Reg's supply of patience, which soon disintegrated to next to nil. The gauleiter, after being told to get dressed immediately, began quoting the Geneva Convention and demanded a servant. 'I'm giving you just five seconds to get changed and get outside,' rapped Seekings. Another stand-off occurred as the German eventually moved, lugging two portmanteaux to the gate. It was there that the gauleiter saw a crowd gathered beyond in the town square. Dropping his cases, the man's face flushed red with fury and he declined to move another inch. He insisted there was no way he was about to be belittled by the townspeople. Seekings took off his beret – by now he wore the red airborne one that revealed his true identity – and brandished it in front of the gauleiter. 'And what order did Hitler give?' asked Reg, referring to the Fuhrer's infamous instructions to execute captured commandos and troops from other Allied behind-the-lines units. The Nazi official made out that he was unaware. 'You're a lying bastard,' growled Seekings, putting his beret back on. Next he drew his Colt .45, inserted a round and gave the bumptious gauleiter an ultimatum. 'I would rather shoot you than march you across that square, so what's it going to be?' The man picked up his cases and moved forward, booed and jeered with every step. 'He must have been a bad bastard,' reflected Reg.

One night, Seekings' sandy-haired appearance and dominant disposition led to him being mistakenly identified as a German. He had requisitioned billets for some of the men at a farmhouse and ended up eating an evening meal with the large family that lived there. The atmosphere in the large kitchen was civil, even convivial, until Reg began to ask the farmer about German troops. All of a sudden the elderly farmer stood up and declared: 'Please shoot me.' A bewildered Seekings responded by outlining that he had no intention of carrying out any such act, but the man remained unconvinced, demanding that his house guest be honest with him. The farmer was certain he was being deceived. 'You are not English. You look like a German, you speak like a German, you act like a German,' he told Seekings. The daughters of the house struggled to persuade their father that he was not about to be seized for treason. 'He thought we were Gestapo or SS trying to trick him,' said Seekings.

Reg came across other German civilians who were similarly wary. 'There was a lot of fear there, no two ways about it,' he

Seekings (l) and Cooper were never far apart as the SAS forged deep into
Germany during March and April, 1945.

said. Many of the older generations he encountered were also
anxious about what the future eventually might look like for their
beleaguered country and longed for an end to hostilities. 'They
could see that Germany was getting hammered.'

Apart from the younger population ('you didn't find many
friendly kids'), Seekings came across fewer and fewer Nazis as
he forged across Germany, but one set of locations proved an
exception – brothels. More than once the Field Security-SAS team
targeted these establishments because of the strong likelihood of
pouncing unawares on SS officers. 'We picked up a lot of these
in brothels,' said Seekings. 'German houses, a lot are connected
up in the ceilings. We used to go there quietly, slip in and get up
in the roof, spread the chaps around and then drop through the
rooms and grab them.' But not every raid proved successful. In
one instance, Seekings had 'bashed in' to a room, only to find a
woman who had been left in 'a hell of a state'. A lieutenant from
the Waffen SS had bitten off her nipples before fleeing through a

window. Seekings was appalled by the actions of the 'animal' who had escaped his clutches.

By early May, 1 SAS had moved on from Lübeck in the direction of Kiel on the Baltic Coast. It was in this port city that a relatively carefree occasion almost turned into deep trouble for Seekings and Cooper as they unwittingly breached the line of an armistice. The episode began with Seekings taking a call in the early hours from a source (whom he never revealed) instructing him to proceed to Kiel and 'take possession' of the town hall before a sweep through the dockyards. Heading off prior to daylight, the journey north proved notable for the hordes of surrendering Germans that packed the roadsides. Once in Kiel, the SAS men faced no resistance at all in completing their business – at which point thoughts turned to pleasure. Before long, Cooper and Seekings were supping on a drink and trying out their best lines on the local girls. But the good times came to an abrupt halt after Seekings received word of a potentially dicey scenario. 'I'd left a chap on my wireless set and he was calling me and said, "Paddy Mayne wants to talk to you … that's Paddy on the buzzer".' Immediately the Irishman demanded to know the whereabouts of Seekings, who admitted to offering up a 'cock and bull story' that clearly didn't wash with his regiment's CO. 'Get the hell out of there fast and don't argue!' Reg was told. Mayne elaborated by explaining that Kiel was about to be sealed off. It turned out that Seekings and Cooper were in danger of falling foul of a freshly negotiated armistice line, the wrong side of which they had unintentionally strayed. 'I got John and we dropped everything – the booze, the girls – and we hared off back to Lübeck.'

It was a rare event indeed for the fun-loving pair to leave a party that was in full swing, but the Kiel drinks proved nothing more than a mere warm-up. In a matter of days the SAS men at last enjoyed the mother of all celebrations.

Chapter 21

FROM WAR TO PEACE

The order for all SAS troops to return to Britain came on 3 May 1945. Seekings duly departed Lübeck in a requisitioned German staff car, a BMW, and began a journey of more than 450 miles to the south-east. A Squadron's destination was a rendezvous point at Poperinge, near Ypres in Belgium. About an hour into the trek, Reg swung off the autobahn at Hamburg. Roadblocks made progress difficult, but he glimpsed enough to recognize that the major city by the Elbe River was a 'terrible bloody mess … it was still burning'. Seekings soon pointed the BMW back towards the autobahn and sped down beyond the German border. By mid-afternoon on 8 May he had motored to the outskirts of Brussels and noticed that the car's fuel tank was almost empty. Stopping to fill up, he debated the possibility of spending a night in the Belgian capital before completing his trip in the morning. As he pondered the matter, a young girl rushed outside from the petrol station. 'The war is finished!' she yelled. An unmoved Seekings dismissed the girl's excitement, informing her that he had heard such talk before. 'It's true,' maintained the girl. 'Your prime minister is speaking now!' Seekings ran after her, ducking indoors to hear the voice of Winston Churchill in a radio broadcast. He was announcing the unconditional surrender of Germany and the end of the war in Europe.

Seekings chose to mark the moment by sitting down for a cup of coffee with the folk from the petrol station. During the conversation, Reg realized where he wanted to be that night – Poperinge. The town nicknamed 'Pop' had been an entry point to the battlefields in the Great War and was a place Albert Seekings had known well from his time fighting against the Germans almost thirty years earlier. With the petrol tank full once again, Seekings left Brussels behind him and motored on for a couple more hours until he reached Poperinge. There he headed for the main square, its buildings draped with red, yellow and black flags. The small town's pavements were packed with SAS troops, many from B and C Squadron, also on their way back from Germany after taking part in Operation Howard, which had been led by Mayne. Another comrade in Poperinge was Bill Fraser, well on the way to recovery from the hand wound sustained in a woodland firefight in late March. Ian Wellsted, downed in the 8 April crossroads shoot-out, was another on the mend. It was his task to organize the SAS's upcoming disembarkation from Ostend.

As the celebrations gathered pace, Seekings felt a warm glow and not just because he was surrounded by mates. Being in Poperinge for VE Day could not have been more fitting as it triggered a strong connection with his dad's own wartime experiences. 'It was just as the old man had described it,' said Reg. The beers flowed long into the night in 'Pop', ensuring high demand for the gents. 'They're just like their fathers,' declared one elderly local woman within earshot of Seekings. 'Drink, drink, drink. Piss, piss, piss.' Reg was amused;

just another emotion in what had been a historic day. Dazed and elated, he also experienced a huge swell of relief and joy – probably more of the former. Indeed, there was a significant part of him that felt 'a bit amazed' that he had somehow survived after an event-packed war. Hardened by all he had seen and done, Seekings must have felt older than his still relatively tender age of twenty-five.

On 10 May Frankforce departed for England, but within days the re-equipped 1 and 2 SAS regiments – jeeps and all – flew out to Norway. In Seekings' words, the men went there 'to take the surrender and clean up the German troops'. Throughout that spring and summer, the SAS handled the disarmament of the large enemy force occupying the Scandinavian country. Johnny Cooper viewed those months spent in Norway as 'a delightful holiday after the rigours of the war years'. Seekings reflected in a similar vein: 'In lots of ways it was flag-flying.' But he also recalled how 'rifle butts and fists' were used to deal with the odd flare-up or two.

When Seekings returned home to the Fens for the first time, he did so unannounced and with a degree of trepidation. Reg had not forgotten his father's warning as he and his brother Bob prepared to leave for the war back in 1939: 'Never darken my door if you're dishonest.' The words flashed across his mind as he knocked at the family's isolated semi-detached (known as the White House, reflecting its exterior colour), aside the Great Fen on the edge of Ely. Albert Seekings answered and, according to his elder son, 'nearly had a fit', but the First World War veteran's shock soon turned to joy. Reg paused after being invited inside. He felt compelled to offer a confession. 'I've got to warn you of one thing,' he said. 'I've not been exactly dishonest, but I have been by your standards.' A grin spread across Albert's face. 'Bloody good show,' he said. 'Glad you're not stupid.'

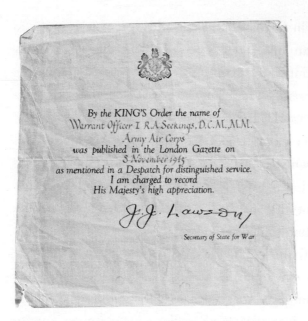

By the KING'S Order the name of
Warrant Officer I R.A.Seekings, D.C.M.,M.M.
Army Air Corps
was published in the London Gazette on
8 November 1945
as mentioned in a Despatch for distinguished service.
I am charged to record
His Majesty's high appreciation.

J.J. Lawson

Secretary of State for War

Seekings' efforts in North-West Europe gained him further recognition.

Reg Seekings' gallantry in the latter stages of the war was recognized in November 1945 with the *London Gazette* documenting that he had been 'mentioned in a Despatch for distinguished service'[12]. But the close of the year was a time of change for him and many others. A month earlier, on 8 October, an order had come to disband the wartime Special Air Service. With fighting in Europe at an end, the decision-makers deemed its dynamic and groundbreaking warfare methods were no longer necessary in the new era of peace, leaving an uncertain future for men such as Seekings. However, he and his brother had already begun to move towards a very different type of life. During the summer, they had married their respective sweethearts.

Bob's wedding to Agnes took place in the Ayrshire village of Catrine, the home of the bride. The younger Seekings had left the SAS shortly after 'HQ SAS Troops' departed Sorn Castle for

12   Mentioned in Despatches is a recognition for bravery in action. It is an official award comprising a certificate and a bronze oak leaf emblem, which is sewn to a designated ribbon (that of the 1939–45 War Medal in Seekings' instance).

southern England in August 1944. With his ongoing foot problems, he was posted to an infantry training centre at Bury St Edmunds in Suffolk. Returning to the Cambridgeshires was not an option at the time as his parent regiment had suffered the fate of captivity in the Fall of Singapore (also known as the Battle of Singapore) in February 1942. The closing months of Bob's war included several consultations about his feet that eventually led to a medical discharge, the details of which are listed in his service records. A typewritten sentence spells out that he had been considered 'permanently unfit' for service. But immediately below the administration, three handwritten words were added. 'Military Conduct: Exemplary'. Bob Seekings had gone to war as a boy and returned a man, albeit one with significant physical and mental scars.

On Saturday 7 July 1945, Reg married Monica Smith at All Saints Church in the bride's home village of Stanton in Suffolk. The date marked the start of what grew into more than fifty years of happy marriage for the couple. Monica was not the only member of her family to wed that summer's day: her younger sister Peggy also walked up the aisle to marry Trooper George Hurrell of the Royal Armoured Corps. Seekings' younger sister Evelyn was present too, serving as one of Monica's three bridesmaids. When her brothers left for war in 1939, Evelyn was not quite in her teens and suffering from tuberculosis. For several years, Reg corresponded with her as if time and circumstance had stood still. That changed in 1943 when Evelyn sent a photo of herself, by now in her mid-teens, and accompanied it with a written message: 'You've been writing to me as though I'm a little child. I'm a grown woman now.' Reg's response was to offer to take her dancing on his return, which he did.

Evelyn, three weeks prior to her eighteenth birthday, wore a green floral taffeta dress for the wedding. She clutched mixed sweet peas and ferns. Monica's bouquet comprised a dozen dark red carnations, which stood out against her white satin dress.

Monica's father Vincent gave her away to an immaculately dressed groom. Seekings, the crown on his right arm a reminder of his Warrant Officer status, dressed for the ceremony in 'best B.D' – best battledress. He wore the uniform's collar open at the neck to reveal a smart shirt and tie in mid-green. Fittingly, Johnny Cooper stood by his side to administer best man duties. Fresh from an uplifting rendition of 'Lead us Heavenly Father', all four of the newlyweds emerged into the daylight to receive family and friends' congratulations before making the short walk to Shepherds' Hall for a reception enjoyed by eighty guests.

As the church bells chimed across the rustic village, bathed in warm sunshine with the temperature reaching a pleasant 70 degrees Fahrenheit, the scenes could hardly have been more idyllic or quintessentially English. They had been preserved by millions of men such as Seekings, who risked their lives to destroy an ideology that had upset the global equilibrium. The war also gave him a platform to redefine who he was. Six years earlier, Seekings had stepped out of the Fenland fields determined to do his duty, but also to make his mark. Strength of mind and body, as well as seemingly endless supplies from a personal reservoir of good fortune, ensured that he ended the war with a long line of medals across his breast. He earned the vast majority when serving in an innovative special operations unit that to this day acknowledges his contribution as one of the fabled band of men known simply as 'The Originals'. Stubborn, cunning, brazen, ferocious and courageous, his feats saw him become one of the most highly decorated Special Forces soldiers of the Second World War.

But when at last the conflict concluded, Seekings greatly prized that he could stand proud in front of any man – regardless of class, upbringing or education. 'I can look the King of England in the eye and say: "I'm as good as you, mate, and probably better, because I've proved it".'

Epilogue

'SEEKINGS WAY'

In one way and another, the SAS never quite left Bob Seekings. 'Use the shadows to your advantage,' he would instruct his three young sons when they ventured out foraging around the fertile Fen fields to help find a bit of extra food. 'Keep calm, don't panic and you'll be all right.' After the harvester had gone through, potatoes left lying close to the surface were fair game, as were gooseberries and apples in the nearby orchards. On one occasion, a local farmer caught Bob picking a few apples on his way home after work. An awkward discussion followed in which the ex-soldier, perhaps trying to diffuse the situation, asked what variety the apples might be. 'You should bloody know – you're eating them!' retorted the fed-up farmer.

Taking a bit of surplus from the land was deemed 'country life', but at times after the war it was also essential for Bob. He and his young Scottish wife Agnes lived in Ely and soon had extra mouths to feed – sons Ian and Kerry came in quick succession, followed a few years later by a third boy, Reg (the same name as his uncle). Times were often tough for Bob, who worked in various jobs, including in the building trade. The cruellest winter of all came in the early months of 1963 when snow and bitter weather resulted in him being laid off for months. With no money coming in and no buffer, the Seekings experienced real hardship, surviving as best they could in a house heated by a single fireplace. 'For a few months we experienced what it's like to be with nothing.' said Bob's youngest son Reg.

When the warmer weather returned, Bob threw himself back into work. Hard graft never bothered him, although he was less inclined to take on responsibility. 'I think the war damaged him quite badly – the experiences,' said Kerry Seekings. 'I think that took away any ambition. He was just happy to survive and look after his family. My mum told me when they first got married, he used to wake up screaming at night, covered in sweat.'

Eventually, the night terrors disappeared, allowing Bob to enjoy more of life. He loved the company of the family's pet dogs and took a close interest in sports such as horseracing and cricket. Kerry reflects on his dad as 'a people person … he had a lot of integrity, taught us right and wrong'. But he outlined how Bob also had his faults. 'He could be selfish,' said Kerry. 'Overall, he tried his best for us, but he didn't have that ambition because the war affected him. He told me when he came back, "That was it, everything just left me".'

Agnes bore a great degree of the parental responsibility in the Seekings' household through the 1950s and beyond. She worked tirelessly to raise her three children, instilling key life skills and a strong behaviour code. 'Mum was the glue in our growing up and she would always put us first, even at her personal sacrifice,' said Kerry,

Later in life, Bob became haunted once again by scenes from his past. There were days when he would become remote and morose. 'Today, I feel he would have been diagnosed with Post-Traumatic

Stress Disorder,' said Kerry Seekings, MBE, and a retired major of the Parachute Regiment.

Bob kept in contact with Eric Musk, who married his pre-war girlfriend Vera Wells on 19 May 1944, in Isleham, a few miles from his home town of Soham. The following June, while based at a transit camp in Dover, Musk received a telegram confirming the birth of his first son, Richard. When Eric's service years concluded, he resumed his role at the local electricity company. Like his Cambridgeshire Regiment, Commandos and SAS friend, it took him a while to recalibrate to civilian life. But Eric returned to the sports field and once again began to make the local news with his football feats. Two more children, Marion and Keith, came along as Musk absorbed himself in the heart of family life. 'He was very, very kind, very, very caring,' said Richard Musk. 'Family meant everything.'

Eric maintained a military discipline regarding his own habits. Not only was the Musk lawn mown in pristine manner, but any early-morning worm casts were swept away. His car always gleamed and his shoes shone. From time to time, he and Bob would catch up. They even appeared side by side in the recording of a DVD, *The Story of the SAS*. Bob lived until ten days after his seventy-ninth birthday in February 2002. Just over a year later, Eric died at the age of eighty-four.

• ● •

Reg Seekings and his wife Monica never had any children (late in life, Reg expressed his regret about this to a friend). The couple settled in Ely where, in 1946, they took on a pub called the Rifleman's Arms. Being a landlord had its moments for Reg, who on one occasion was forced to remove two troublemaking American servicemen from his hostelry. Polite requests to leave met with a hostile response, so he ducked under the counter to sort the matter out. Within seconds, he had the two men propped up against an outside wall after landing two well-placed punches.

Seekings' connection to the SAS lived on. Indeed, his Service Record shows that in the middle of July 1952 he reported for two weeks' training in Otley in Yorkshire with the 21st SAS Regiment of the Army Reserve.

Closer to home, Reg eventually sought change from his usual daily routine. Trade in the Rifleman's Arms had slowed to the point that one year he needed to find farmhand work to bolster his income and, around the same time, old aspirations became rekindled. A draft letter, found among his personal papers, to Colonel Franks showed that Seekings had liaised with David Stirling and also a Rhodesian farmers' organization about employment in the African country's farming district. 'I feel this is the chance of a lifetime for me,' wrote Reg. 'I have been connected with farming all my life and my heart is in it.' Giving up the licence to the Rifleman's Arms in 1954, he relocated to Southern Rhodesia for a future as a tobacco farmer.

If the world of farming marked a return to his roots, a strong connection to a more recent past also resurfaced during his years in Southern Rhodesia. In his adopted country, Seekings joined the British South Africa Police as a reserve and became a regular sight around the force's Morris Depot in Harare. He would pop into The Copper Pot, the pub frequented by fellow reservists and regular BSAP men.

Seekings worked very closely with Chief Superintendent Bill Bailey, who established the Police Anti-Terrorist Unit (PATU) in 1966. The pair had plenty in common as Bailey had served in the Long Range Desert Group during the Second World War. With the Rhodesian Bush War (1964–79) escalating, he called on Seekings, an auxiliary inspector, to assist with training PATU 'sticks' for counter-insurgency purposes.

Old allies (l to r) Pat Riley, Reg Seekings, Bob Bennett and Mike Sadler deep in conversation at an event in the 1980s.

Reg delivered renowned weaponry instruction to young conscripts and passed on his experience at gruelling battle camps. At a classified location not far outside Harare, he would stage exercises in which his pupils had to either attack or defend a machine-gun post. There was a fair amount of schlepping up and down hills while Reg roared out instructions. 'He pushed us really hard, but in a very fair way,' said 'Steven', a National Service Patrol Officer who undertook a three-month training course in the second half of the 1970s. 'His style was, "You listen to me, do what I say because your life is depending on this. If you do what I say, you stand a better chance of surviving out there when deployed".'

Steven noted how Reg's eyes narrowed as he spoke as if to emphasize how important his words were. 'We soon realized that he knew what he was doing when it came to military strategy and tactics.' Not that Seekings boasted about his past or referenced his SAS credentials. 'He was very modest – he never talked about that,' said Steven. After one expert weaponry session, curiosity got the better of Steven and other conscripts who started asking questions regarding the identity of their instructor. 'He's ex-British Army, very experienced,' they were told. 'Little did I know how experienced he was and what he had done,' said Steven. 'I remember him well as a tough and highly competent professional.'

In 1982, the year of his sixty-second birthday, Seekings returned home to England, settling down into retirement in Monica's home village of Stanton. As had been the case in Southern Rhodesia, largely he kept his own counsel when it came to his previous life. He would enjoy a pint of bitter with folk in both the local pubs, The Angel and The Cock Inn, but he was just as content to walk his dachshund dogs Toffee and Fudge, as well as spend time digging in his garden. For a period, a few local youngsters took to teasing the still powerful-looking, but by now portly figure; a local woman spoke of how eggs were hurled. Seekings remained undaunted and once even chased after his tormentors with a shovel. Thereafter, he experienced no further problems, which might also have been down to the fact that the miscreants had their cards marked about exactly whom they had been hounding.

After his father Albert had died in 1968, Reg had made little effort while in Rhodesia to stay in touch with his relatives back home. That changed after he came back as he re-established contact with friends and family. One of the first catch-up visits he made was to the Essex home of Johnny Cooper, while he also saw many other familiar SAS faces at Regimental Association get-togethers. In his seventies, he reacquainted with his cousin and old boxing corner man Stan Pearce. They spoke often in lengthy telephone calls. And then there was the other S-A-S – Seekings and Seekings. Brothers Reg and Bob met up from time to time in Cambridge where they would talk over fish and chips.

Monica proved to be the anchor point for most of Reg's life. The bullet that had lodged at the base of his skull he had made into a brooch for her – she lost it, apparently. But their love for one another remained intact until Monica died just before Christmas in 1996. When he rang to let a friend know the news, Reg broke down in tears, shattered by his loss.

Just over two years later, at home on his own in his bungalow in Suffolk, he prepared himself a meal. It was the last he would ever make. Reg Seekings, a one-man force field, had gone through life withstanding punches, bullets and bombs, but he was human all the same and died of heart failure. His death certificate references chronic heart disease and is dated 17 March 1999, just two days before what would have been his seventy-ninth birthday.

Twenty-two years later a bypass bridge over the Great River Ouse was named in his honour. The road, which opened to traffic in 2018, skirts the south side of Ely and swings around close to Quanea Drove, the stomping ground of Seekings' youth. From its apex, the bridge offers stunning views of the historic Ely Cathedral, surrounded by the rich fields of the Fens.

The bypass bridge is a fine and perfectly located tribute to a man who left an imprint wherever he ventured. Also, it could hardly carry a more fitting name for a man who backed himself at every turn.

The signs at either end of the bridge read 'Seekings Way'.

ACKNOWLEDGEMENTS

A book such as this calls for considerable research and long days writing, but it would never have got off the ground without the support and encouragement of so many people. I am hugely grateful to everyone that I have corresponded with, either in person, in conversations on the phone or via email. Without the input of so many, *SAS: Duty Before Glory* would not have been written.

From the start the Seekings family have been unfailingly helpful. Not only are Ian, Kerry and Reg the nephews of Reg Seekings, they are also the sons of Bob Seekings, who served in the wartime Special Air Service. I met with them in the summer of 2021 to discuss the prospect of this book; they were hospitable and friendly in sharing their memories, as well as showing me photographs and other mementoes. It was a great starting point and served to spur me on. We have spoken or emailed in a cordial manner on a regular basis ever since and I would like to offer a massive thank you to them for all their assistance.

Mel Morley, Reg Seekings' niece and executor of his will, has been every bit as helpful since I met her with her another of Reg's relatives, Sheila Palmer, in the middle of 2021. From the outset, Mel showed great trust in my ability to write the book and that never changed, for which I can't thank her enough.

The Musk family have been valuable allies since I first became acquainted with them in the autumn of 2021. Eric's elder son

Richard and daughter Marion gave valuable insights into their father. Eric's grandson Stuart Palmer generously allowed me to see his grandfather's handwritten account of the Termoli invasion. It was a pleasure to meet with all three of them.

In the same vein, I later became acquainted with two more of Eric's grandchildren, Alison and Nigel Musk, along with Ali's partner Liam Munt. Not only did Ali and Nigel provide me with photos and details of Eric's war years, but they were also the most wonderful supporters during the book's development. Eric Musk was 'a bloody good bloke' according to the Seekings' boys. Without doubt, the genes have been passed down through the generations to Ali and Nigel.

The very first person I made contact with to discuss writing Reg's story was Gil Boyd, BEM. He has been invaluable over the last three years and I will always be grateful for his help and friendship. A keen historian and ex-soldier from 2 Para (the 2nd Battalion, The Parachute Regiment), Gil met Reg Seekings and carried out research before writing documents of his own about the first men of the SAS. As well as being a hive of information, Gil possesses a seriously good contacts' book. He put me in touch with a string of people, including Mel Morley (who was a former police colleague of his) and Kerry Seekings (a fellow ex-Para). Gil also introduced me to Anna Lewes (her husband John was Jock Lewes' nephew), who kindly agreed to the reproduction of two pages from Jock Lewes' original notebook in which Seekings' name appears.

Through Gil, the door also opened to the SAS Regimental Association. In the summer of 2021 I received a very positive email from its secretary, John Allcock in which he made the point that a book on Reg's exploits was 'well overdue'. Since that initial correspondence, John, Tracy, Rebecca and the Regimental Archivist have been helpful and friendly in equal measures. I would like to thank John for allowing me to make several visits to the Association's office for research purposes, including to view the original SAS War Diary. Also, I am grateful to the Association for making available a series of photographs that have been used in the book.

Along with the research undertaken at the Regimental Association's headquarters, I went on three occasions to the National Archives at Kew. What a place it is. I could visit every week and never run out of folders and files to explore. I also attended other first-class research facilities, including the Liddell Hart Centre for Military Archives at King's College London and the Research Room at the Imperial War Museum (IWM). The employees at all three locations were ultra-efficient and helpful. I am especially grateful to Dave McCall for his assistance with regard to the licensing of the extensive Seekings interview material that is held in the IWM Sound collections. Thanks, too, to Jane Fish (IWM).

That I was able to use the Seekings reels was down to journalist and author Gordon Stevens, who facilitated access to his superb interviews with Reg, conducted in the mid-1980s. I enjoyed immensely listening to him speak with Seekings, who proved a willing and thoughtful interviewee in Gordon's expert hands. Indeed, Gordon interviewed many key figures from the wartime SAS and wrote a fascinating book, *The Originals: The Secret History of the Birth of the SAS in Their Own Words.*

One of the best aspects of writing this book was that I got to spend time with SAS great Mike Sadler. Through the Regimental Association and Simon H, I first spoke with Mike during the summer of 2021. The phone call was so long that it required a break to brew up at the halfway point. A few months later, Mike moved close to where I live and, in 2022 and 2023, I had the good fortune of visiting him on a string of occasions. It amazed me just how much he recalled, not just about his experiences in the war, but also from his youth. What a life that man lived and what an honour it was to listen to him talk of the North Africa raids, his night-time parachute jump behind the lines in France and his memories of men such as David Stirling, Paddy Mayne, Johnny Cooper and Seekings. Those hours were all the more pleasurable for many of them being spent in the company of his daughter Sally. Thank you Mike, Sally and Simon H for those visits, all of which I will never forget.

I would also like to thank Stephen Mosely of the Orders and Medals Research Society (Hong Kong Branch) for the significant amount of original materials that he provided for inclusion in this book. I owe him a similar amount of gratitude for the military expertise, advice, encouragement and friendship he has given since we first became acquainted early in the book's life. For more than fifty years, Stephen has found the story of Reg Seekings to be a most inspiring, absorbing and enjoyable narrative of the Second World War generation, and his extensive knowledge of his subject reflects this.

Since the end of August 2021, I have enjoyed an endless series of emails with Alan Orton, whose father John was an L Detachment/SAS Original, previously in 11 (Scottish) Commando. Alan has answered hundreds of questions from me since we first corresponded. He also shared his own information-packed works. I would like to thank him for his patience and all of his interest in this book. If we ever manage to meet in person, he deserves much more than a pint of Adnams for putting up with all of my novice questions and habitual forays down rabbit holes.

Another to whom I am indebted is Alan Hoe, who served for many years in the SAS and later wrote the authorized biography of David Stirling. Alan kindly read and commented on my work as I wrote it. His constructive assessment of my words was always illuminating and much appreciated.

I corresponded with a series of other authors who have written authoritatively about the Special Air Service. In particular, I would like to thank Gavin Mortimer, who has interviewed dozens of wartime SAS soldiers and possesses an enviable knowledge of his specialist subject matter. When I started work on the book, Gavin was generous with his advice and support. On several occasions since, when I've emailed with a question or two, he has been quick to help, for which I'm very appreciative.

I extend similar thanks to bestselling SAS author Damien Lewis, who has taken a great interest in my book. I am very grateful to him for offering to write a cover note. Tom Petch (thanks for the photo, Tom), Josh Levine and Stewart McClean are three further authors of fine SAS works, who have been there to assist and encourage me through the writing process.

Boxing historian Miles Templeton (www.boxinghistory.org. uk) was incredibly helpful in sourcing newspaper reports of Reg Seekings' key bouts and giving additional insights into the sport in the 1930s. Miles kindly also sourced an article by Major Vivian Street ('Some men have nine lives', *Blackwood's Magazine*, 1947) at the National Newspaper Library at Boston Spa in North Yorkshire, for which I was very grateful.

At times, the book has moved in mysterious ways, including the making of new friendships. I hope Martin Boswell does not mind me referring to him as a friend, but he has really been an absolute star since I first got in touch with him. The sheer weight of his experience has meant he has been a huge asset to my efforts as I've worked to get the words down on the page. Martin served in the Royal Anglian Regiment, is a former Chairman and Historian of the Cambridgeshire Regiment Collection, was Exhibitions Coordinator of IWM Duxford (1990–2003) and Curator of Uniforms, Personal Equipment and Flags, IWM London (2003–17). His wisdom, guidance, knowledge and passion when it comes to the Cambridgeshire Regiment and all round kindness has been greatly appreciated. Also, he has provided materials and photography.

What a pal he has been.

Another new acquaintance with whom I am keen to remain in contact is Nigel Wood, who lives at the farm where Reg Seekings was born. Nigel gave me lots of details regarding the wider Seekings' lineage and also offered astute feedback when reading the book's draft chapters.

John and Nick Sinden spent many happy times with Reg in his later years. They offered a fount of stories and insights. I am very appreciative of Nick making the initial contact and for both he and his father being readily available to answer my questions on subsequent occasions.

Two other valued readers were Jon West and Matt Ramsay. They raised many valid points, as well as flagging up inconsistencies on style and spotting spelling errors. A heartfelt thank you to both – I owe you a day at the cricket.

My father Christopher Rushmer and my wife Julie Rushmer read every single word. They often re-read sections and also gave suggestions on how the work could be improved. Both of them have had to put up with me regularly interrupting whatever they were doing to discuss 'the book'. Julie even came up with a plan of how I could get the words written in time to meet my publisher's deadline. I can't thank enough either her or my dad for their seemingly limitless tolerance, patience and encouragement.

My literary agent David Luxton worked tirelessly to find the right publisher for *SAS: Duty Before Glory* and I am delighted that Michael O'Mara Books believed in its potential. Many thanks to my two editors Jo Stansall and Louise Dixon, as well as the rest of the team at MOM Books, who have got behind my work.

I would also like to extend thanks to the following: Bob Abel, Lorna Almonds-Windmill, Bruce B, John Baker and Ben Hill at the Airborne Assault Museum, Christina Barnes, Trevor Benton, Mick Bispham, Chris Brennand, Gordon Cawthorne, Graeme Cooper,

Paul and Lisa Davis, John Edwards, Simon Fletcher, John Fordham, Tony Gimbert, Ben Hill, Andrew K, Stella Leeks, Nabil Lawrence, Anna Lewes, Pierce Noonan, Carol Palmer, Thelma Pearce, Mike Petty, Steven, Steve Pittaway, Pete Rogers (Commando Veterans Archives), Mike Rouse, Julie Seekings, Ronnie Smith, Bob Terry, Kim Terry, Malcolm Tudor.

If I have thoughtlessly forgotten anyone, I apologize. Please get in touch and I will seek to remedy the situation for future editions.

SOURCES

The principal sources for this book are audio interviews with Reg Seekings held by the Imperial War Museum (reference: Reg Seekings audio IWM/Gordon Stevens/IWM) and Seekings' handwritten papers that were kindly made available to me from a private Hong Kong collection. In the following chapter-by-chapter breakdown, these prime sources are referred to first when material from either of them has been used in a chapter. Similar prominence has been given to private papers relating to Eric Musk and also the Service/Pay Books of Reg and Robert Seekings and Monica Seekings (née Smith).

The following are then also listed in this order: the bibliography for each chapter; author interviews; research centre details, along with the number/name applying to specific papers used; print and digital articles; miscellany, including unpublished works/papers and additional Seekings audio held by the Airborne Assault Museum and ParaData archives.

A note on abbreviations: After first use, NA = National Archive and IWM stands for Imperial War Museum. Also, WO = War Office.

PREFACE
Soldier's Service and Pay Book of A. R. Seekings
Stevens, Gordon. *The Originals: The Secret History of the Birth of the SAS in their Own Words.* Ebury Press, 2005

Hoe, Alan. *David Stirling: The Authorised Biography of the Creator of the SAS*. Warner Books, 1994

'Packed House for Excellent Programme', *Wisbech Standard*, 3 February 1939

SAS Rogue Warriors: https://www.bbc.co.uk/programmes/p0cb6sm8

CHAPTER 1

Reg Seekings audio IWM/Gordon Stevens/IWM

Stevens, Gordon. *The Originals: The Secret History of the Birth of the SAS in their Own Words*. Ebury Press, 2005

Author interview with Nigel Wood, current owner of Quanea Farm – Reg Seekings' birthplace

Author interview in 2021 with Trevor Benton, Stuntney villager who met Reg Seekings as a young man

Author interview with sons of Bob Seekings – Ian Seekings, Major Kerry Seekings (MBE) and Reg Seekings, 2021

Author interview with boxing historian Miles Templeton, 2021

Author interview in 2021 with Thelma Pearce, wife of Reg Seekings' cousin, Stan Pearce

Author correspondence with Martin Boswell, former chairman of the Cambridgeshire Regiment Association

TVS, SAS Interviews, Imperial War Museum, Documents 21759, Box 62/137/1

'From the Editor's Chair', *Boxing magazine* (known now as *Boxing News*), 22 February 1939

'Territorials in the Ring. Individual Championships at Bury', *Bury Free Press Post*, 11 February 1939

'Ely's New Drill Hall', *Ely Weekly Guardian*, 21 April 1939

Unpublished papers gathered by the late Major Dennis Hutt (kindly supplied by Martin Boswell, former chairman of the Cambridgeshire Regiment Collection)

A. R. Seekings interview with John Kane c.1998 – transcript kindly supplied by Gavin Mortimer (parts of the original audio are also held by the Airborne Assault Museum and ParaData.org.uk: Archive box number 5B1 1/8/1)

CHAPTER 2

Reg Seekings audio: IWM/Gordon Stevens/IWM

The Service Records of Robert W. Seekings (From the private papers of Bob Seekings)

Beevor, Antony. *Crete.* John Murray, 1991

Davy, Michael, ed. *The Diaries of Evelyn Waugh.* Phoenix, 2009

Durnford-Slater, Brigadier John. *Commando: Memoirs of a Fighting Commando in World War Two.* Greenhill Books, 2002

Liddell Hart, B. H., ed. *The Rommel Papers.* Arrow, 1987

Mead, Richard. *Commando General, The Life of Major General Sir Robert Laycock.* Pen & Sword, 2016

Messenger, Charles. *Commandos: The Definitive History of Commando Operations in the Second World War.* William Collins 2016

Messenger, Charles with Colonel George Young DSO and Lt Colonel Stephen Rose OBE. *The Middle East Commandos.* William Kimber & Co Ltd, 1988

National Archives WO 218/166 War Diary, Headquarters, Layforce

NA WO 218/166 Report on Raid on Bardia Appendix VIII 26 April

NA WO 218 168 7 Commando/A Battalion Layforce War Diary

Author interview with sons of Bob Seekings – Ian Seekings, Major Kerry Seekings (MBE) and Reg Seekings, 2021

Author interview with Richard Musk and Marion Palmer, son and daughter of Eric Musk, 2021

Author interview with Nigel and Alison Musk, grandchildren of Eric Musk

Author correspondence with Martin Boswell, former chairman of the Cambridgeshire Regiment Collection

British Army Casualty List 869, page 3

British Army Casualty List 584, page 21

'Ten Days in Open Boat: Little Water, No Food', *Cambridgeshire Times*, 25 July 1941

Seekings audio: Airborne Assault Museum and ParaData.org.uk; Archive box number 5B1 1/8/1

Article written by the late David Langton, available at https://www.cofepow.org.uk/armed-forces-stories-list/2nd-battalion-cambs-regiment

The Rhodes to Nowhere – Layforce and the Middle East Commando, unpublished work of Alan Orton

Unpublished papers gathered by the late Major Dennis Hutt (kindly supplied by Martin Boswell, former chairman of the Cambridgeshire Regiment Collection)

CHAPTER 3

The private papers of Reg Seekings

Reg Seekings audio: IWM/Gordon Stevens/IWM

Hoe, Alan. *David Stirling: The Authorised Biography of the Creator of the SAS*. Warner Books, 1994

Lewes, John. *Jock Lewes: Co-Founder of the SAS*. Pen & Sword, 2023

Mortimer, Gavin. *Stirling's Men: The Inside History of the SAS in World War II*. Cassell Military Paperbacks, 2005

Petch, Tom. *Speed, Aggression, Surprise; The Untold Secret Origins of the SAS*. WH Allen, 2022

Pittaway, Jonathan. *Long Range Desert Group, Rhodesia – The Men Speak*. Privately published c. 2006

Ross, Hamish. *Paddy Mayne*. Sutton Publishing Ltd., 2003

Stevens, Gordon. *The Originals: The Secret History of the Birth of the SAS in their Own Words*. Ebury Press, 2005

King's College London: Liddell Hart Centre for Military Archives, Laycock Papers – 'Employment of Special Service Troops in the Middle East' Box 3/19

King's College London: Liddell Hart Centre for Military Archives, Laycock Papers – L243/A Layforce Terms of Service, Box 3/19

Operation Squatter, unpublished work by Alan Orton

Original Jock Lewes notebook, courtesy of Anna Lewes and Gil Boyd, BEM

CHAPTER 4

The private papers of Reg Seekings

Reg Seekings audio: IWM/Gordon Stevens/IWM

Cooper, Johnny. *One of the Originals: The Story of a Founder Member of the SAS*. Pan, 1991

Hoe, Alan. *David Stirling: The Authorised Biography of the Creator of the SAS*. Warner Books, 1994

Lewes, John. *Jock Lewes: Co-Founder of the SAS*. Pen & Sword, 2023

Macintyre, Ben. *SAS Rogue Heroes*. Viking, 2016

Stevens, Gordon. *The Originals: The Secret History of the Birth of the SAS in their Own Words*. Ebury Press, 2005

https://heartheboatsing.com/2022/11/10/jock-lewes-from-tideway-to-tobruk-part-ii-oxford-1933-1937/

CHAPTER 5

The private papers of Reg Seekings

Reg Seekings audio: IWM/Gordon Stevens/IWM

Ross, Hamish. *Paddy Mayne*. Sutton Publishing Ltd., 2003

Stevens, Gordon. *The Originals: The Secret History of the Birth of the SAS in their Own Words*. Ebury Press, 2005

Operation Number One: *The Original SAS War Diary* (SAS Regimental Association)

King's College London: Liddell Hart Centre for Military Archives, McLeod Papers (General Sir Roderick McLeod) – 'Memo on the origins of the SAS by Colonel David Stirling, 1948' p3, 1/10

Original Jock Lewes notebook, courtesy of Anna Lewes and Gil Boyd, BEM

Operation Squatter, unpublished work by Alan Orton

NA WO 201/811 LRDG 'Recce Report No.20 'R' 1' Patrol 26 Nov: Report by Captain Easonsmith

Report by RSM Pat Riley (SAS Regimental Association)

CHAPTER 6

The private papers of Reg Seekings

Reg Seekings audio: IWM/Gordon Stevens/IWM

Soldier's Service and Pay Book of A. R. Seekings

Asher, Michael. *The Regiment: The Definitive Story of the SAS*. Viking, 2007

Cowles, Virginia. *The Phantom Major: The Story of David Stirling and the SAS Regiment*. Pen & Sword, 2016

Pittaway, Jonathan. *Long Range Desert Group, Rhodesia – The Men Speak*. Privately published c. 2006

Shaw, W. B. Kennedy. *Long Range Desert Group, Reconnaissance and Raiding Behind Enemy Lines*. Frontline Books, 2021

Author interview with Mike Sadler

Operation Number Two (B), *The Original SAS War Diary* (SAS Regimental Association)

NA WO 201/811 L.R.D.G S1 Patrol Operation Instruction No.10

NA WO 218/90 L.R.D.G's Part in the 8 Army's Offensive – The Third Phase Dec 25-8 Feb

NA WO 373/18/141, MacDonald, DCM, *London Gazette*, 24 February 1942

'28k for footballer's war medals', 3 July 2008, *Express and Star* newspaper https://www.expressandstar.com/sport/2008/07/03/28k-for-footballers-war-medals/

Silent Courage: The Story of the SAS, DVD (release date, unclear)

CHAPTER 7

Reg Seekings audio: IWM/Gordon Stevens/IWM

The private papers of Reg Seekings

Cooper, Johnny. *One of the Originals: The Story of a Founder Member of the SAS*. Pan, 1991

Almonds-Windmill, Lorna. *Gentleman Jim: The Wartime Story of a Founder of the SAS and Special Forces*. Robinson, 2002

Cowles, Virginia. *The Phantom Major: The Story of David Stirling and the SAS Regiment*. Pen & Sword, 2016

Hoe, Alan. *David Stirling: The Authorised Biography of the Creator of the SAS*. Warner Books, 1994

Lewes, John. *Jock Lewes: Co-Founder of the SAS*. Pen & Sword, 2023

Shaw, W. B. Kennedy. *Long Range Desert Group, Reconnaissance and Raiding Behind Enemy Lines*. Frontline Books, 2021

Stevens, Gordon. *The Originals: The Secret History of the Birth of the SAS in their Own Words*. Ebury Press, 2005

Operation Number Four (A), *The Original SAS War Diary* (SAS Regimental Association)

Author interview with Mike Sadler, 2022

NA WO 218/90 'LRDG's Part in the 8 Army's Offensive – The Third Phase', 25 December 1941–8 February 1942

IWM 24562 HOE/David Stirling private papers

Seekings audio: Airborne Assault Museum and ParaData.org.uk; Archive box number 5B1 1/8/1

CHAPTER 8

The private papers of Reg Seekings

Reg Seekings audio: IWM/Gordon Stevens/IWM

Cooper, Johnny. *One of the Originals: The Story of a Founder Member of the SAS*. Pan, 1991

Cowles, Virginia. *The Phantom Major: The Story of David Stirling and the SAS Regiment*. Pen & Sword, 2016

Pittaway, Jonathan. *Long Range Desert Group, Rhodesia – The Men Speak*. Privately published c. 2006

Operation Number Six, *The Original SAS War Diary* (SAS Regimental Association)

NA WO 218/90 LRP/G/6 L.R.D.G Operation Instruction No.24

CHAPTER 9

The private papers of Reg Seekings

Reg Seekings audio: IWM/Gordon Stevens/IWM

Asher, Michael. *The Regiment: The Definitive Story of the SAS*. Viking, 2007

Cooper, Johnny. *One of the Originals: The Story of a Founder Member of the SAS*. Pan, 1991

Cowles, Virginia. *The Phantom Major: The Story of David Stirling and the SAS Regiment*. Pen & Sword, 2016

Hoe, Alan. *David Stirling: The Authorised Biography of the Creator of the SAS*. Warner Books, 1994

Lewis, Damien. *SAS Brothers in Arms*. Quercus, 2022

Shaw, W. B. Kennedy. *Long Range Desert Group, Reconnaissance and Raiding Behind Enemy Lines*. Frontline Books, 2021

Stevens, Gordon. *The Originals: The Secret History of the Birth of the SAS in their Own Words*. Ebury Press, 2005

Operation Number 10 (B), *The Original SAS War Diary* (SAS Regimental Association)

Author interview with Mike Sadler, 2022

NA WO 218/90 LRP/G/6 L.R.D.G Operation Instruction No. 38

NA WO 218/90 Long Range Desert Group War Diary, Fifth Phase, 19 April to 26 May 1942

NA WO 218/90 Long Range Desert Group War Diary, Sixth Phase, 27 May to 28 June 1942

'Operations in the Middle East from 1 November 1941 to 15 August 1942', despatch by General Sir Claude Auchinleck from 27 January 1943, published in *London Gazette*, 15 January 1948

CHAPTER 10

Reg Seekings audio: IWM/Gordon Stevens/IWM

The Service Records of Robert W. Seekings (From the private papers of Bob Seekings)

Almonds-Windmill, Lorna. *Gentleman Jim: The Wartime Story of a Founder of the SAS and Special Forces*. Robinson, 2002

Asher, Michael. *The Regiment: The Definitive Story of the SAS*. Penguin, 2018

Cooper, Johnny. *One of the Originals: The Story of a Founder Member of the SAS*. Pan, 1991

Cowles, Virginia. *The Phantom Major: The Story of David Stirling and the SAS Regiment*. Pen & Sword, 2016

Hoe, Alan. *David Stirling: The Authorised Biography of the Creator of the SAS.* Warner Books, 1994

James, Malcolm (Malcolm Pleydell). *Born of the Desert: With the SAS in North Africa.* Greenhill, 2001

Mather, Carol. *When the Grass Stops Growing.* Leo Cooper, 1997

Stevens, Gordon. *The Originals: The Secret History of the Birth of the SAS in their Own Words.* Ebury Press, 2005

Thompson, Julian. *Imperial War Museums' Book of War Behind Enemy Lines.* Pen & Sword, 2018

Author interviews with Mike Sadler, April and December 2022

Author interview with Ian, Kerry and Reg Seekings, 2021

'Operations in the Middle East from 1 November 1941 to 15 August 1942', despatch by General Sir Claude Auchinleck from 27 January 1943, published in *London Gazette*, 15 January 1948

Seekings audio: Airborne Assault Museum and ParaData.org.uk; Archive box number 5B1 1/8/1

CHAPTER 11

The private papers of Reg Seekings

Reg Seekings audio: IWM/Gordon Stevens/IWM

Almonds-Windmill, Lorna. *Gentleman Jim: The Wartime Story of a Founder of the SAS and Special Forces.* Robinson, 2002

James, Malcolm (Malcolm Pleydell). *Born of the Desert: With the SAS in North Africa.* Greenhill, 2001

Maclean, Fitzroy. *Eastern Approaches.* Penguin, 2009

Mather, Carol. *When the Grass Stops Growing: A War Memoir.* Leo Cooper, 1997

Shaw, W. B. Kennedy. *Long Range Desert Group: Reconnaissance and Raiding Behind Enemy Lines.* Frontline Books, 2021

Stevens, Gordon. *The Originals: The Secret History of the Birth of the SAS in their Own Words.* Ebury Press, 2005

Author interviews with Mike Sadler, May 2022

NA WO 201/735 'Report on Operation – Benghazi – Sep '42'

Commando Veterans Archive (www.commandoveterans.org/ Drongin8Commando)

CHAPTER 12

The private papers of Reg Seekings

Reg Seekings audio: IWM/Gordon Stevens/IWM

Letter from David Stirling's office, June 1954, SAS Regimental
  Association archives
Churchill, Winston. *The Second World War*. Pimlico, 2002
Hoe, Alan. *David Stirling: The Authorised Biography of the Creator of the SAS*.
  Warner Books, 1994
James, Malcolm (Malcolm Pleydell). *Born of the Desert: With the SAS in
  North Africa*. Greenhill, 2001
Liddell Hart, B. H., ed. *The Rommel Papers*. Arrow, 1987
Ranfurly, Hermione. *To War with Whitaker*. Pan Books, 2018
NA WO 201/732 Paper on 'Special Units Sep '42'
NA WO 201/756 28 September paper 'Meeting regarding plans for
  Lt.Col Stirling's Force'
NA WO 218/96 16 November paper 'Formation of Special Unit MEF'
NA WO 201/756 8 October paper G.H.Q M.E.F Operation Instruction
  No.146
NA WO 201/756 November 1942 paper 'Programme for S.A.S. Regt'
NA WO 201/756 17 November G.H.Q M.E.F Operation Instruction
  No.150
NA WO 201/756 25 November G.H.Q M.E.F Operation Instruction
  No.151
NA WO 201/756 'Notes on Arrangements Made for Stirling's Operation'
NA WO 201/756 'Intentions of Lt.Col Stirling 1 SAS Regt up to
  2 December 42'
AND 'Appendix A'
NA WO 218/96 SAS War Diary, November 1942
NA WO 218/97 SAS War Diary 'Report by Sgt Seekings A.R.B Sqn SAS
  Regt'

CHAPTER 13

The private papers of Reg Seekings
Reg Seekings audio: IWM/Gordon Stevens/IWM
Farran, Roy. *Winged Dagger: Adventures on Special Service*. Cassell Military
  Classics, 1998
Hoe, Alan. *David Stirling: The Authorised Biography of the Creator of the SAS*.
  Warner Books, 1994
Liddell Hart, B. H., ed. *The Rommel Papers*. Arrow, 1987
Author interviews with Mike Sadler, April 2022
IWM 24562 HOE/David Stirling private papers
NA WO 218/97 SAS War Diary 'Report by Sgt Seekings A.R. B Sqn SAS
  Regt'

NA WO 218/97 SAS War Diary, March 1943

NA WO 373/46/40 – Recommendation for Award for Reginald Seekings, 26 November 1942

'Some Men Have Nine Lives' by Vivien Street, *Blackwood's Magazine*, March 1947

CHAPTER 14

Reg Seekings audio: IWM/Gordon Stevens/IWM

The private/personal papers of Eric Musk

The Service Records of Robert W. Seekings

Churchill, Winston. *The Second World War.* Pimlico, 2002

Davis, Peter MC. *S.A.S. Men in the Making.* Pen & Sword, 2015

Harrison, Derrick. *These Men Are Dangerous – The Early Years of the SAS.* Grafton, 1990

Holland, James. *Sicily '43, The First Assault on Fortress Europe.* Corgi, 2021

Messenger, Charles. *Commandos: The Definitive History of Commando Operations in the Second World War.* William Collins 2016

Mortimer, Gavin. *Stirling's Men: The Inside History of the SAS in World War II.* Cassell Military Paperbacks, 2005

Author interviews with Mike Sadler, August 2021

Author interview with sons of Bob Seekings – Ian Seekings, Major Kerry Seekings (MBE) and Reg Seekings, 2021 and subsequent correspondence

Notes Relating to Special Raiding Squadron, 1st SAS Regiment, July–October 1943, IWM, Documents 25504

IWM 24562 HOE/David Stirling private papers

NA WO 218/97 SAS War Diary, March 1943, National Archives

NA WO 218/99 SAS War Diary, July 1943, 'First Operation' report

NA WO 373/18/126 – Recommendation for Award for Jack Terry, announced 24 February 1942

NA WO 373/3/539 – Recommendation for Award for John Wiseman, announced 21 October 1943

NA WO 373/3/199 – Recommendation for Award for Reginald Seekings, announced 18 November 1943

NA WO 373/3/104 – Recommendation for Award for Harold Poat, announced 18 November 1943

https://www.commandoveterans.org/JackTerry11Commando

CHAPTER 15

Reg Seekings audio: IWM/Gordon Stevens/IWM

The private/personal papers of Eric Musk

Mortimer, Gavin. *Stirling's Men: The Inside History of the SAS in World War II.* Cassell Military Paperbacks, 2005

Davis, Peter MC. *S.A.S. Men in the Making.* Pen & Sword, 2015

Durnford-Slater, Brigadier John. *Commando, Memoirs of a Fighting Commando in World War Two.* Greenhill, 2002

Harrison, Derrick. *These Men Are Dangerous – The Early Years of the SAS.* Grafton, 1990

Holland, James. *Sicily '43, The First Assault on Fortress Europe.* Corgi, 2021

McClean, Stewart. *SAS: The History of the Special Raiding Squadron 'Paddy's Men'.* Spellmount Ltd, 2006

Mortimer, Gavin. *The SAS in World War II.* Osprey, 2011

Author interview with sons of Bob Seekings – Ian Seekings, Major Kerry Seekings (MBE) and Reg Seekings, 2021 and subsequent correspondence

Notes Relating to Special Raiding Squadron, 1st SAS Regiment, July–October 1943, IWM, Documents 25504 1943 'Second Operation' report

NA WO 218/99 SAS War Diary, July–September 1943 and appendices reports

https://www.loquis.com/en/loquis/1081175/Bagnara+Calabra+le+Bagnarote

CHAPTER 16

The private/personal papers of Eric Musk

Reg Seekings audio: IWM/Gordon Stevens/IWM

Davis, Peter MC. *S.A.S. Men in the Making.* Pen & Sword, 2015

Durnford-Slater, Brigadier John. *Commando, Memoirs of a Fighting Commando in World War Two.* Greenhill, 2002

Farran, Roy. *Winged Dagger, Adventures on Special Service.* Cassell 1999

Harrison, Derrick. *These Men Are Dangerous – The Early Years of the SAS.* Grafton, 1990

Lewis, Damien. *SAS Forged in Hell, From Desert Rats to Dogs of War.* Quercus, 2023

McClean, Stewart. *SAS: The History of the Special Raiding Squadron 'Paddy's Men'.* Spellmount Ltd, 2006

Messenger, Charles. *Commandos: The Definitive History of Commando Operations in the Second World War.* William Collins, 2016

Mortimer, Gavin. *The SAS in World War II.* Osprey, 2011

Mortimer, Gavin. *Stirling's Men: The Inside History of the SAS in World War II.* Cassell Military Paperbacks, 2005

Stevens, Gordon. *The Originals: The Secret History of the Birth of the SAS in their Own Words.* Ebury Press, 2005

Author interview with sons of Bob Seekings – Ian Seekings, Major Kerry Seekings (MBE) and Reg Seekings, 2021 and subsequent correspondence

Notes Relating to Special Raiding Squadron, 1st SAS Regiment, July–October 1943, IWM, Documents 25504 1943 'Operation Devon' report

NA WO 218/99 SAS War Diary, October 1943 and appendix reports

Roll of Honour, SAS Regimental Association

https://www.royal-irish.com/events/38-irish-brigade-land-at-termoli

https://www.londonirishrifles.com/ (Termoli 1943)

CHAPTER 17

Reg Seekings audio: IWM/Gordon Stevens/IWM

Soldier's Service and Pay Book of Reg Seekings

Cooper, Johnny. *One of the Originals: The Story of a Founder Member of the SAS.* Pan, 1991

Harrison, Derrick. *These Men Are Dangerous – The Early Years of the SAS.* Grafton, 1990

McCue, Paul. *SAS Operation Bulbasket.* Pen & Sword, 2010

McLuskey, J. Fraser. *Parachute Padre: Behind German Lines with the SAS France 1944.* Spa, 1985

Stevens, Gordon. *The Originals: The Secret History of the Birth of the SAS in their Own Words.* Ebury Press, 2005

Wellsted, Ian. *SAS: With the Maquis in Action with the French Resistance.* Frontline Books, 2016

Author interview with sons of Bob Seekings – Ian Seekings, Major Kerry Seekings (MBE) and Reg Seekings, 2021 and subsequent correspondence

Seekings audio: The Airborne Assault Museum and ParaData.org.uk; Archive box number 5B1 1/8/1

King's College London: Liddell Hart Centre for Military Archives, General Sir Roderick McLeod collection – McLeod 2, Notes on the Organisation, History and Employment of Special Air Service

NA WO 331/7 Report No. FF2175 'German Order to Kill Captured Allied Commandos and Parachutists'

NA WO 218/192 SAS Brigade Instruction No.15, Operation Overlord, 1 SAS Regt, June 2

NA WO 218/192 – Report on Operation 'Houndsworth 102' by Major Fraser M.C.

NA WO 218/192 – Report of Advance Recce Party 2–14 June by Lt. I.G. Wellsted

NA WO 218/192 – Report B, Report of the Phantom Section's journey, June 10–17 44 by Lt Moore

NA WO 218/192 – Report C, Report on Operation 'Houndsworth 102' by Captain A. D. Muirhead, 2 Troop

NA WO 218/192 – Report on operations covering the period 21 Jun to 29 Sep 44 by the chaplain to the 1st SAS Regiment

NA WO 218/114 – Headquarters, Special Air Service Troops War Diary, Feb, 1944

NA WO 218/2389 – SAS/SF Operations in Overlord, 'Strategic Use of SAS Troops', 19 May, 1944

NA WO 218/2389 – SAS/SF Operations in Overlord, 10 August report by Director of Tactical Investigation

Roll of Honour, SAS Regimental Association

CHAPTER 18

Reg Seekings audio: IWM/Gordon Stevens/IWM

Cooper, Johnny. *One of the Originals: The Story of a Founder Member of the SAS*. Pan, 1991

McLuskey, J. Fraser. *Parachute Padre, Behind German Lines with the SAS France 1944*. Spa, 1985

Stevens, Gordon. *The Originals: The Secret History of the Birth of the SAS in their Own Words*. Ebury Press, 2005

Wellsted, Ian. *SAS: With the Maquis in Action with the French Resistance*. Frontline Books, 2016

King's College London: Liddell Hart Centre for Military Archives, General Sir Roderick McLeod collection – McLeod 2, Notes on the Organisation, History and Employment of Special Air Service 2/1

NA WO 218/114 – Headquarters, Special Air Service Troops War Diary, August, 1944– page/sheet '5'

NA WO 218/192 – Report on Operation 'Houndsworth 102' by Major Fraser M.C.

NA WO 218/192 – Battle of Vermot 'D' by Capt Wiseman

NA WO 218/192 – Report C, Report on Operation 'Houndsworth 102' by Captain A. D. Muirhead, 2 Troop

NA WO 218/192 –Report on Operation 'Houndsworth 102' by Lieut C. R. Moore, 2 Patrol SAS Phantom

NA WO 218/192 – Report on operations covering the period 21 Jun to 29 Sep 44 by the chaplain to the 1st SAS Regiment

Reg Seekings audio: The Airborne Assault Museum and ParaData.org. uk, Archive box number 5B1 1/8/1

'The Parachuting Padre' by Lord Ashcroft, www.dailymail.co.uk/news/ article-8395059/, 6 June 2020

CHAPTER 19

Reg Seekings audio: IWM/Gordon Stevens/IWM

Service Record of Monica Seekings (née Smith), Auxiliary Territorial Service

Mortimer, Gavin. *The SAS in World War II*. Osprey, 2011

Mortimer, Gavin. *Stirling's Men: The Inside History of the SAS in World War II*. Cassell Military Paperbacks, 2005

Wellsted, Ian. *With the SAS Across the Rhine: Into the Heart of Hitler's Third Reich*. Frontline Books, 2020

Author interview with Ronald Smith, November 2022

Author interview with Mike Sadler, October 2022

NA WO 218/117 'HQ SAS Tps' War Diary March 1945

NA WO 218/117 'HQ SAS Tps' War Diary April 1945

NA WO 218/119 – Operation Archway 'General account of operations'

NA WO 218/117 – Handwritten note recording operational strengths in April 1945

NA WO 218/117 – 'Operation Archway, Report on action of 27 March 1945 by Capt Muirhead'

NA WO 218/117 – 'Operation Archway, Report on action by Capt Cooper'

NA WO 218/119 – 12 April Letter from HQ Squadron 1st SAS detailing 8 April battle

NA WO 218/119 War Diary of SAS 'HQ' Norway, May to November 1945

NA WO 218/119 'Report on SAS in Norway' Page 3

TVS, SAS Interviews, IWM, Documents 21759, Box 62/137/1

CHAPTER 20

Reg Seekings audio: IWM/Gordon Stevens/IWM

Cooper, Johnny. *One of the Originals: The Story of a Founder Member of the SAS*. Pan, 1991

Mortimer, Gavin. *The SAS in World War II*. Osprey, 2011

Mortimer, Gavin. *Stirling's Men: The Inside History of the SAS in World War II*. Cassell Military Paperbacks, 2005

Randall, John and M. J. Trow. *The Last Gentleman of the SAS*. Mainstream, 2014

Wellsted, Ian. *With the SAS Across the Rhine: Into the Heart of Hitler's Third Reich*. Frontline Books, 2020

NA WO 218/117 'HQ SAS Tps' War Diary March/April 1945

NA WO 218/119 – Operation Archway 'General account of operations'

'The liberation of Belsen', www.nam.ac.uk

'The gate of Hell', by Alexander van Straubenzee, www.telegraph.co.uk, 10 April 2005

'The liberation of Bergen Belsen', https://www.iwm.org.uk

CHAPTER 21

Reg Seekings audio: IWM/Gordon Stevens/IWM

Service Records of Robert W. Seekings

Cooper, Johnny. *One of the Originals: The Story of a Founder Member of the SAS*. Pan, 1991

Stevens, Gordon. *The Originals: The Secret History of the Birth of the SAS in their Own Words*. Ebury Press, 2005

Wellsted, Ian. *With the SAS Across the Rhine: Into the Heart of Hitler's Third Reich*. Frontline Books, 2020

NA WO 218/119 'Report on SAS in Norway'

NA WO 218/119 'HQ SAS Tps' War Diary September–November 1945

NA WO 218/119 'Disbandment – HQ SAS Tps' 8 October 1945

NA WO 218/119 – Operation Archway 'General account of operations'

NA WO 218/114 – 'Report of Move, HQ SAS Tps (Main)'

TVS, SAS Interviews, IWM, Documents 21759, Box 62/137/1

'Monica and Peggy Wed Together', *Bury Free Press*, 20 July 1945

Met Office Digital Library and Archive 'Daily Weather Report: DWR_1945_07'

EPILOGUE

The Service Records of A. R. Seekings

Ashton, Patrick. *Ely Inns, A History of Ely Inns and Beer Houses.* The Ely Society, 2007

Author interview/correspondence with Ian, Kerry and Reg Seekings

Author interview with Richard and Marion Musk and Stuart Palmer, October 2021

Author interview with Alison and Nigel Musk, November 2022

Author interview with 'Steven', former National Service Patrol Officer, PATU, May 2024

Author interviews with John Sinden

Author interview Gordon Cawthorne

Author interview with Thelma Pearce

Author interview with John Fordham

Author interview with Mel Morley and Sheila Palmer, 2021

The private papers of Reg Seekings

'Second World War and SAS hero remembered with new street signs', *Ely Standard*, 5 May 2021

'In Pictures, Ely bypass is open', *Ely Standard*, 31 October 2018

'Force Branches', www.bsapolice.org

Obituary, Reg Seekings, *The Independent*, 3 May 1999

TEXT PICTURE CREDITS

Page 23	Photo by courtesy of Martin Boswell
Page 31	Photo supplied by courtesy of the family of Bob Seekings
Page 38	Photo by Tony Rushmer
Page 47	Photo supplied by courtesy of the SAS Regimental Association
Page 51	From the original notebook of Jock Lewes, courtesy of Anna Lewes and Gil Boyd, BEM
Page 57	As above, courtesy of Anna Lewes and Gil Boyd, BEM
Page 67	Photo supplied by courtesy of the family of the late Lieutenant-Colonel 'Jake' Easonsmith, DSO, MC
Page 89	Photo supplied by courtesy of the Cooper family
Page 142	Photo supplied by courtesy of the SAS Regimental Association
Page 239	Photo supplied by courtesy of the family of Peter Davis MC
Page 245	Photo supplied by courtesy of the Cooper family
Page 261	Photo supplied by courtesy of the SAS Regimental Association
Page 266	Photo supplied by courtesy of Nick Sinden
Page 273	Photo supplied by courtesy of the SAS Regimental Association
Page 275	Photo by Tony Rushmer

INDEX